WILLIAMS FW14B
1992 (all models)

COVER CUTAWAY: Williams FW14B.
(Goodyear Dunlop Motorsport)

For Dad.

The Williams name and logo are trademarks of Williams Grand Prix Engineering Limited and are used under licence. All rights reserved. © 2016.

© Haynes Publishing 2016

Steve Rendle has asserted his right to be identified as the author of this work.

All rights reserved. No part of this publication may be reproduced or stored in a retrieval system or transmitted, in any form or by any means, electronic, mechanical, photocopying, recording or otherwise, without prior permission in writing from Haynes Publishing.

Published in May 2016

A catalogue record for this book is available from the British Library

ISBN 978 0 85733 825 9

Library of Congress control no. 2014957432

Design and layout by James Robertson

Published by Haynes Publishing,
Sparkford, Yeovil, Somerset BA22 7JJ, UK
Tel: 01963 440635
Int. tel: +44 1963 440635
Website: www.haynes.co.uk

Haynes North America Inc.,
861 Lawrence Drive,
Newbury Park, California 91320, USA

Printed in the USA by Odcombe Press LP,
1299 Bridgestone Parkway, La Vergne, TN 37086

WILLIAMS FW14B

1992 (all models)

Owners' Workshop Manual

An insight into the design, engineering, maintenance and operation of Williams's World Championship-winning F1 car

Steve Rendle

Nigel Mansell puts the FW14B through its paces during its first official test at Estoril in February 1992. *(John Townsend)*

Contents

6	**Introduction**	
Acknowledgements		7

8	**The Williams story**
Frank Williams (Racing Cars) Ltd – the early years	10
Williams Grand Prix Engineering – the start of something big	13
FW15C – a worthy successor to the FW14B	21
Subsequent Williams team history	21

28	**Design and development of the Williams FW14B**
The FW14 and the 1991 season	30
The Williams active suspension story	38
The development of the FW14B – the car that nearly wasn't!	47

50	**The Williams FW14B in action**
Pre-season testing	52
The 1992 championship season	52

74	**Anatomy of the Williams FW14B**
Introduction	76
Chassis	76
Fuel tank	79
Bodywork	79
Aerodynamics	82
Suspension	87
The FW14B active-ride system	90
Steering	97
Brakes	98
Engine	99
Transmission	112
Wheels	115
Tyres	116
Electronics	116
Hydraulic system	122
Safety equipment	122
Cockpit controls	123

128	**The engineers**
Patrick Head	130
Adrian Newey	132
Paddy Lowe	132
Brian O'Rourke	135
Chris Dietrich	135
Steve Wise	135
Dave Lang	136
Simon Wells	138
David Brown	139
John Russell	140
Dickie Stanford	140
Bernard Dudot	140
Jean-Jacques His	141
Philippe Coblence	141

142	**The drivers**
Nigel Mansell	144
Riccardo Patrese	147
Damon Hill	151
Mark Blundell	151
Gil de Ferran	152
John Robinson	152
Alain Prost	152
Karun Chandhok	153
Valtteri Bottas	153
Private owners	153

154	**Williams Heritage**

158	**Appendices**
1 – The rival cars	158
2 – FW14B 1992 race results and statistics	166
3 – FW14B specifications	167
4 – FW14B individual chassis histories	168

171	**Index**

173	**Bibliography**

Introduction

BELOW A familiar sight during 1992, as the two FW14Bs lead in formation – Mansell ahead of Patrese – and leave the rest of the field in their wake. *(John Townsend)*

Approaching 25 years after its competition debut, at the 1992 South African Grand Prix, the Williams FW14B is still one of the most iconic grand prix cars of all time, and frequently features in 'top-ten' selections of the most successful F1 cars through the years. The car's white, blue and yellow livery became synonymous with Williams's success from the mid-1980s to the early 1990s, and of course has become inseparably linked to the race number 'Red 5' and Nigel Mansell's distinctive helmet colours.

The FW14B dominated the 1992 season, thanks in part to its active suspension system, which provided a stable platform to exploit Adrian Newey's unrivalled flair for aerodynamic

design. However, the active suspension was just one element in the 'package' that brought the FW14B and Williams so much success. The car was powered by a peerless Renault V10 engine, and featured a blown diffuser and traction control, plus pioneering electronic control systems that would soon become commonplace in F1.

With the exception of the Renault engine, all of the engineering technology employed on the car was developed in-house by the relatively small engineering teams at Williams, and the active suspension in particular only saw the light of day thanks to the perseverance of a small R&D team working behind the scenes as the race squad went about its business of winning grands prix. Williams is a team that has always had an engineering focus, and today the Williams name is synonymous with engineering excellence, which in recent years the company has applied, through its Advanced Engineering division, to new projects outside F1, including advanced lightweight materials, hybrid power systems, electronics, aerodynamics and vehicle dynamics for the motorsport, automotive, aviation, defence, sports science and energy sectors.

I was one of the many thousands of partisan fans who watched Nigel Mansell in the FW14B win the 1992 British Grand Prix, one of ten victories for the car during a season in which it made its indelible mark on the record books. Expectation at Silverstone that July afternoon was high, and neither the car nor the drivers disappointed, Riccardo Patrese finishing second in the sister FW14B to complete a perfect weekend for the 'home' team. Although the focus for many of the fans present was Nigel Mansell, there was a huge amount of pride, affection and respect for the Williams team as a whole, and it continues to this day.

Nearly 50 years after Frank Williams first fielded a racing car as an entrant and nearly 40 years after he introduced his own car, Williams today is arguably the only F1 team that exists purely to go racing, and it remains under the guidance of its irrepressible, enthusiastic founder. The team is almost an extension of the passion displayed by the many F1 enthusiasts – both in the UK and around the world – who are not only fascinated by the cutting-edge engineering of an F1 car but also have a hunger for pure *racing*!

Here is the story of a World Championship-winning racing car, designed, manufactured and raced by a team of highly talented engineers – a human story as well as an engineering story, and the story of a car that, as later chapters will reveal, was never intended to be!

ACKNOWLEDGEMENTS

I am indebted to many people for lending their support to this project. A number have helped beyond the call of duty, and without their time and dedication it would not have been possible to complete this book. To everybody involved, I would like to express my heartfelt thanks.

I would like to offer special thanks to all at Williams for making me feel so welcome during my visits to Williams Heritage at Grove, and in particular to the following people for their enthusiasm and willingness to share their knowledge and experiences: Chris Dietrich, Dave Lang, Toby Norrell, Brian O'Rourke, Dickie Stanford, Simon Wells, Steve Wise and Jonathan Williams. Also Angela Burt, James Francis and Mark Loasby.

Special thanks are also due to Philippe Coblence, formerly of Renault Sport, for his tireless enthusiasm and help in providing details of the engines used in the FW14B, and thanks too to Bernard Dudot and Jean-Louis Lefebvre.

Special thanks also to Sir Patrick Head and to Paddy Lowe, for their enthusiasm in sharing their recollections and anecdotes of their time at Williams working with the FW14B.

Many thanks to both Nigel Mansell and Riccardo Patrese for taking time out of their busy schedules to talk about their reminiscences of developing and racing the FW14B, and for providing fascinating insight from the driver's perspective.

Thanks to Lucy Genon and Nathalie Fiancette at Renault Sport for their support and research in supplying material from the Renault Sport archive; to John Colley of John Colley Photography for his patience and professionalism in taking the photographs of the 'project' car; and to John Townsend for his quick responses to my research requests, and for supplying period photographs from his splendid F1 Pictures archive.

Thanks are also due to Victoria Preston, Iain Wakefield and Mark Hughes, and to everybody involved in transforming my words and picture selection into a finished book, in particular James Robertson.

And finally, to Barbara, Tom and Emily, for your sacrifices and uncomplaining understanding during the time my focus was on this book.

Steve Rendle
March 2016

Chapter One

The Williams story

The foundations for future success of the Williams F1 team were laid in 1977, when Frank Williams formed a partnership with young designer Patrick Head, and Williams Grand Prix Engineering was born, the team's first World Championship title coming three years later with Alan Jones. Since the International Cup for F1 Manufacturers was first awarded, in 1958 (19 years before Williams Grand Prix Engineering was formed), only Ferrari has won more constructors' titles than Williams. This remarkable feat is testament to the enthusiasm, commitment and skills of Williams team members past and present.

OPPOSITE Winner Alan Jones, in the Williams FW07, leads John Watson's McLaren M26 at the 1979 Austrian Grand Prix. Jones's Austrian win was the third of four consecutive wins for Williams, starting with the team's first-ever victory, with Clay Regazzoni, at the British Grand Prix. *(LAT Photographic)*

Frank Williams (Racing Cars) Ltd – the early years

Frank Williams first ventured into motorsport in 1961, as a driver, when he bought his very first car, a road-legal race-tuned Austin A35, which he campaigned in a few club events before moving up to an Austin A40 in 1962, with mixed results.

In 1964, Frank moved into single-seater racing when he teamed up with Anthony 'Bubbles' Horsley (who would later come to prominence with Lord Alexander Hesketh's F1 team and James Hunt) to drive a Brabham F3 car in return for working as a mechanic and 'gopher'. Once again, Frank's results were mixed, and although he displayed obvious potential, he also had his fair share of off-track excursions. Frank's finances were in a perilous state, and to make ends meet he began to supply and deliver parts to drivers competing in the F3 championship, eventually progressing to buying and selling complete cars.

The business proved successful, and financed the purchase of a Cooper F3 car for 1965. The car proved tricky to drive, and Frank's best result was a fourth place, in Sweden, towards the end of the season.

The 1966 season continued in similar vein, but Frank was now selling new cars bought direct from the manufacturers – F3 Brabhams and Lolas. Frank drove a Brabham himself and continued to have mixed results along the way, although he did win a race at Knutstorp in Sweden. At the end of the 1966 season, he decided to concentrate on building up his business in order to finance a more competitive car for 1967. The hard work paid off, and the business flourished, with Frank deciding to postpone his return to racing for a year to focus on the continued growth of what was to become Frank Williams (Racing Cars) Ltd for the start of the 1968 season.

Over the previous few years, Frank had formed a strong friendship with up-and-coming English driver Piers Courage, who had shown flair in junior series to briefly make it to F1 with BRM, before competing in the Tasman series in Australia and New Zealand. After Frank was left with a cancelled customer order for an F2 Brabham BT21, Courage talked him into entering the car in the 1968 European Formula Two Championship, as a team owner. As Courage's performances in the Tasman series had secured him another drive with BRM in F1, Jonathan Williams (no relation to Frank!) stood in when Courage was at grands prix and it was Jonathan who secured Frank's first victory as a team owner, at the 1968 Monza European Formula Two Championship round.

After Courage took a spectacular win at Longford in Tasmania during the 1968 season, the organisers of the Tasman series were keen for him to return to their races for 1969. The Tasman regulations effectively permitted F1-spec cars, but with 2.5-litre engines rather than the 3-litre units used in F1 at the time. The Tasman organisers offered Frank a fee to run Courage in the series and he accepted. Frank bought a BT24 chassis, which Brabham had run in F1 in 1968, along with two Cosworth DFV 3-litre V8 engines. The design of the DFV allowed for it to be easily reduced in capacity to meet the Tasman regulations.

BELOW Piers Courage, in the Frank Williams Racing Brabham BT26A, at Montjuïc Park for the 1969 Spanish Grand Prix, the second round of the championship. Note the high wings introduced at the start of 1969, and banned from the Monaco Grand Prix. *(LAT Photographic)*

The fact that Williams now had an F1 car and two F1-spec engines sitting in his workshop made him think that perhaps the time had come to form a Grand Prix team, especially bearing in mind the potential of his driver. So, after persuading Courage to drive for his fledgling team in F1, as well as the Tasman series, Frank set about the task of arranging deals with various suppliers for his F1 effort.

Using a new Brabham BT26A bought via a third party, as Jack Brabham was not keen to have a rival F1 team running one of his latest cars, the Williams team's first F1 race was the non-championship 1969 Race of Champions at Brands Hatch. Various problems meant that Courage had to start from the back of the grid and in the race the immaculate blue Brabham had to retire. The first season for Williams had its ups and downs but, impressively, Courage finished second at both Monaco and Watkins Glen – an astonishing feat for the team's first season.

The Williams/Courage partnership continued for 1970, with a Cosworth DFV-powered De Tomaso 505 car designed by Gian Paolo Dallara. Tragically, Piers Courage lost his life in a fiery crash at the Dutch Grand Prix. Frank was devastated by his loss as he was very close to his driver, but he vowed to carry on racing. Brian Redman and then Tim Schenken drove the De Tomaso for the rest of 1970.

For 1971, Williams switched to a Cosworth DFV-powered March 701, later upgraded to a 711, driven by Frenchman Henri Pescarolo. The team's best result was fourth place in the British Grand Prix at Silverstone.

In both 1970 and 1971 Frank also mounted F2 championship challenges, but for 1972 he concentrated purely on F1. The initial plan was to build a car himself, with finance from the Politoys model-car company, after which the car would be named. As this car, designed by Len Bailey and built by Maurice Gomm, took longer than expected to produce, the team ended up using a customer March 721, again for Pescarolo although, significantly, Williams now became a two-car team, with the previous season's March 711 entered for Brazilian driver Carlos Pace. It was a challenging year, with no results to speak of. The Politoys FX3 car finally made its debut at the British Grand Prix, but Pescarolo wrote it off in a heavy accident and

LEFT Frank Williams and Piers Courage in the pits at Clermont Ferrand for the French Grand Prix in July 1969. Courage retired from the race with a loose nosecone. *(Sutton Motorsport Images)*

BELOW Carlos Pace in the Frank Williams March 721 gives March works driver Ronnie Peterson a lift during practice for the French Grand Prix at Clermont Ferrand in July 1972. *(Sutton Motorsport Images)*

ABOVE The Frank Williams (Racing Cars) Ltd factory at Slough in 1973, with ISO-Marlboro transporter parked outside the workshop. *(LAT Photographic)*

RIGHT Frank Williams looks contemplative sitting in one of his ISO-Marlboro cars at the Austrian Grand Prix at Zeltweg in August 1974. *(Sutton Motorsport Images)*

had to switch back to the March, which he also damaged from time to time.

The Politoys design was resurrected for 1973 and rebranded as an ISO-Marlboro FX3B, with support from Italian sports car manufacturer ISO-Rivolta and Marlboro cigarettes. Two cars were entered in the championship, for Italian Nanni Galli and New Zealander Howden Ganley. Galli's money ran out after only five races, and he was replaced by a succession of drivers, including Pescarolo, and single outings for Schenken and Jacky Ickx. An updated car, the ISO-Marlboro IR01, was introduced later in the season in order to comply with new regulations that required all cars to be fitted with crash structures, but results failed to improve.

The ISO-Marlboro cars were used again in 1974, but now redesignated 'FW' (Frank Williams's initials). Flamboyant Italian Arturio Merzario drove the 'lead' car, with various drivers again taking the wheel of the second car. Three chassis were built during the season, FW01, FW02 and FW03, a series that led eventually to the FW14B, and then to today's cars. The best result was fourth place at Monza for Merzario, who also qualified a remarkable third for the South African Grand Prix, where he finished sixth.

For 1975, the first car to bear the Williams name was introduced – the Williams FW04. Merzario was retained to drive it, joined by Frenchman Jacques Laffite, who scored a memorable second place at the Nürburgring, admittedly aided by various retirements. This result earned the team sufficient points for Williams to be entitled to FOCA (Formula One Constructors' Association) travel subsidies for the 1976 season – a major boost to the team's finances. During 1975 no fewer than nine other drivers made one-off appearances for Williams, including Ian Scheckter, Lella Lombardi and Damien Magee.

Towards the end of 1975, a major change took place in the way Frank Williams (Racing Cars) Ltd operated, which set the course for the future, albeit via a tortuous route. Frank had hired a talented young designer, Patrick Head, who had effectively served his apprenticeship at Lola, and shortly after

LEFT Jacques Laffite in the FW04 on his way to second place in the 1975 German Grand Prix at the Nürburgring. *(LAT Photographic)*

this Frank formed an alliance with Austro-Canadian businessman Walter Wolf, who was keen to make his mark in F1 as a team owner. After much deliberation, Frank agreed to Wolf becoming a shareholder in his company, whereby Wolf would settle the team's significant debts in return for a 60 per cent stake.

With Frank as team manager, the team acquired the remaining assets of Hesketh Racing, the team that brought James Hunt to prominence during 1975 but then went into liquidation. For 1976, the Hesketh 308C became the Wolf-Williams FW05, the team was renamed Walter Wolf Racing and Ickx became the lead driver, with backing from Marlboro. The inherited Hesketh proved to be a disaster, modifications failing to improve the overweight car's form. Ickx qualified for only four races before being replaced by the returning Merzario, but the results failed to improve, with the year's best finish a seventh place, for Ickx, in Spain.

Williams Grand Prix Engineering – the start of something big

With Walter Wolf calling the shots, Frank was effectively sidelined, and to his dismay was no longer directly involved in racing (or attending races), Wolf having brought in Peter Warr as team manager for 1976. For Frank, a born racer who had strived though hard times to keep his dream alive, this was too much to take, and he decided to go it alone.

Frank contacted Patrick Head, who had effectively been demoted in his season

ABOVE Jacky Ickx aboard the Williams FW05 (a reworked Hesketh 308C) at the 1976 season-opening Brazilian Grand Prix, where he finished eighth. *(Sutton Motorsport Images)*

BELOW Patrick Nève in the March 761 on his way to 12th place at the very first race for Williams Grand Prix Engineering – the 1977 Spanish Grand Prix at Jarama. Note the 'Fly Saudia' sponsorship and race number 27, both of which became inextricably linked with the team's early success. *(LAT Photographic)*

RIGHT Frank Williams and Patrick Head with the FW06, the first car of Williams Grand Prix Engineering's own design, outside the team's factory at Didcot in March 1978. *(Sutton Motorsport Images)*

BELOW At Silverstone, Clay Regazzoni in the FW07 crosses the finish line at the 1979 British Grand Prix to take the very first F1 win for Williams. *(Williams)*

with Wolf following the arrival of Harvey Postlethwaite, to ask if he would be interested in becoming the designer for a new venture. And so, in 1977, Williams Grand Prix Engineering was born. With insufficient resources to build a new car, the team acquired a customer March 761, with French driver Patrick Nève bringing sponsorship. The first race for Williams Grand Prix Engineering was the 1977 Spanish Grand Prix, where Nève qualified 22nd and finished a creditable 12th in the race. The team's best result in its first season was seventh place at the Italian Grand Prix.

In late 1977, Head designed the first of Williams Grand Prix Engineering's own cars – the FW06 – powered by the ubiquitous Cosworth DFV. The car was unveiled to the press at the team's new premises in Didcot, Oxfordshire, in December 1977 and, significantly, the car displayed sponsorship from Saudia Airlines. Australian Alan Jones was recruited as the driver, and a single car was entered in all 16 rounds of the 1978 World Championship, with the best results a fourth place at Kyalami in South Africa and an excellent second place, behind Carlos Reutemann's Ferrari, at Watkins Glen in the US.

The FW06 continued for the first four rounds of the 1979 championship, for which Williams ran a two-car team, with Swiss driver Clay Regazzoni joining Jones. The 1979 Spanish Grand Prix saw the debut of the all-new ground-effect FW07, which proved to be a turning point for the team. Both FW07s retired from their first two races, but then in Monaco Regazzoni finished second, and at the British Grand Prix at Silverstone he took a famous first victory for Williams.

The team secured a 1–2 finish in Germany, Jones ahead of Regazzoni, and then Jones went on to complete a hat-trick, with consecutive further wins in Austria and Holland, before adding one more victory in

LEFT Carlos Reutemann on his way to victory in the 1980 Monaco Grand Prix in the FW07B – the car that would take Williams to its first Constructors' World Championship. *(Williams)*

CENTRE Alan Jones lifts the winner's trophy for the 1980 Dutch Grand Prix on the podium at Zandvoort as second-placed Jody Scheckter (Ferrari) and third-placed Jacques Laffite (Ligier) look on. *(Williams)*

BELOW Mario Andretti made a one-off appearance for Williams in the FW07C in the 1982 United States West Grand Prix at Long Beach. *(Williams)*

Canada. A decade after Frank Williams's first F1 race as an entrant, Williams Grand Prix Engineering had made its indelible mark on F1, winning five races and finishing second in the 1979 Constructors' World Championship, behind Ferrari.

The FW07 evolved into the FW07B for 1980, with Argentine driver Carlos Reutemann replacing Regazzoni. Jones remained with the team for a third year and was wonderfully successful, winning five races to take the team to its first Drivers' World Championship. With Reutemann also winning in Monaco, and a further 12 podium positions during the season for the two drivers, Williams Grand Prix Engineering secured a landmark first Constructors' World Championship.

The FW07 was further developed for 1981, Reutemann, in the FW07C, proving the main challenge to Brabham's Nelson Piquet for the drivers' championship. Reutemann narrowly lost out to Piquet at the final round at Caesars Palace in Las Vegas – a race won by Jones. With two wins apiece for the two drivers, Williams again took the constructors' championship.

The FW07C was used for the first three races of 1982 before being replaced by the FW08. As Jones retired at the end of 1981, Finnish driver Keke Rosberg arrived at the team. Reutemann drove the second car in the opening

two races but then moved on, to be replaced for a single race (United States West, at Long Beach) by Mario Andretti before Irishman Derek Daly was recruited for the rest of the year. The 1982 season was famously one of the closest fought in F1 history, with no fewer than 11 drivers winning races. At the final round, at Caesars Palace, Rosberg was crowned World Champion, having taken a single win at the Swiss Grand Prix, plus five further podium places during the season. Williams finished fifth in the constructors' championship.

Rosberg, who remained with Williams for four years, was joined for 1983 by Jacques Laffite, returning to drive for Frank again.

ABOVE Keke Rosberg in the FW08 at the 1982 Swiss Grand Prix – his first F1 win and his only victory on the way to becoming that year's World Champion. *(Williams)*

CENTRE AND RIGHT The six-wheel FW07D was tried only once, by Alan Jones at Donington in November 1982 (centre), before it was superseded by the FW08B (right), tested by Keke Rosberg. The cars showed great promise, but the six-wheel concept was outlawed before Williams could develop the idea further. *(Sutton Motorsport Images/Williams)*

RIGHT Ayrton Senna sits in the FW08C during his very first F1 test, at Donington on 9 July 1983. *(Williams)*

Jonathan Palmer made a one-off appearance in a third car at the European Grand Prix at Brands Hatch. Although the new FW08C used the trusty Cosworth DFV engine throughout the season, the Honda-powered FW09 appeared at the final round in South Africa. Rosberg took the team's only win of the season, in Monaco, and finished fifth in the drivers' championship, with the team fourth in the constructors' championship. In a portent of things to come, Ayrton Senna drove an FW08 for a test at Donington during the summer.

The 1984 season saw Rosberg and Laffite drive the FW09, with Williams the only team to be supplied with Honda's turbo V6. For a second year in succession, Rosberg took Williams's only victory, this time at the Dallas Grand Prix. The Honda engine proved powerful, but fragile, the FW09s posting 21 retirements during the season. Rosberg finished a disappointing eighth in the drivers' championship, with Laffite 14th, while the team was only sixth in the constructors' championship. During the year Williams moved to new purpose-built premises in Didcot.

The Honda-powered FW10 was the challenger for 1985 and to drive it Frank signed Nigel Mansell as effective number two to Rosberg, much to the surprise of many in the pitlane and press corps. At the time, Mansell had a reputation for making mistakes, and had found life difficult during his final year with Lotus, with little support from many members of the team. However, this was the beginning of a spectacularly successful partnership between Williams and Mansell, who went on to become the team's British hero – albeit punctuated by his two-year sojourn at Ferrari.

That season Rosberg took two wins at the wheel of the FW10 – in Detroit and Australia – to finish third in the drivers' championship,

BELOW Keke Rosberg on his way to Williams's only victory of 1984, at the Dallas Grand Prix, in the FW09C. *(Williams)*

RIGHT Nigel Mansell en route to his first F1 win, in the FW10 at the 1985 European Grand Prix at Brands Hatch. *(Williams)*

RED 5

During 1985, Mansell used the race number 'Red 5' for the first time. It became synonymous with his time at Williams.

For the season's first four races, both FW10s carried white race numbers on their noses, but the team concluded that it was difficult to distinguish Rosberg's car from Mansell's from the front, so Mansell's car carried a red number 5 from the Canadian Grand Prix onwards.

ABOVE AND BELOW Mansell carried a white number 5 on his Williams for the final time at the 1985 Monaco Grand Prix (above – seen battling with Alain Prost in the McLaren MP4/2B), before becoming 'Red 5' for the first time in Canada (below – seen after stopping with an engine problem during Saturday qualifying). *(Sutton Motorsport Images)*

while Mansell, after finishing second in Belgium, achieved his first F1 win, in the European Grand Prix at Brands Hatch, along with a second victory at the following race in South Africa.

Rosberg decided to leave Williams at the end of 1985, and he departed on a 'high' after winning the end-of-season Australian Grand Prix. Brazilian Nelson Piquet, a double World Champion, replaced him for 1986.

In March 1986, Frank Williams was driving with the team's new PR manager, Peter Windsor, from Nice airport to the Paul Ricard circuit, where the team was testing the new FW11. During the journey, Frank lost control of his hire car, sustaining life-threatening injuries. His dogged determination and passion for life ensured that he refused to succumb, but he has had to live ever since as a quadraplegic. Patrick Head temporarily took the reins, but in time Frank returned to lead his beloved team.

The Williams-Honda FW11 proved to be the class of the field in 1986, Piquet and Mansell challenging each other for the championship lead throughout the season, with four wins for the Brazilian and five for the Englishman. Ironically, the fact that the two Williams drivers had been battling each other for points worked against them at the season finale in Australia. Famously, with Piquet leading the race, Prost second and Mansell third – finishing positions that would have given Mansell the championship – the third-placed Williams suffered a puncture at high speed, extraordinary TV images showing Mansell fighting to maintain control of the car as it slewed to a halt. This put Piquet in a championship-winning position, but the team elected to call him in for a precautionary tyre stop to reduce the risk of a repeat of Mansell's drama. Prost, who simply needed to finish ahead of Piquet to become World Champion, now led and, despite a late charge from Piquet, the Frenchman took victory in both the race and the drivers' championship. Defeat had been cruelly snatched from the jaws of victory for Williams, the only consolation being that the team's success in the constructors' championship was comprehensive.

For 1987, the FW11 evolved into the FW11B, and again there was a season-long duel between the two Williams drivers, and

ABOVE The two FW11s line up second and third on the grid at the 1986 Mexican Grand Prix, behind pole-position man Ayrton Senna in the Lotus 98T. *(Williams)*

again the team dominated the constructors' championship. By the Japanese Grand Prix in November, Mansell had won six races to Piquet's three, but the Brazilian, significantly, had scored seven second places, which gave him a 12-point lead in the championship. Mansell crashed heavily in practice at Suzuka, leaving him sidelined not only from the Japanese race but also the final round in Australia, where Italian Riccardo Patrese stood in, so Piquet duly became World Champion.

Significantly, the FW11B was the first Williams to run in a race with 'reactive' suspension, Piquet using it on his car to dominate the Italian Grand Prix. The Brazilian driver got on well with the system, but Mansell did not and therefore raced a conventional car everywhere except in Portugal.

Piquet left the team at the end of 1987, to be replaced by Patrese, and Williams also parted company from Honda, having to go over to normally aspirated Judd V8 engines for 1988. That year the team struggled with the FW12, unable to compete on equal terms with the Honda-powered McLaren MP4/4, which won all but one round of the championship in the hands of Ayrton Senna and Alain Prost.

The FW12 was designed from the outset to

LEFT In a taste of what was to come in 1992, Nelson Piquet dominated the 1987 Italian Grand Prix at Monza in the 'reactive' suspension FW11B. *(John Townsend)*

ABOVE Nigel Mansell took a well-earned second place in the 1988 British Grand Prix at Silverstone in an FW12 which, remarkably, had been converted overnight to passive suspension.
(John Townsend)

run with the reactive suspension system used on the Honda-powered FW11B and the car also featured Williams's first transverse gearbox. However, the reactive system sapped power from the Judd engine and the car's outright pace was compromised, while various other difficulties resulted in inconsistent handling. At Silverstone for the British Grand Prix, following problems in Friday practice, Mansell refused to use the reactive suspension any more and the system was abandoned. Overnight, Williams's engineers improvised a conventional suspension set-up (see pages 44–45) and on race day, in treacherous conditions, Mansell brought the car home in second place, his first finish of the year. Later, at the Spanish Grand Prix, he added another second place, his only other finish of the year. Patrese's best result was fourth place at the final round in Australia.

Owing to chicken pox, Mansell missed the Belgian and Italian Grands Prix. He was replaced by Martin Brundle at Spa and by Jean-Louis Schlesser at Monza, where Schlesser famously clashed with race leader Ayrton Senna and effectively prevented McLaren from taking a clean sweep of race victories in 1988. At the end of the year Mansell left Williams for Ferrari.

In an attempt to control ever-increasing power outputs and reduce costs, turbocharged engines were outlawed from F1 at the end of 1988. Williams was able to agree an exclusive engine-supply contract with Renault, and during 1988 developed the FW12B as a test-bed for the new V10 engine. The team started the 1989 season with the FW12C, an updated version of the FW12B, and used it until the new FW13 appeared at the Portuguese Grand Prix in September.

Belgian driver Thierry Boutsen was recruited to partner Patrese. Boutsen took two wins, both in wet conditions, in Canada (where Patrese backed him up for a 1–2 for Williams) and in Australia, ending up fifth in the drivers' championship. Patrese was third in the drivers' championship, thanks to more points-scoring finishes, his season bringing four second places and two thirds. Williams finished second in the constructors' championship, behind dominant McLaren.

Although there were teething troubles with the Renault engine installation, the new Williams-Renault partnership got off to a solid start, especially with both drivers taking podium finishes in each of the final two rounds of 1989. In another significant development for the future, testing of the team's active suspension system intensified, with Englishman Mark Blundell carrying out the bulk of the driving duties using a Renault-powered FW12 test hack.

The Patrese/Boutsen partnership continued for 1990. The FW13B was ready for the first race, the US Grand Prix in Phoenix, and

LEFT Thierry Boutsen on his way to victory in the FW12C at the 1989 Canadian Grand Prix – the first win for a Renault-powered Williams.
(Williams)

featured an all-new Renault V10 engine (the RS2) mounted lower in the chassis than its predecessor. During the season, Patrese and Boutsen scored a single win apiece – Patrese in San Marino and Boutsen at the Hungarian Grand Prix – with only two other podium positions, both for Boutsen, who was third in the US Grand Prix and second at Silverstone. The team concluded that neither driver, on the strength of their 1990 performances, had the 'extra something' required to return Williams to the top step of the podium on a regular basis, and there were changes afoot.

For 1991, the team ran the Adrian Newey-designed FW14. Details of the development and race history of the FW14 and FW14B are provided in Chapters 2 and 3.

FW15C – a worthy successor to the FW14B

Into 1993 the Williams-Renault partnership continued for a fifth successive season. As explained in Chapter 2, it was originally intended that the FW14B's successor, the FW15, would be introduced during 1992, but its debut was postponed until 1993 owing to the continuing dominance of the FW14B. As several amendments to the FISA regulations were introduced for 1993 – narrower rear tyres, reduced track dimensions, raised front-wing endplates and a lower rear wing – with the intention of reducing cornering speeds, the FW15 had to be modified and became the FW15B for pre-season testing, while the race car for the start of the season was further refined and designated FW15C.

With the new driver line-up of triple World Champion Alain Prost and Damon Hill (promoted from his test-driving duties), the FW15C emulated the dominance of its predecessor. The car featured evolutions of the semi-automatic gearbox, traction control system and active suspension system used on the FW14B, and also featured anti-lock brakes.

Williams again dominated both World Championships, the FW15C taking ten race victories – seven for Prost and three for Hill – with Prost winning the drivers' championship and Williams taking a comfortable victory in the constructors' championship. In spite of the technological superiority of the FW15C, Ayrton Senna and McLaren mounted a strong challenge, Senna taking five victories – including a famous one in treacherous conditions at the European Grand Prix at Donington Park – to finish second in the drivers' championship ahead of Hill.

Subsequent Williams team history

After the successes of 1992 and 1993, the 1994 season proved to be one of the most difficult in Williams's history. FISA regulations were amended to outlaw 'driver aids' such as active suspension, traction control and ABS, and the new FW16 was effectively a passive-suspension evolution of the FW15C, although it was the first Williams to feature power steering. Ayrton Senna was recruited from McLaren as lead driver to partner Hill.

The FW16 proved tricky to master in the early part of the season, and Senna spun out from the first two races before tragically losing his life at Imola during the San Marino Grand Prix in May. This was a crushing blow to the team, but Damon rose admirably to the challenge of becoming lead driver, while the second car was shared by test driver David Coulthard and the returning Nigel Mansell in between his IndyCar commitments. In the first half of the season Hill took three second places, and a win in Spain, as the FW16 was steadily improved. Mansell drove in France but

ABOVE Damon Hill in the FW15C at the 1993 Monaco Grand Prix, where he finished second to Monaco master Ayrton Senna. *(John Townsend)*

ABOVE At his home race, the Brazilian Grand Prix at São Paulo, Ayrton Senna qualified the FW16 on pole in 1994, but spun out of the race when pushing hard to reel in eventual winner Michael Schumacher. *(John Townsend)*

BELOW Nigel Mansell returned for four races in 1994 as 'Red 2' aboard the FW16. He is seen here winning the final race of the season, at Adelaide in Australia – his last F1 victory. *(John Townsend)*

retired with transmission failure. The revised FW16B was introduced for the German Grand Prix in July and Hill went on to win with it in Belgium, Italy and Portugal, with second places in Hungary and at the European Grand Prix at Jerez. By the end of the season he was in a position to challenge Michael Schumacher (Benetton) for the drivers' title at the final round in Australia, where the constructors' championship would also be decided.

During the Australian race Schumacher ran wide, brushing the wall and allowing Hill to close on him. Controversially, as Hill took the inside line, Schumacher appeared to turn in aggressively, damaging the Benetton and retiring on the spot. Hill continued, only to retire a few laps later with a broken wishbone, handing the drivers' title to Schumacher by a single point. With the IndyCar season finished, Mansell returned to drive the second car for the final three races and won memorably in Australia to help Williams to the constructors' championship – a very welcome result after the early-season trauma.

For 1995, when the regulations introduced new safety measures as a result of the Imola tragedy and also stipulated a reduction in engine capacity to 3.0 litres, Hill and Coulthard continued with the new Renault-powered FW17, upgraded to FW17B specification later in the season. Hill took four wins and Coulthard achieved his first F1 victory, in Portugal, but despite these successes a series of retirements for both drivers prevented them from taking the challenge to defending champion Schumacher. The two Williams drivers were second and third in the drivers' championship, Hill ahead of Coulthard, while the team was second in the constructors' championship, behind Benetton.

Fresh from his 1995 IndyCar Championship victory, French-Canadian Jacques Villeneuve was recruited to replace Coulthard for 1996, driving alongside Hill. That year's FW18 proved to be the class of the field, Williams taking the constructors' championship after the drivers won all but four races between them. With eight

victories, Hill was crowned World Champion, and Villeneuve, with four wins, was runner-up, ahead of Schumacher.

Villeneuve continued with Williams for 1997, driving the FW19, but the team, controversially, elected not to retain the services of Hill, signing German Heinz-Harald Frentzen to replace him. Villeneuve fought a season-long battle with Schumacher (now driving for Ferrari) for the drivers' title, the contest going to the final round at Jerez in Spain. In a repeat of the 1994 championship finale, the outcome was again decided by an incident involving Schumacher, who blatantly turned his Ferrari into the side of the Williams as Villeneuve drew alongside to pass. Schumacher retired immediately, but Villeneuve raced on to finish third, taking sufficient points to become World Champion. Villeneuve's tally of wins for the season was seven, while Frentzen, who was third in the drivers' championship, took a single victory in San Marino. Williams successfully defended the constructors' championship despite a strong challenge from Ferrari.

The driver pairing for 1998 remained unchanged, but Williams had to use a Mecachrome V10 engine – a 'rebadged' derivative of the 1997 Renault power unit – in the new FW20, Renault having withdrawn from F1 as an official 'works' engine supplier at the end of 1997. In a winless season, the team managed only three third places – two for Villeneuve and one for Frentzen – on the way to finishing third in the constructors' championship.

The 1999 season brought two new faces, Ralf Schumacher and Alex Zanardi, to drive the FW21, which again used rebadged Renault engines, now carrying the 'Supertec' moniker. Despite lifting the CART championship in 1997 and 1998, Zanardi struggled to adapt to the driving style required on newly introduced grooved tyres and had a poor season, but the younger Schumacher brother ran consistently towards the front of the field, taking second place at the Italian Grand Prix, and two thirds. The team finished fifth in the constructors' championship.

Williams secured an exclusive five-year BMW engine deal for 2000 and recruited F1 rookie Jenson Button to replace Zanardi. Schumacher took three third places in the FW22, with Button scoring points in six races to help the team to third place in the constructors' championship.

ABOVE Damon Hill on his way to securing the 1996 Drivers' World Championship in the FW18 at Suzuka in Japan. *(John Townsend)*

BELOW Alex Zanardi, in the Supertec-powered FW21, leads Giancarlo Fisichella at Imola during the San Marino Grand Prix. *(Williams)*

23
THE WILLIAMS STORY

ABOVE The 2003 FW25 took Juan Pablo Montoya to the first Monaco victory for Williams since Keke Rosberg's win 20 years earlier. *(Williams)*

For 2001, Colombian Juan Pablo Montoya replaced Button and the BMW V10-powered FW23 took the team back to the front of the field, with a total of four wins – three for Schumacher and one for Montoya – along with a further five podium finishes. However, the BMW engine proved to be fragile and the FW23 suffered 18 retirements, but the team repeated its previous year's third place in the constructors' championship, behind Ferrari and McLaren.

The driver line-up remained unchanged for 2002, and the new FW24 emulated its predecessor, both cars running consistently at the front of the field and allowing Williams to take the fight to the dominant Ferraris. Ralf Schumacher won in Malaysia and finished second in Brazil, and regular podium positions, including four second places for Montoya, helped to secure second place in the constructors' championship.

Williams's consistent form continued in 2003 with the FW25 and the team took four wins – two each for Schumacher and Montoya – plus four pole positions and four fastest laps, resulting in second place in the constructors' championship, behind Ferrari, for the second successive year. Montoya took a stunning win in Monaco, Williams's first victory in the principality for two decades. Spaniard Marc Gené deputised for Schumacher at Monza, after Ralf had a hefty testing accident there.

For the 2004 season, Williams fielded the distinctive 'walrus-nosed' FW26 for the unchanged pairing of Schumacher and Montoya. The car proved very quick in pre-season testing, but was tricky to set up over a race weekend, leading to a redesign of the nose, with a more conventional solution appearing from the Hungarian Grand Prix in August. To add to the team's woes, Schumacher suffered a heavy accident at the US Grand Prix at Indianapolis that put him out of action until the Chinese Grand Prix, Gené and Brazilian Antonio Pizzonia standing in for him. In an inconsistent season, Schumacher took pole in Canada and finished second in Japan, while Montoya, who was second in Malaysia and third in San Marino, finished the season on a high, winning the final round in

RIGHT Ralf Schumacher in the 'walrus-nosed' FW26 on his way to seventh place in the 2004 San Marino Grand Prix. *(John Townsend)*

Brazil to take the team to fourth place in the constructors' championship.

The FW27, introduced for 2005, was the last Williams powered by BMW, and the team had two new men – Australian Mark Webber and German Nick Heidfeld – to drive it. Results again proved inconsistent, with the highlights a double-podium finish in Monaco – second for Heidfeld and third for Webber – plus pole position and second for Heidfeld at the European Grand Prix (held at Nürburgring), and third for Heidfeld in Malaysia. Heidfeld was replaced by Pizzonia for the final five races after suffering an injury in a mountain-bike accident. The team finished fifth in the constructors' championship.

Williams teamed up with Cosworth as engine supplier for the 2006 FW28, with rookie Nico Rosberg replacing Heidfeld. Poor reliability and tricky handling compromised the car's performance, and the best results were two sixth places for Webber. In a low-key season, the team finished eighth in the constructors' championship.

The 2007 season was the first year of a new engine partnership with Toyota, and Austrian Alex Wurz was recruited to drive alongside Rosberg, with Webber departing for Red Bull Racing. It was another challenging year for the team, but frequent points finishes for Rosberg, and a single podium – for Wurz in Canada – secured fourth place in the constructors' championship. Following Wurz's announcement of his retirement from F1 after the Chinese Grand Prix, the penultimate round, test driver Kazuki Nakajima took his seat for the final race, in Brazil.

The Toyota-powered FW30 for 2008 was an evolution of its predecessor, and Nakajima continued alongside Rosberg. At the opening race, in Australia, third place for Rosberg and sixth for Nakajima lifted the team's hopes, but thereafter the only visit to the podium was an unexpected second place for Rosberg in Singapore, where Nico was able to challenge winner Fernando Alonso, whose victory came in controversial circumstances following the deployment of a safety car precipitated by his team-mate Nelson Piquet Jnr crashing out. Williams finished eighth in the constructors' championship.

Rosberg and Nakajima continued with Toyota power in 2009 and Rosberg scored points consistently with the FW31 throughout the season. Nakajima, however, failed to score, and the team finished eighth in the constructors' championship.

A return to Cosworth power for 2010, and new drivers in the shape of Brazilian Rubens Barrichello and German Nico Hülkenberg, failed to help the team challenge for podium positions. Hülkenberg took pole position with the FW32 in damp conditions at the penultimate round in Brazil, but the best race result was a fourth place for Barrichello at the European Grand Prix in Valencia, taking the team to sixth

BELOW Nico Rosberg in the Toyota-powered FW30 during the 2008 Singapore Grand Prix. Rosberg finished second in a controversial race won by Fernando Alonso in the Renault.
(John Townsend)

ABOVE The Williams mechanics tend to Nico Hülkenberg's FW32 in the pole-position slot on the grid for the 2010 Brazilian Grand Prix. *(John Townsend)*

place in the constructors' championship.

Williams had a South American driver pairing for 2011 when Venezuelan Pastor Maldonado lined up alongside Barrichello. The underpowered Cosworth-engined FW33 suffered poor reliability, and ninth places in Monaco and Canada for Barrichello, and ninth place in the constructors' championship, was scant reward for the unrelenting effort of all in the team. 2011 also saw the team race a car with a KERS (Kinetic Energy Recovery System) for the first time. The origins of the Williams KERS dated back to 1996, when the team worked with Newcastle University on a project to develop a flywheel-based system. Soon afterwards, the FIA revised the regulations to restrict the amount of energy which could be stored outside of the fuel, bringing the original project to an end. For 2009, the regulations were opened up to allow KERS, although Williams did not run the system during 2009, and none of the teams used it in 2010. When KERS was installed on the FW33 in 2011, once again Williams had developed all the system components (motor, inverter, battery pack and control system) in-house – the only team to do so.

For 2012, the Williams-Renault partnership was revived, and Barrichello was replaced by fellow Brazilian Bruno Senna, driving alongside Maldonado. Although the FW34 proved little more competitive than the FW33, Maldonado raised the team's spirits considerably by taking pole position for the Spanish Grand Prix, converting his grid slot into a well-deserved victory in the race – the team's first win since 2004. The Spanish victory, the team's only podium finish, was a major highlight in an otherwise difficult season that saw Williams finish eighth in the constructors' championship.

The team continued with Renault power for 2013, when Finnish test driver Valtteri Bottas was promoted to race alongside Maldonado in the FW35. It proved to be another frustrating season, as the car lacked pace, scoring points in only two races, with the best result an eighth place for Bottas in the US Grand Prix, resulting in ninth place in the constructors' championship.

RIGHT Pastor Maldonado celebrates on the top step of the podium having won the 2012 Spanish Grand Prix. *(John Townsend)*

LEFT The team celebrates finishing second and third at the 2014 Abu Dhabi Grand Prix, taking Williams to third place in the constructors' championship. Frank Williams was unable to travel to the race, hence the team sent him good wishes by spelling out "P3 4 Frank" on the celebratory pit board. *(Williams)*

The F1 rules underwent major changes for 2014 with the introduction of 1.6-litre V6 turbocharged engines and Energy Recovery Systems (ERS). Williams inked a deal to use Mercedes engines in the FW36, and with Martini signed as new title sponsors, the cars featured striking new livery. Experienced Brazilian Felipe Massa was recruited to drive alongside Bottas, and the car set the pace in pre-season testing. With a new management structure and technical team, the FW36 proved to be highly competitive, transforming the team's fortunes with nine podium finishes, including second place for Massa in Abu Dhabi (where Bottas joined him on the podium in third) and two second places for Bottas (at the British and German Grands Prix). The team finished a well-deserved third in the constructors' championship.

Continuity throughout the team from 2014 to 2015 saw Williams continue to challenge at the front end of the grid, the Mercedes-powered FW37 performing strongly to take four podiums – two third places for Bottas and two for Massa. The team successfully defended its third place in the constructors' championship, behind the dominant Mercedes and a resurgent Ferrari, Bottas and Massa finishing fifth and sixth respectively in the drivers' championship.

LEFT Valtteri Bottas on his way to third place in the 2015 Mexican Grand Prix in the Mercedes-powered FW37, helping Williams to take third place in the constructors' championship. *(Williams)*

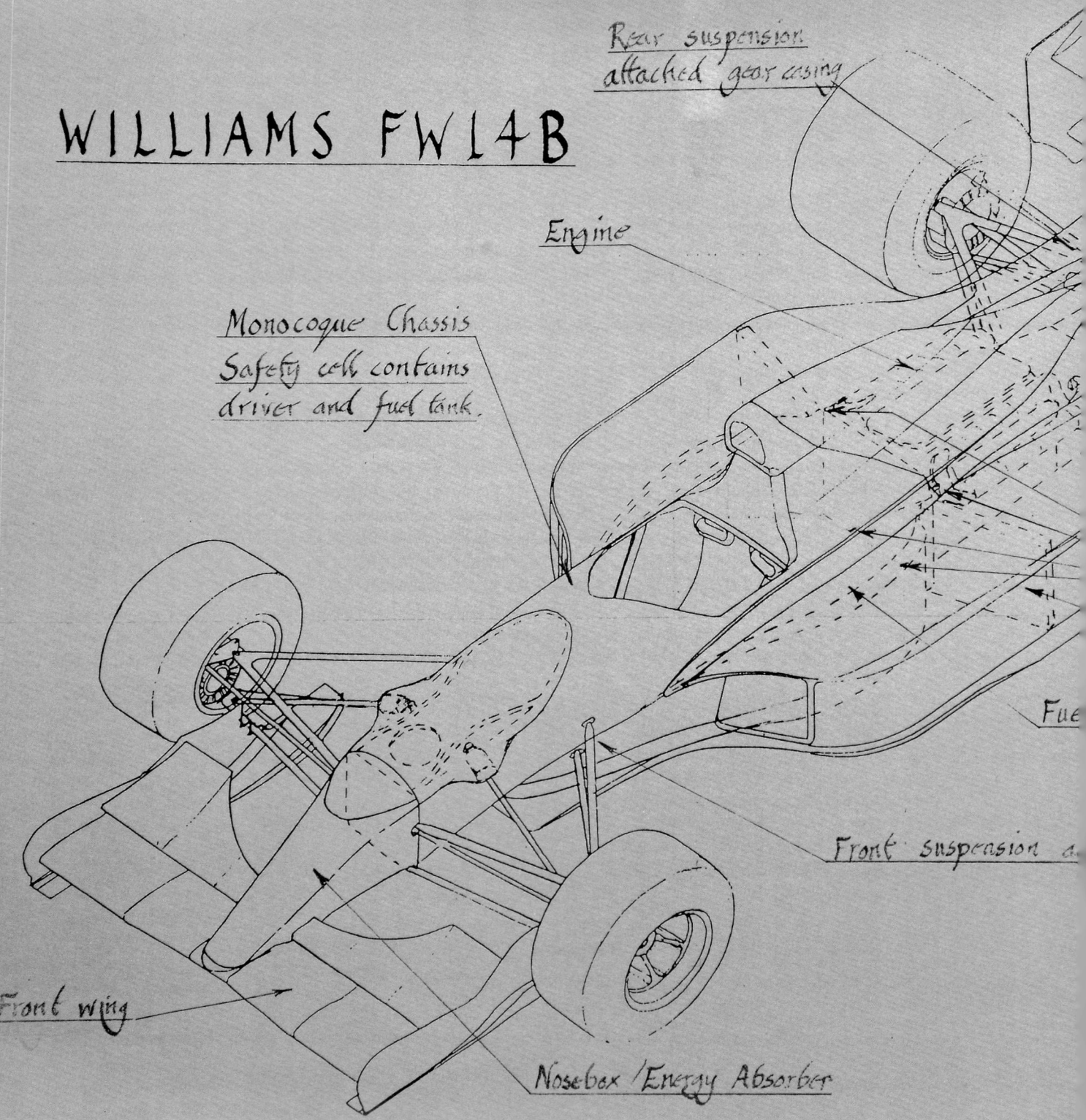

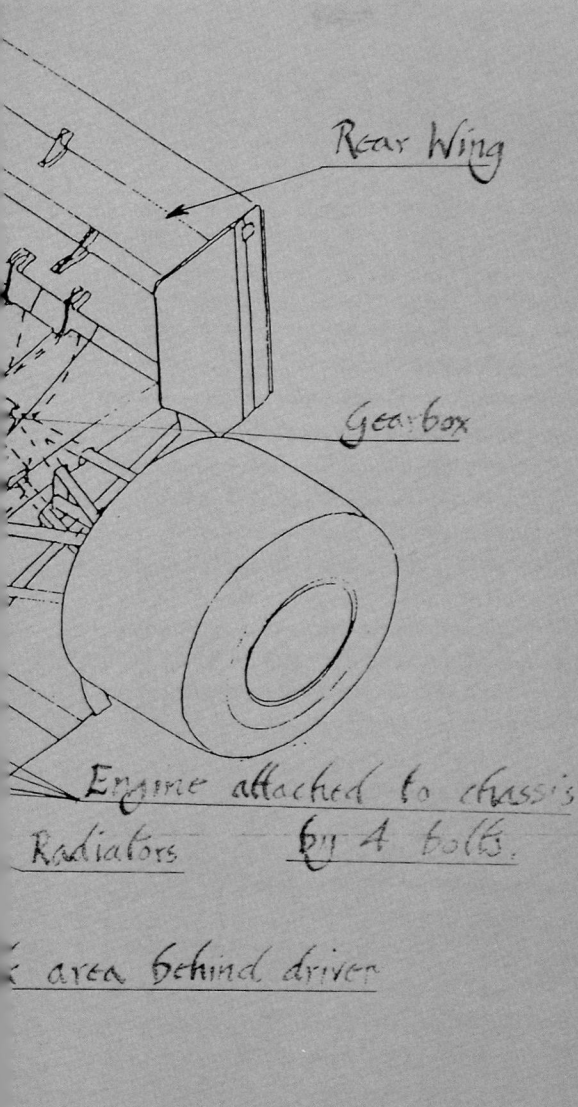

Chapter Two

Design and development of the Williams FW14B

In the eyes of many commentators, the defining feature of the FW14B was its active suspension system, although in reality this was just one element of the package that gave the car the edge over its rivals, the other factors being its Renault engine, semi-automatic gearbox, fuel, tyres, aerodynamics, traction control and, of course, two talented drivers. The FW14B's active suspension system was the culmination of several years' work by the engineering team at Williams, going back to 1984, while the car itself was essentially an adaptation of the 1991 FW14, modified to run with active suspension.

OPPOSITE A basic layout diagram for the FW14B, drawn by Williams's Head of Composites, Brian O'Rourke, in October 1991. *(Williams Heritage Archive/John Colley)*

The FW14 and the 1991 season

Although Williams won races during the first two years of its agreement with engine partner Renault, 1989 and 1990, there was a feeling at the time that the combination had yet to reach its full potential. It became apparent that the team needed to bolster its efforts for 1991 by acquiring a potential World Championship-winning driver, reviewing its management structure, and strengthening its engineering resources.

The first step in this plan to challenge for the World Championship was the recruitment of Adrian Newey in mid-1990. Newey had already forged a reputation as a highly successful designer, with a CV that included championship-winning IMSA GTP cars in 1983 and 1984, followed by championship-winning IndyCar and CART designs (which also won two successive Indianapolis 500 races) in 1985 and 1986. After a brief spell with the Newman-Haas CART team, Newey returned to March, where he had previously worked during 1981 as race engineer in the European F2 championship.

Newey's first F1 car, the 1988 March 881, punched well above its weight and troubled the front-running teams on occasion, despite the team's relatively modest budget. The March 881's successors, the CG891 and the Leyton House CG901, continued to impress, notably with their aerodynamics, and the CG901 in particular won many admirers with its aesthetically pleasing lines. When his relationship with the March team deteriorated, Newey left midway through 1990 and was rapidly hired by Williams to work on its challenger for the 1991 season.

Patrick Head and Newey worked together on the design of the FW14. Head provided an overall guiding hand, while Newey's role as chief designer meant that he took charge of the car's overall mechanical design and its aerodynamic packaging. Head personally handled the design of an ambitious transverse semi-automatic gearbox, which was mated to a significantly revised Renault V10 engine, the RS3, and featured an electro-hydraulic gearchange similar to the system introduced by John Barnard, Ferrari's chief designer, on the 1989 Ferrari 640.

After driving for Williams from 1985 to 1988,

BELOW Before moving to Williams, Adrian Newey had masterminded the design of the Leyton House CG901, which shared broad visual similarities with the FW14. Mauricio Gugelmin is seen here in the car at the 1990 Belgian Grand Prix. *(LAT Photographic)*

Nigel Mansell signed for Ferrari for two seasons from the beginning of 1989, becoming the first driver to win an F1 race in a car with a semi-automatic gearbox – on his Ferrari race debut at the 1989 Brazilian Grand Prix – in spite of a near-disastrous pre-season testing programme, plagued by unreliability. Unreliability problems continued to characterise Mansell's time at Ferrari, and as political issues within the team came to a head at the 1990 British Grand Prix, *Il Leone*, as he had become affectionately known among the Italian *tifosi*, felt that he had been outmanoeuvred by team-mate Alain Prost and announced that he would retire from F1 at the end of the season.

Frank Williams was keen to bring Mansell back to his team. He had come to admire the gritty Brit's 'all or nothing' driving approach during his previous spell at the team and so he set out to reverse Mansell's decision to retire. Williams was also eager to retain its existing driver, Riccardo Patrese, who had been with the team for three seasons, having joined as Mansell's team-mate, and was fiercely loyal. Mansell, however, was initially reluctant to sign, and Frank faced a challenge in trying to tempt him out of retirement. The British driver was insistent that certain terms be met if he were to rejoin the team, including undisputed number-one status.

At first, it appeared that it would be difficult for Williams to agree to all the requirements of various parties, including specific commitments of support from Renault and Elf, both of which would be vital partners in Williams's quest for World Championship glory. Long-time Williams commercial director Sheridan Thynne, who had known Frank since the early 1960s and had joined the team in an official capacity in 1979, played an important role in negotiations with sponsors and partners to bring Mansell back to the team, and to the surprise of some doubters a deal was signed on 1 October 1990. Mansell would return to drive the new FW14 for 1991, with Patrese as his team-mate.

Mansell reacquainted himself with a Williams car during a test at Paul Ricard with an FW13B at the end of 1990. After a couple of laps, he returned to the pits to suggest various suspension changes, after which he went back out and significantly improved his lap times over

LEFT Adrian Newey pictured at the Japanese Grand Prix in 1992. *(Sutton Motorsport Images)*

LEFT Sheridan Thynne talks to Nigel Mansell during a quiet moment in the pit garage in 1992. Thynne played a major part in bringing Mansell back to Williams for 1991. *(John Townsend)*

ABOVE Nigel Mansell during his first post-Ferrari test for Williams, driving an FW13B at Paul Ricard in late 1990. Note the 'all-white' engine cover and upper nose, and the 'Camel' decal in front of the cockpit. *(LAT Photographic)*

those previously set at the circuit in the FW13B – a very positive start for the renewed Williams/Mansell alliance.

Among the personnel changes at Williams was the appointment of Peter Windsor as team manager. Windsor had previously worked at the team as manager of sponsorship and public affairs, before leaving for a spell at Ferrari.

The FW14 was unveiled to the world's press at a wet and windy Silverstone South Circuit on 21 February 1991 – a little over two weeks before the start of the grand prix season – with Mansell behind the wheel. Newey's influence on the FW14 had led to the adoption of the distinctive 'high-nose' concept, as used successfully on the Leyton House CG901, and there was no disputing the fact that the FW14 was one of the most attractive designs on the grid in 1991.

As Mansell drove his first few cautious laps at the Northamptonshire circuit, initial impressions were favourable, although the returning British hero found the characteristics of the semi-automatic gearbox significantly different from the Ferrari system that he had experienced for the previous two seasons, and a harmless off-track excursion into a pool of mud curtailed his first tentative laps. At the end

RIGHT Nigel Mansell gives the FW14 its debut at a test and press launch at Silverstone on 21 February 1991. *(John Townsend)*

LEFT **Riccardo Patrese in the FW14 battles with Ayrton Senna at the wet start of the 1991 San Marino Grand Prix.** *(Williams)*

of the test, the car had run with no significant problems and showed much promise, although in the damp conditions, and running on full-wet tyres, it had been impossible to explore its performance potential.

The team had less time than it would have liked to test and develop the FW14 prior to the US Grand Prix at Phoenix, Arizona on 10 March 1991, but at the end of qualifying at the season opener the FW14s were third and fourth on the grid – Patrese ahead of Mansell – behind Ayrton Senna's McLaren and Alain Prost's Ferrari. In the early part of the race, Mansell ran third, with Patrese in close pursuit. Unfortunately, Mansell retired after 25 laps with gearbox failure, when still lying third. Some 15 laps later a similar fate befell Patrese, who was running second behind Senna, although Patrese's retirement was somewhat more dramatic, as he spun and stopped sideways across the circuit after an unexpected downchange from the semi-automatic gearbox. The Benetton of Roberto Moreno made contact with Patrese's car, but fortunately neither driver was injured, and the FW14 emerged relatively unscathed.

Battle recommenced two weeks later in Brazil, where the FW14s moved a little further up the grid, Patrese lining up second behind home-town hero Senna, with Mansell third. Mansell passed Patrese at the start, but after 50 laps chasing Senna, gearbox gremlins once again intervened and Mansell's car spun to a halt in a cloud of tyre smoke. The Englishman's retirement promoted Patrese to second, and the Italian took up the chase, Senna now suffering from his own gearbox problems. At the end of the race, Patrese was just two seconds behind Senna, who won his home grand prix for the first time.

Reliability problems continued for Williams in San Marino, Mansell retiring on the first lap after gearbox issues resulted in him getting hit by Martin Brundle's Brabham, while Patrese retired from the lead with a misfire, leaving Senna to take his third victory.

Monaco saw another retirement for Patrese, this time due to Stefano Modena's Tyrrell (a remarkable second on the grid, behind Senna) blowing its engine in the tunnel, depositing oil that caused Patrese to crash out. Mansell finished his first race of the season in a worthy second place, after a combative pass on Prost's Ferrari. For the fourth race in succession, Senna was the victor.

As the F1 teams reached Montréal for the Canadian Grand Prix, the FW14 showed its full potential, Patrese taking pole, ahead of his team-mate. Mansell led the race until he allowed the engine revs to drop on the final lap, which precipitated an engine stall, due to a known trait whereby the alternator could not put out sufficient power to maintain the engine-management system baseline voltage at low engine revs. The Englishman was classified

ABOVE The FW14s of Mansell and Patrese lead away at the start of the 1991 Canadian Grand Prix. *(Williams)*

BELOW Williams was the class of the field at the 1991 Mexican Grand Prix, Patrese eventually winning, ahead of Mansell. *(Williams)*

sixth. Patrese finished third, despite further gearbox maladies.

In Mexico, the two Williams again qualified 1–2, Patrese ahead of Mansell, and the order was maintained in the race, Patrese taking the first win for the FW14 while second-placed Mansell set the fastest lap.

At the French Grand Prix at Magny-Cours, Patrese made it a hat-trick of pole positions as he lined up ahead of Prost and Senna, Mansell starting fourth. However, Patrese made a poor start, dropping to tenth, but pressed hard to recover to an eventual fifth place at the finish. Meanwhile, Mansell fought a race-long battle with Prost, passing the Frenchman with 18 laps to go and pulling away to take his first victory of the season.

The next round was the home race for both Williams and Mansell, at Silverstone, and the crowd's undisputed favourite delighted his loyal fans by taking a comfortable pole position and dominating the race to take victory. He famously stopped his car on the slowing-down lap to pick up his closest challenger, Senna, who had run out of fuel on the final lap when lying second, dropping to fourth in the final classification. Patrese retired at the start after his FW14 was hit by Gerhard Berger's McLaren.

Mansell continued his winning ways in Germany, taking another dominant win ahead of team-mate Patrese for another Williams 1–2. This three-race winning streak also made Mansell the first British driver to take a hat-trick of victories since Jackie Stewart won the same three events – in France, Britain and Germany – 20 years previously. At the halfway point of the season, the drivers' championship had developed into a two-way fight between Senna

ABOVE Nigel Mansell crosses the line to win the 1991 French Grand Prix – his first win of the season. *(Williams)*

BELOW An iconic image – winner Nigel Mansell gives Ayrton Senna a lift on his FW14 after the Brazilian ran out of fuel on the final lap of the 1991 British Grand Prix. *(Williams)*

ABOVE The sparks fly from Riccardo Patrese's FW14 at the 1991 Portuguese Grand Prix. *(Williams)*

BELOW Mansell, in the FW14, battles wheel-to-wheel with Ayrton Senna for almost the entire length of the straight in Barcelona, before passing the Brazilian into Turn 1 – a battle that would enter the annals of F1 folklore. *(Williams)*

the Hungaroring, Mansell ahead of Patrese, who let 'Red 5' pass in order to give his team leader a chance to attack Senna. Mansell retired with electrical failure in Belgium, where Patrese finished fifth after more gearbox woes.

Mansell took another win at Monza for the Italian Grand Prix, passing Senna for the lead after 34 of 51 laps. Patrese was again on the receiving end of gearbox trouble, retiring from the lead at half-distance after passing Berger, Mansell and Senna in impressive style.

The Portuguese Grand Prix saw Patrese win from pole position, although early in the race he let his team-mate through to lead in order to help Mansell's championship challenge. Unfortunately for the Englishman, after pulling away to establish a comfortable lead, he was black-flagged 20 laps from the finish. His pit crew had accidentally released him from his pitstop with a loose wheel, and after Mansell was left stranded in the pitlane, the crew went to the car to fit a replacement wheel, breaking safety regulations in the process.

At the following round in Spain, Mansell won again after an eventful and exciting race in changing conditions, with Patrese third and Senna fifth. Now 16 points behind

and Mansell, with Senna on 51 points, thanks to his run of four straight victories in the first four races, and Mansell on 43, while Patrese was third with 24.

Senna won again in Hungary and Belgium. The two Williams cars were second and third at

championship leader Senna, Mansell had a chance of the title with two races to go, but, bearing in mind the impressive form of Senna and McLaren, it was a mountain to climb.

The penultimate round of the championship, in Japan, saw Mansell qualify third, with Patrese fifth. Crucially, the McLarens qualified on the front row of the grid, Berger ahead of Senna. As the race got underway, Berger led from Senna, who allowed his team-mate to pull away while he concentrated on holding up Mansell, who needed to win the race to keep his slim championship hopes alive. Mansell chased Senna relentlessly, but a mistake on lap 10 resulted in him spinning into retirement – which confirmed Senna as World Champion. Earlier in the race, McLaren had asked Berger to allow Senna through to lead, thus protecting his championship position, on the condition that the two would swap positions back again on the final lap if they were still running 1–2. Senna kept his word, allowing Berger through to win.

The two McLarens again qualified on the front row for the final race in Australia, ahead of the two Williams, Senna taking pole from Berger, Mansell and Patrese. At the start of the race, in torrential rain, Senna led away from Berger and Mansell, Patrese dropping to sixth. The difficult conditions worsened, resulting in a number of incidents, Mansell becoming a victim when he spun off into a wall on lap seven while lying second. As more drivers spun out, including Patrese, a decision was taken to stop the race, and the result was counted back two laps, with Senna winning from Mansell, Berger, Piquet and Patrese. Half points were awarded for the shortened race.

And so, at the end of the season, Mansell finished second in the Drivers' World Championship, with Williams runner-up to McLaren in the Constructors' World Championship. The FW14 had proved to be an impressive challenger, and had it not been for the early-season gearbox problems Williams very likely would have pushed Senna and the fast, reliable McLaren MP4/6 much harder for the drivers' and constructors' championships.

Efforts now were concentrated on the 1992 championship challenge.

BELOW Nigel Mansell tackles the treacherous conditions at the season-closing 1991 Australian Grand Prix at Adelaide – the final race for the FW14. *(Sutton Motorsport Images)*

The Williams active suspension story

A major contributor to the success of the FW14B was its active suspension system. Although the FW14B was the first Williams to use active suspension from its debut race, the system had been under development for several years, and the first Williams to race with an active system was the 1987 FW11B.

THE DEBUT OF THE FW14B – ALMOST

An active suspension-equipped FW14 – chassis FW14/06, soon to be redesignated as FW14B/06 – was taken to the Australian Grand Prix in 1991, although Paddy Lowe recalls: "We never were going to race it, as it was just an exercise to see what problems it might throw up by putting it into a race-weekend environment."

Chris Dietrich, now Lead Engineer – Car Systems, Sensors and Wiring at Williams, takes up the story: "We did take the FW14B to Adelaide in '91. I'd gone out to Adelaide because for the last few races we'd introduced a new VCM [Vehicle Control and Monitor module], which was used to control the gearbox and also the active ride. We were just basically looking after it for the last few races. Paddy [Lowe] was coming out, so it was then decided that as we had some people out there, let's send the active car out, as it would be a good opportunity to run it and see how it performed. It ran in Friday pre-practice, went really well, and Nigel [Mansell] was keen to run it. But because the constructors' championship was still possible, mathematically, Renault didn't want to take the risk, so it didn't do the race."

In the event, Mansell was second in Adelaide, in the passive FW14, with Patrese fifth, which resulted in Williams finishing second to McLaren in the constructors' championship.

BELOW Paddy Lowe (left) and Simon Wells (right, sitting on front tyre) with the active-suspension-equipped FW14/06 in the pitlane at Adelaide during the 1991 Australian Grand Prix weekend. *(Paddy Lowe)*

As the active suspension system is such an integral part of the FW14B story, the following pages provide an overview of the history and development of the system used to such good effect during 1992. The system was further refined for use on the 1993 FW15C, before active suspension was outlawed from the beginning of the 1994 season.

The theory

In the early 1990s, the dominant factor affecting the performance of an F1 car was aerodynamics, as remains generally the case today. An F1 car is aerodynamically very sensitive to its attitude and ride height. With a conventional mechanical suspension system, using springs, dampers and anti-roll bars, the car's attitude and ride height is directly related to the load on the suspension, and that load comprises both mechanical and aerodynamic components. As the car travels faster, the aerodynamic load increases, and the ride height of the car reduces as the suspension compresses. In the 1990s (and more recently in 2015 with the introduction of titanium skidplates), cars could often be seen creating spectacular showers of sparks on high-speed straights, when the car was at its fastest and the ride height at its lowest.

Ideally, it is advantageous to run a car with low ride height all the time, but with a conventional (passive) suspension system a compromise has to be made. The suspension has to be very stiff to enable it to carry increased load at high speed, but the downside of this is that the car can be nervous over bumps, due to the reduced suspension compliance. In order to provide a driveable set-up, a car's ride height is likely to be higher than ideal, at both low and high speeds.

The aim of the Williams active suspension system was to provide a consistent ride height at both low and high speeds, which in turn provided a stable aerodynamic platform, helping to optimise downforce throughout a lap. The active system achieved this by effectively separating the load-bearing ability of the suspension from its movement.

The movement of the suspension was controlled by four hydraulic actuators (struts), one at each corner of the car, fitted at the tops of the pushrods. The load-bearing ability of the

LEFT Note the flat angle of the FW14B, with no perceptible roll, thanks to the active suspension doing its job, as Riccardo Patrese turns left through the chicane at the 1992 Mexican Grand Prix. *(John Townsend)*

suspension was provided by mechanical spring packs – originally gas springs, but later in the development process a change was made to disc-spring packs – with the bump and rebound damping provided by adjustable hydraulic valves. Whereas the pushrod (or pullrod) at each corner of a car with conventional suspension was mechanically linked to the damper and spring, on the Williams active system each pushrod was hydraulically linked to the remotely mounted damper valve and spring pack. As the load on a pushrod increased, the hydraulic fluid pressure in the relevant actuator was increased, pushing fluid through the damper valve and compressing the remotely mounted spring, which resisted the load, just as in a conventional suspension system. In effect, the hydraulic fluid was providing a coupling between the pushrods and the springs. Using a pump and a system of valves, hydraulic fluid was transferred around the system in order to control the ride height at each corner of the car. By providing a hydraulic link between the opposite corners of the car (front left/rear right, and front right/rear left), an anti-roll function, with fixed balance (determined by the hydraulic actuator piston ratios), was built in. Significantly, because the suspension's warp stiffness was effectively decoupled from its other modes, the car had zero warp stiffness, which gave the car very strong traction, particularly on uneven surfaces such as kerbing or banked corners.

By using an electronic control unit (integral with the Vehicle Control and Monitor module – see page 117) to control the valves that regulated the flow of hydraulic fluid around the system, the movement of the suspension, and hence the ride height, could be very precisely controlled.

To adjust the balance of a car with conventional (passive) suspension, various suspension adjustments can be made, but on an F1 car, once a base set-up has been found, generally the preferred method for fine adjustments is aerodynamic – ie, adjustment of the front and rear wing settings. On the FW14B, active suspension enabled adjustment of the balance of the car to change the oversteer/understeer characteristics by altering the angle of attack of the aerodynamic platform – the rake of the car. This was achieved by making adjustments to the front and rear target ride height, which was done continuously by the electronic control system constantly applying corrections. Inevitably, the control system resulted in a small amount of lag in the corrections being implemented, so to counteract this lag Williams developed a 'feed-forward' system, which had a partly predictive function and also responded to inputs received from lateral and longitudinal accelerometers mounted on the floor of the cockpit (see page 95).

The Williams system is often referred to as 'reactive' or 'semi-active', as it retained a spring/damper system, unlike the Lotus-developed 'active' suspension that did away with springs and dampers to provide a fully active system.

Origins

In the early 1980s, Automotive Products (AP) developed a hydraulic 'active' suspension system with the aim of marketing the system to manufacturers for use on road cars. The system was demonstrated on a test-hack Ford Granada.

AP's concept was relatively crude, and relied on a hydraulic system in which the four corners of the car were interconnected, with a hydraulic actuator at each corner (double-acting at the rear and single-acting at the front), three control valves (two at the front and one

ACTIVE OR REACTIVE SUSPENSION?

The nomenclature of the Williams active suspension system has an interesting history...

Originally, Williams intended to refer to the system as 'active ride', but Lotus took exception to this, having already used the term for its 'active' suspension system. So, initially, Williams referred to its system as 'reactive', and in early testing the FW14 featured a decal proclaiming 'Williams Reactive Suspension'.

Brian O'Rourke, now Chief Composites Engineer at Williams, remembers: "I seem to recall that Lotus got a bit sad about us calling our system 'active' ride because theirs – which went back several years and was very clever, albeit heavy – was completely active. Ours wasn't, since it used a compressible spring, but with a hydraulic actuator. I don't know whether this fed into it or not, but I remember, about that time, showing some RAF people round the factory, and the subject got on to fly-by-wire aircraft systems, which are fully active. I mentioned the way our suspension worked to them and they said that it was, then, really a 're-active' system. When I heard Patrick Head talk about the problem with the naming of our installation, I threw in the suggestion of 'reactive ride' instead. I don't know whether that had any effect, but some while later our 'Reactive' badges appeared."

In 1992, the FW14B carried 'Williams Active Suspension' decals on the monocoque sides, between the front wishbones. In an *Autosport* interview with Giorgio Piola in 1992, Patrick Head explained: "Reactive is not a term with a proper meaning and I wanted to go back to using the word 'active'. Lotus has the term 'active ride', so we say 'Williams active suspension'."

And talking about the decal, Head went on to remark: "We are not trying to sell it [the active suspension system], but we do it all in-house, together with the control system, the control strategy and the computer – everything. I like to have a little sticker on the car because it is good for the guys in the factory to see that they have done it all themselves."

BELOW During the 1992 season, the FW14Bs sported this 'Williams Active Suspension' decal. *(John Colley)*

at the rear, mechanically connected to the suspension arms), a hydraulic fluid pump, a reservoir and an accumulator, and three gas spring/damper units (two at the front and one at the rear). The hydraulic system was controlled entirely mechanically, with no electronic control, and the scope of the system was limited to controlling the ride height of the car, rather than optimising ride quality and tyre load. Partly due to its limitations, AP decided not to develop the system further for use in road cars.

However, AP was already working with Williams as a supplier of brake and clutch components for its F1 cars, and asked the team in early 1984 if the active ride system might be of interest. At this time, F1 cars were running with extremely stiff suspension, originally due to the use of ground-effect aerodynamics, but even after ground-effect cars were banned (from the start of the 1983 season) the use of extremely stiff springs continued in order to handle the high aerodynamic loads and to provide the optimum aerodynamic platform by minimising changes in ride height. AP felt that the use of its system might allow a softer – and therefore more compliant – set-up, which would help to improve grip, particularly on a bumpy track surface, without compromising ride-height control.

Williams decided to begin a development programme to assess the potential of AP's system, under the guiding hand of Frank Dernie, who had joined Williams towards the end of 1978 to assist Patrick Head with aerodynamic development, playing a part in the success of the FW07. Dernie later became Head of Research and Development, leaving the team in 1988 to become Technical Director at Lotus, later returning to Williams in a consultancy role for the period 2003–07. Speaking about the ride-quality compromise in an interview with Keith Howard for *Motor Sport* magazine in December 2001, Dernie commented: "I didn't give a damn about ride quality. The driver was paid to deal with bumps, all I wanted to do was make the car quicker."

The team modified an FW09 chassis to use for the active-suspension development programme and this test 'mule' ran for the first time at Abingdon airfield during 1985. The driver was Tony Trimmer, who entered six F1 races between 1975 and 1978, and won the British

RIGHT An FW11 active-suspension test car during a test session at Abingdon airfield in late 1986. Note the simple front wing, with no endplates. *(Dave Lang)*

Aurora F1 Championship in 1978. Simon Wells, now Williams Operations Director, recalls the occasion: "Tony only ran it up and down in a straight line, then Patrick [Head] had a go, and then Frank Dernie had a go. The hydraulics were really crude – it was just a test to see whether or not it was going to work."

The FW09 test mule ran in its first proper circuit test at Silverstone in late 1985, in the hands of Nelson Piquet. Williams Chief Composites Engineer Brian O'Rourke recalls that in the debrief after the test Piquet commented: "It rides like a Cadillac, but handles like one too!" Unfortunately, this first test was cut short when a turbo failure caused a major fire at the rear of the car.

This very first test car was fitted with an entirely mechanical control system, with the control valves operated by the suspension arms. Despite the limited mileage completed at the test, it became apparent that the team would need to develop an electronic control system to maximise the potential of the active suspension.

At this early stage, the active system was clearly insufficiently developed to consider using it on a race car. Although the team had no intention of racing an active car during 1986, a year that saw both Williams drivers, Mansell and Piquet, challenge for the championship with the FW11, development continued behind the scenes with both FW10 and FW11 test cars.

Significant work was carried out on the electronic control system, which was originally supplied by US company Motion Technology, owned and run by Kurt Borman. To provide a control function, Borman adapted what was effectively the first electronic data-logging system to be fitted to an F1 car, and in developed form this control system was used on all the active-suspension development and race cars up to and including the 1988 Judd-engined FW12. In a 1992 interview with Gordon Kirby in *Autosport*, Borman explained: "In 1986 we decided that some simple modifications to the more-or-less proven electronics of the data logger, along with

BELOW An interesting comparison, showing the evolution of the active suspension system components and their layout on the FW11 between 1986 (top) and 1987 (bottom). *(Williams Heritage Archive)*

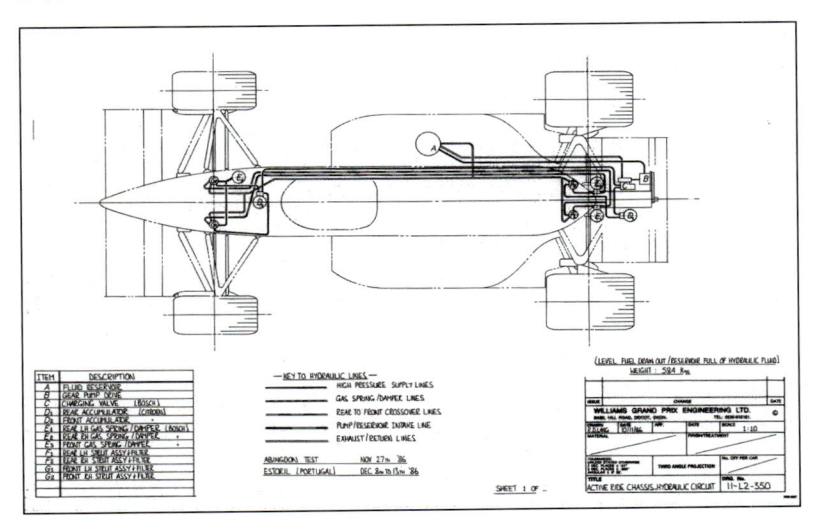

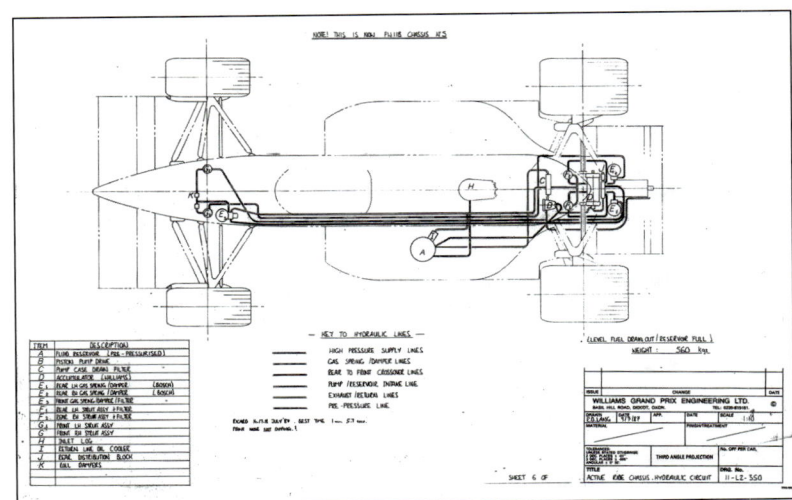

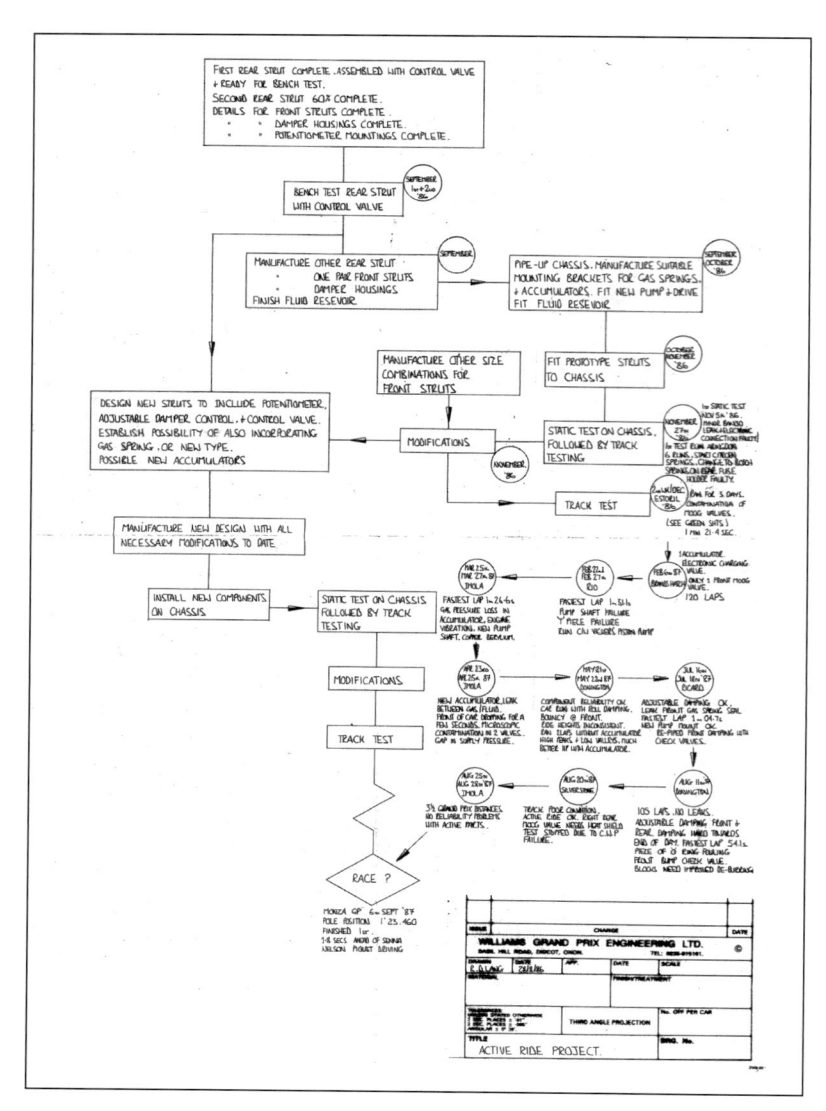

ABOVE An interesting document originally prepared by Dave Lang in August 1986, showing the initial active-suspension programme development plan for late 1986 to 1987, and subsequently annotated (circles and notes) with the progress achieved up until the system was first raced at Monza in September 1987. *(Williams Heritage Archive)*

some new software, would allow it to function as a crude but viable interim electronic controller for the suspension. Obviously, being able to make changes in software would greatly speed up the development process. I never thought we'd race it so soon, but it all went along better than expected."

During pre-season testing of the new FW11B in Brazil in early 1987, an active car was tested alongside a car with conventional suspension. It became clear that the active system offered advantages. Interestingly, Piquet carried out all the test driving, as Mansell's faith in active suspension had been shaken by less-than-favourable experiences during his time at Lotus, where on several occasions the system had let him down, as explained in the panel on page 46.

Development of the active FW11B continued, and Piquet gave the car its race debut at Monza in September 1987, where it proved significantly faster than Mansell's sister car with conventional suspension. Piquet took pole position and victory ahead of the active-suspension Lotus 99T of Ayrton Senna, who spun out of the lead while pushing hard on worn tyres (he ran the race on a single set), but recovered to finish second. Mansell was third.

Originally, it was intended that the active FW11B's appearance at Monza would be a one-off, but Piquet used it for the next two races, in Portugal and Spain, finishing third and fourth respectively. Mansell also qualified an active car in Portugal but had to retire it from the race. At the final round in Australia, Piquet tried an active car in the practice sessions and race-day warm-up, but raced a passive car. A small development team travelled to the races with the active cars, as the regular race engineers were not familiar with the active system.

Before the introduction of active suspension, the FW11B had already dominated the 1987 season, with six wins – two for Piquet and four for Mansell – prior to the success of the active car at Monza. Piquet became World Champion, ahead of Mansell, by dint of fewer retirements, more podium finishes, and the fact that Mansell was forced to miss the last two races following a back injury sustained in a practice accident at the penultimate round in Japan.

For 1988, Williams designed the FW12 to run with active suspension from the outset, but the season was dominated by McLaren-Honda, with the MP4/4s of Ayrton Senna and Alain Prost famously winning all but one race. Ironically, at Monza, Senna was leading when he came to lap Frenchman Jean-Louis Schlesser, who was standing in for the injured Mansell in the FW12, the Brazilian clashing with the Williams and denying McLaren a perfect score. This left the two Ferraris to take a historic 1–2, with Gerhard Berger winning from Michele Alboreto on hallowed home ground.

Talking about the developments made to the active suspension system between the FW11B and FW12, Williams Design Engineer Dave Lang recalls: "When we first ran the FW11B, we were using a gear-type pump for the active ride. By the time we went to the FW12, we'd introduced the variable swash-

PADDY, WE'VE GOT A LEAK!

Williams engineers Dave Lang and Chris Dietrich both recall that, during the 1989 active-suspension test programme, Paddy Lowe was paranoid about hydraulic leaks. A cunning plan was hatched to exploit Lowe's fears during a test at the Pembrey circuit, in South Wales, on 23 August 1989. Dave Lang (DL) and Chris Dietrich (CD) take up the story.

DL: "We used to enjoy going to Pembrey, and because we were in Wales, we thought, well, why don't we have a leek in the cockpit?"

CD: "Because Paddy was paranoid about hydraulic leaks, and there'd been one whenever Patrick was around…"

DL: "Every time Patrick turned up, something would happen. If something was going to go wrong, it would go wrong the moment he drove up to the circuit!"

CD: "A couple of weeks before, he'd gone down to P&T [Williams Prototype and Testing workshop], and I think Ian Anderson, who was in charge of the prototype and test area, was playing around with the hydraulics, and Patrick said: 'Turn it on, I want to see something happen', and he did. There was a pipe that hadn't sealed properly, and it sprayed out red fluid everywhere. Patrick had a white shirt on – it was really obvious! So Paddy was sensitive to problems with hoses…"

DL: "We went to a greengrocer and bought a nice leek, and told Mark Blundell what we were going to do. JC [John Cadd – No.1 Mechanic on the test team] buried it down under his feet, and the plan was to do one or two laps and then for him suddenly to come on the radio and say: 'I'm going to have to come in, I'm going to have to come in, I've got a leak – it's all over my feet, it's all over my feet.' Paddy went all sort of red, and panicked. So Mark drove in, and then JC took the inspection hatch off and reached down and said: 'Oh yeah, it's really wet down here – oh, maybe this is the problem!' and then he pulled the leek out."

CD: "We only did the one lap, and Paddy was a bit suspicious."

DL: "Afterwards we stuck the leek in the airbox and took another picture."

CD: "It was a very small group of people going to these tests, only around half-a-dozen people, so it was all a bit laid back. It was serious, but you had to keep the mood a bit light with all the late nights."

ABOVE The moment when John Cadd pulled a leek from the footwell of the FW12 at the Pembrey test in August 1989. Paddy Lowe, sitting on the car's tyre, bows his head in disbelief!
(Dave Lang)

LEFT An extract from the team's 'Green Sheet' used to record details of the Pembrey test in August 1989. Note the entry for lap 31 – 'LeEk in footwell'!
(Williams Heritage Archive)

DESIGN AND DEVELOPMENT OF THE WILLIAMS FW14B

plate pump from Vickers (see page 91). We'd gone from taking an off-the-shelf gear pump and trying to control that, to taking an aircraft-spec hydraulic pump and putting it into an application that it had never actually been designed for. The other main thing was learning the penalties for not keeping the fluid clean all the time, which is when we developed the off-car flushing pack ['washing machine'], having moved the Moog valves remote from the struts, into a control-valve assembly. We were flying by the seat of our pants when we were doing it, because we were taking bits and pieces off the shelf from standard suppliers, like pipe fittings, and all of a sudden putting 3,000psi through them, and fitting them on a race car with massive accelerations and decelerations on the engine, and also all these vibrations that were coming because we were changing the fuel spec. It would cause havoc in a certain rpm range, with resonant frequencies that we hadn't seen before. So we were developing all our hardware around what we were learning all the time."

RIGHT An engineering drawing by Dave Lang for the original front active suspension strut fitted to the FW12 up until the end of Friday qualifying at the 1988 British Grand Prix. *(Dave Lang/Williams Heritage Archive)*

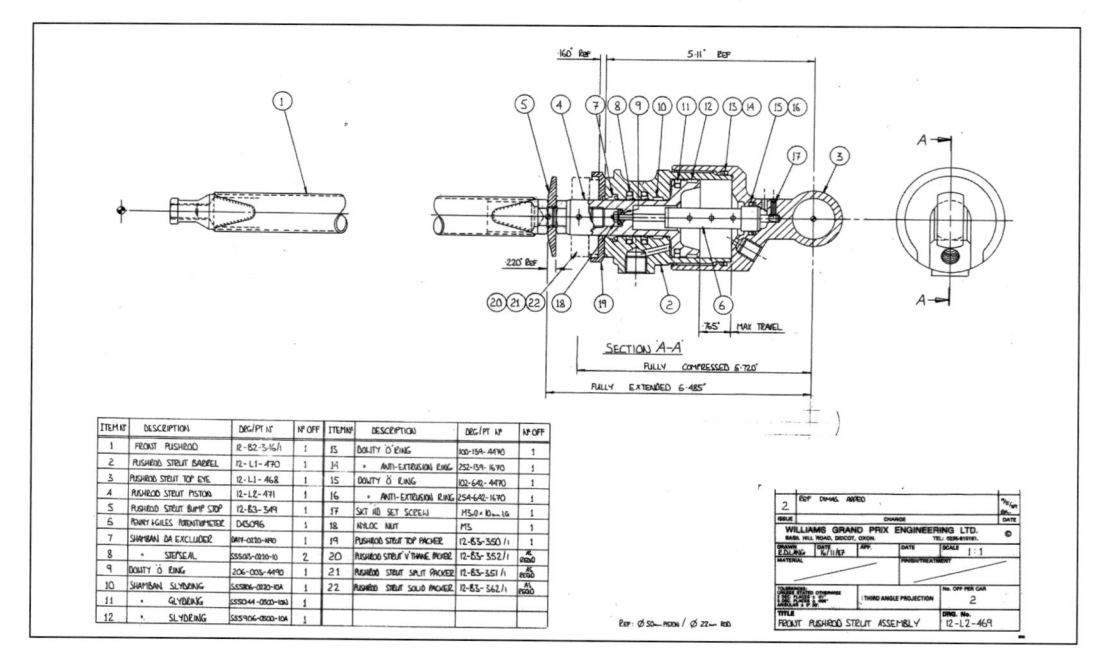

RIGHT The engineering drawing originated by Dave Lang for the passive front suspension strut assembly designed overnight after practice for the 1988 British Grand Prix. *(Dave Lang/Williams Heritage Archive)*

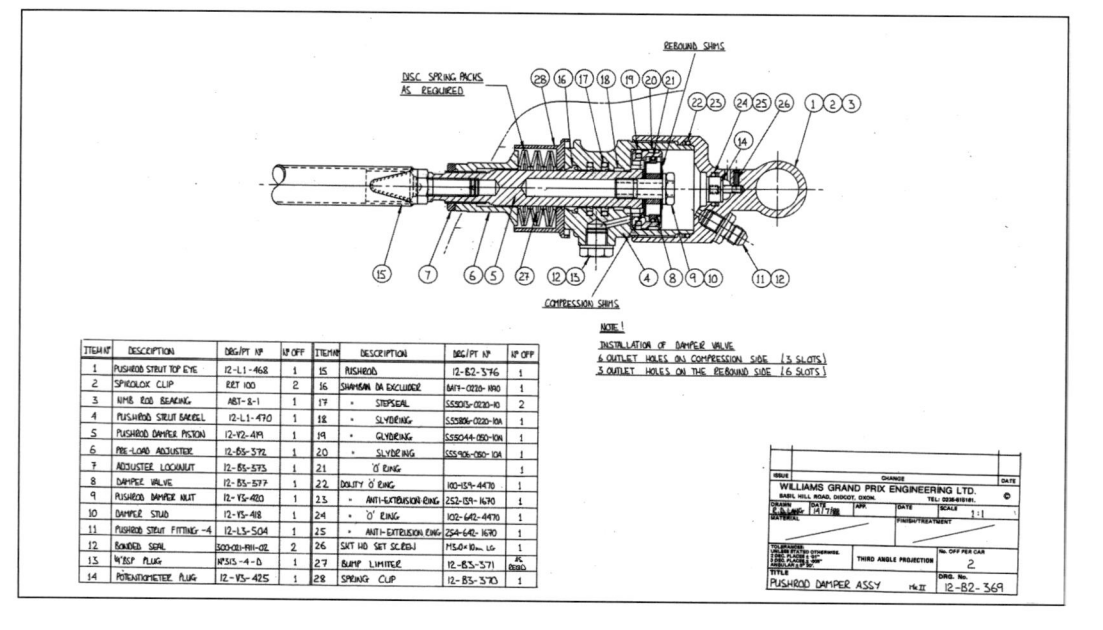

As the team's relationship with Honda had come to an end, the FW12 used a Judd 3.5-litre V10 engine during 1988. The car proved problematic in the first half of the season, the main difficulties being handling instability caused by the active suspension system, lack of pace due to the hydraulic system sapping engine power, and inadequate engine-oil cooling. The problems came to a head at the British Grand Prix at Silverstone, where Mansell encountered handling problems during Friday's track running, and insisted that the team convert the cars to use conventional suspension if he were to take any further part in the weekend.

The team rose to the challenge, and overnight a group of engineers, including Dave Lang, designed and built a completely new passive suspension system – an astonishing achievement! Essentially the active strut housing was used to accommodate a damper, and an in-line disc-spring pack was fitted. This was a massive compromise, as no anti-roll coupling was available with the hastily engineered arrangement, but the solution solved the immediate problem in time for the following day. The hard work paid off as Mansell finished second to Senna in the wet race, and set fastest lap.

The hastily improvised passive-suspension solution was used for the next few races, until the front suspension components and monocoque were reworked to include pull-rods, bellcranks and a conventional coil spring/damper arrangement mounted further rearward than the temporary components introduced at Silverstone. Dave Lang's recollections of the engineering challenges during that Silverstone weekend are presented on pages 136–138.

The team elected not to use active suspension during the 1989 season, on the FW12C and FW13, although active testing

LEFT A cartoon drawn in 1989 by Enrique Scalabroni (who worked on the design team at Williams from 1985 to 1989) after the team's Chief Mechanic at the time said that pigs would fly if they ever got the active system working! *(Dave Lang)*

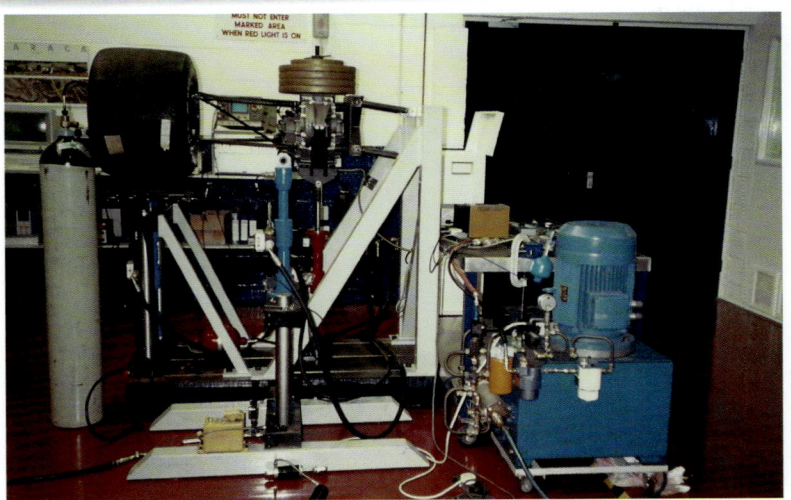

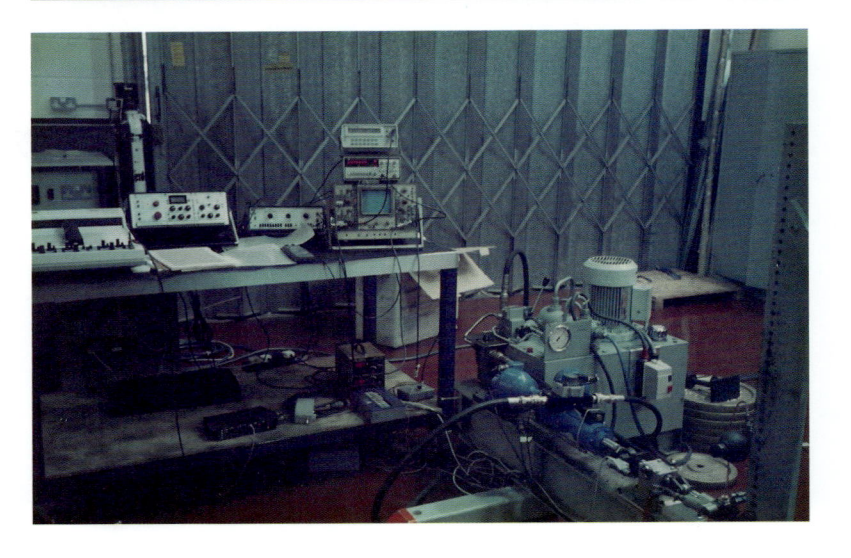

CENTRE A view of a quarter-car rig – comprising a gearbox and rear left-hand suspension assembly – developed by Simon Wells to test active-suspension components between 1989 and 1992. *(Simon Wells)*

RIGHT Early active-suspension hydraulic-system components under test on another rig developed by Simon Wells. *(Simon Wells)*

LOTUS, MANSELL AND EARLIER F1 ACTIVE-SUSPENSION EXPERIMENTS

Williams was not the first F1 team to experiment with active suspension. In 1980, Team Lotus discovered a problem with the handling of its Lotus 80. Developed at the height of the ground-effect era, this car produced so much downforce that the engineers struggled to harness its potential. The whole car had been designed with the goal of optimising ground effect, in order to produce sufficient downforce to dispense with front and rear wings. The engineers achieved this with spectacular success, but a serious flaw was discovered during testing and the early part of the 1979 season.

This problem occurred as the car pitched and rolled under braking, acceleration, cornering and over bumps. Even a small fluctuation in ride height caused a significant loss of downforce, which would then be regained just as suddenly. Additionally, the car's centre of pressure – a key aerodynamic set-up parameter – was moving as the car pitched and rolled. The sum of these effects was to cause the car to 'porpoise' violently, particularly through corners, which was alarming for the drivers and also negated any lap-time gains made when the car was handling properly.

After experimenting unsuccessfully with even stiffer suspension (the suspension used on ground-effect cars was already very nearly solid!), and the use of various front and rear wing designs, Lotus aerodynamicist Peter Wright realised that an alternative solution was required. Wright enlisted the help of the Cranfield Institute of Technology, and Professor David Williams, who had been developing a 'synthetic-spring' system to provide feedback to the pilot in a control system designed for use in an experimental 'fly-by-wire' aircraft.

The engineers realised that in order to solve the Lotus 80's handling problems, it would be necessary to control the car's ride height accurately and consistently, and it was possible that the synthetic-spring concept could be adapted to fulfil exactly those requirements. Initially, the plan to develop the active suspension system was set aside while development for 1981 proceeded on the revolutionary Lotus 88B, which potentially offered a mechanical solution to the ride-height-control problem, with its twin-chassis, dual suspension. When the 88B was outlawed before it had even raced, Lotus's focus shifted back to active suspension.

Lotus boss Colin Chapman could see the potential of the active system and pushed development with the aim of racing an active car in 1983. Developed using a road-going Lotus Esprit test hack, the active system first appeared on the Lotus 92 F1 car in December 1982 during an initial test at Snetterton. In an unfortunate coincidence of timing, Colin Chapman died from a heart attack that same day, a profound loss that understandably had a considerable impact on the momentum of the Lotus 92 active programme.

The Lotus 92 was raced with active suspension at the 1983 Brazilian and United States West (Long Beach) Grands Prix, Mansell finishing 12th on both occasions. However, there were teething problems with the active system, including several instances when the base of the car dropped to the ground with all four wheels in the air! In addition, the introduction of active suspension coincided with Lotus's new deal to run Renault turbo engines – in the adapted 92T – and Team Lotus's resources were in danger of becoming over-stretched. Mansell was among those who wanted to abandon active suspension and its development was once again shelved, the 92 running thereafter with conventional suspension.

Almost a decade later, Mansell took the active Williams-Renault FW14B to World Championship victory.

Lotus ran an active-suspension car again four years later, in 1987, when Ayrton Senna in the 99T took the first-ever victory for a car with active suspension, in the Monaco Grand Prix, following that with another victory a month later in the United States (Detroit) Grand Prix. Both were bumpy street circuits, where the advantages of active suspension came to the fore. That same year, Williams also debuted its active suspension system, on the FW11B.

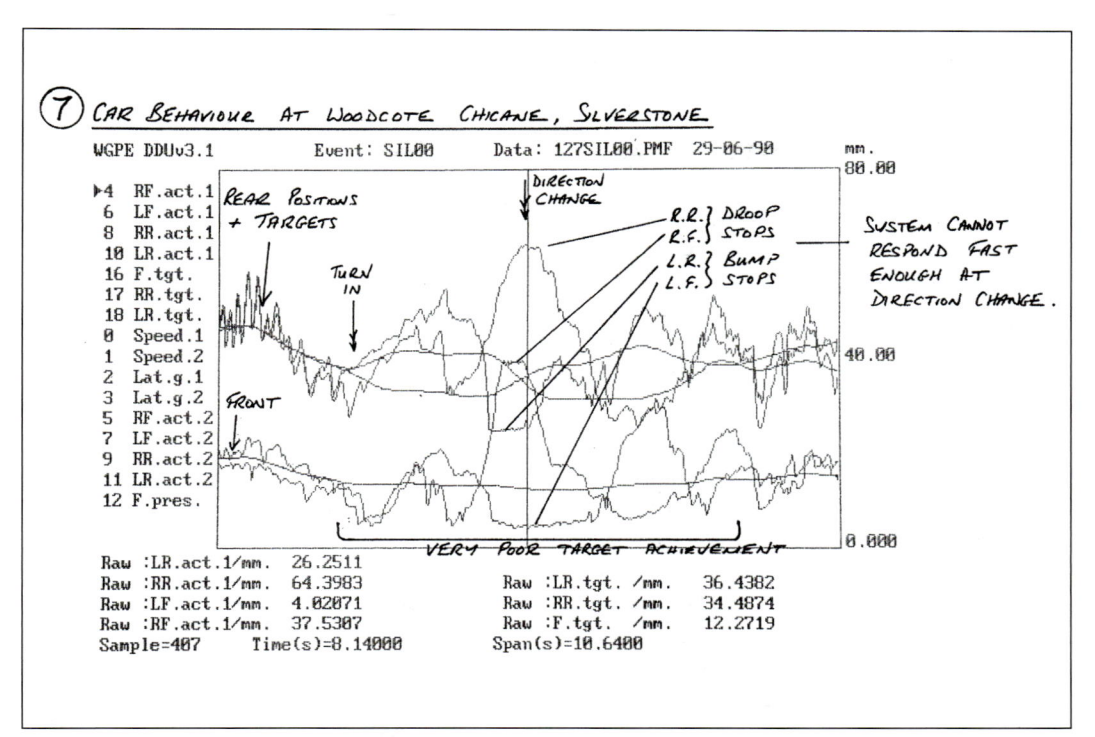

LEFT An annotated telemetry trace, from an active-suspension test with the FW12 at Silverstone in June 1990, shows that there was still much work to do, as the system failed to respond quickly enough to direction changes at the Woodcote Chicane (no longer used on today's Silverstone track configuration). *(Williams Heritage Archive/John Colley)*

continued during the year using an FW12 test car, with test driver Mark Blundell carrying out much of the development driving. At the end of the 1988 season, Frank Dernie left Williams for Lotus. Paddy Lowe – later to become Technical Director at McLaren and then Executive Director (Technical) at Mercedes-Benz – and Steve Wise, who had both been recruited by Williams towards the end of 1987, worked on further developing the electronic control system for the active ride. Meanwhile, Dave Lang worked on the design and development of the mechanical components, with Simon Wells carrying out R&D and component testing.

For 1990, a separate test programme was established to refine and develop the active system using an FW13 mule. Mark Blundell was retained as test driver, and in mid-1990 Adrian Newey joined the team, focusing on the development of the new FW14 to be raced during the 1991 season.

In a report from a two-day test session at Pembrey on 7–8 June 1990, using active-equipped chassis FW13/1, Paddy Lowe noted: "After the last test at Croix-en-Ternois three weeks ago, several modifications have been made to the car in the hydraulics to improve oil flow and reduce damping. Some different front struts were also manufactured to allow different car balance. With these modifications it was possible to achieve good set-up for the car, overcoming many of the traction and bump-absorption problems experienced at Croix."

Lowe went on to report: "A total of 141 laps were covered (94 on Thursday, 47 on Friday) in dry conditions, with intermittent light drizzle on Friday causing some delays. The car was totally reliable, apart from the loss of an experimental rear light lens! The best time set was 44.2s (Thursday) and 43.6s (Friday) on race tyres. This compares favourably with some previous best times of 44.7s (FW12A – Judd – Reactive – MB [Mark Blundell]) and 45.9s (FW12C – [Renault] RS01 – Passive – TB [Thierry Boutsen])."

The development of the FW14B – the car that nearly wasn't!

The key issue to be addressed for Williams over the winter of 1991/92 was reliability, and in particular gearbox reliability.

While the race team had been working with Mansell and Patrese to challenge for the 1991 championship with the FW14, the dedicated test team had been working independently throughout the season, carrying out development work on various systems with a view to racing them when their reliability and lap-time advantage had been proved. As well as active suspension, these systems included an anti-lock braking system and traction control. The engineering team working on these developments during 1991 included Dave Lang, Steve Wise, Simon Wells and Paddy Lowe.

Damon Hill was now employed as Williams's test driver, Mark Blundell, test driver during 1990, having secured a race seat with Brabham, although he was invited back to test with Williams again during the year. Hill was recommended by the Middlebridge F3000 team's John MacDonald, for whom he drove in 1990. Damon played a key role in the development of the active suspension system eventually adopted for the FW14B, and during the 1991 and 1992 seasons he completed extensive test mileage for Williams.

For the development programme, chassis FW14/06 was converted to active suspension in the early summer of 1991, followed by a second chassis, FW14/07, towards the end of the year. It was intended that these chassis would be used purely for development of the active system prior to potentially fitting it to the planned new car for the 1992 season – the FW15.

During this programme, Patrick Head worked on refining the semi-automatic transmission and improving its reliability, one initiative being the addition of an option for automatic (driver-initiated) sequential upchanges and downchanges, both of which were introduced during the 1992 season.

In an interview in *Motor Sport* magazine published in 2012, Head gave some insights into the development of the active system at this time: "Through 1991 the active ride car was developed, moving from gas springs, with associated high rising rates, to linear packs of disc springs with little or no rising rate. This cured the high-speed bouncing on the tyre sidewalls as the suspension was now sufficiently compliant at high load. Through the winter of '91–'92, we worked hard on reliability." The linear packs of disc springs that Head mentions are Belville spring packs, as used on the FW14B – see page 94.

The test programme during 1991 and 1992 was almost certainly the most intensive ever undertaken by an F1 team up to that point, much of it concentrating on the development of active suspension. During 1991, the two FW14 chassis used for active testing covered an estimated 4,000 miles (7,000km) between them. By the end of 1992, FW14/06 – a chassis that was never raced – had completed over 8,500 miles (14,000km) of test mileage. A conservative estimate suggests that during 1992 the six FW14B chassis covered a total of around 27,000 miles (44,000km), including testing and racing.

In a fax to Renault Sport's Bernard Dudot in April 1992, Patrick Head stated: "The FW14B has no right to its current reliability record, as, not having been designed for active suspension, it has a number of messy areas which require much attention – the 11,500kms of active testing miles over the winter is a large part of the reason."

Talking about a forthcoming Silverstone test, Head continued: "We have a number of small items to evaluate at this test, mainly concerned with the active suspension. We have developed some theories at the first three races which require testing on the circuit. I had initially thought that we should cover chassis testing with Nigel on Chassis 7 and the engine testing mainly with Damon on Chassis 10. If you wish to do this differently then we can change that. Because of Damon's large feet the car he drives has very different pedals and a different steering rack, so the changeover takes about 1 hour."

Interestingly, an FW14 equipped with active suspension was taken to Australia for the final race of the 1991 season, but was not raced.

After his confidence-shaking experiences at Lotus (see panel on page 46), Mansell had been reluctant to participate in the development of Williams's active suspension during 1987 and 1988, and remained hesitant in 1991 until it became obvious that the active car was setting impressive lap times in the hands of Hill.

Early in December 1991, the team ran a four-day test at Barcelona at which a final decision was to be made on whether or not to run active suspension for 1992. At this test, Mansell drove for the first two days, and the potential of the active system was obvious both to him and to the team. As a result, Williams took the decision to run with active cars from the start of the 1992 season.

As the winter progressed, for various reasons – not least the promise shown by the FW14 active test car – progress on the design of the new FW15 slowed, and a decision was taken to further develop the active FW14 as the race car with which to start the 1992 season. In late January/early February 1992, the two FW14 chassis used for active-suspension testing during 1991 were redesignated FW14B, and over the following weeks four additional new FW14B chassis were constructed, ready for the start of the season.

And so the FW14B was born, with the intention that it would be used as a stop-gap until the introduction of the FW15, the initial target for the debut of the new car being the Monaco Grand Prix. The main obvious visual distinguishing feature between the FW14 and FW14B is the fairings or 'ears' on each side of the car at the upper ends of the front pushrods, added to accommodate the active-suspension struts.

Thanks to the extensive test programme and the hard work of the development team, the performance of the active suspension looked extremely promising for the start of the racing season. The first race, the South African Grand Prix at Kyalami, provided justification for the team's faith in the system.

The FW14B, as it transpired, saw out the whole of the 1992 season, and the FW15 was never raced. After the FW14B proved to be the class of the field, winning the first five races, the pressure to push on with the FW15 was reduced. Although significant progress had been made with the FW15's development, the new car did not hit the track until mid-September 1992, at a three-day test at Silverstone in Hill's hands. Williams suspected that the introduction of a car that was likely to surpass the performance of the already-dominant FW14B might provoke FISA to implement regulation changes to rein in the performance of Williams's cars, and so a decision was made to delay the introduction of the FW15 until 1993.

With hindsight, it is difficult to believe that the car that dominated the 1992 season, taking Williams to the Constructors' World Championship and Nigel Mansell to the Drivers' World Championship, was never intended to be!

ABOVE At the Renault Sport headquarters at Viry-Châtillon, Bernard Dudot shows Nigel Mansell the new RS3C engine at the end of January 1992, as Sheridan Thynne looks on. *(Renault Sport/DPPI)*

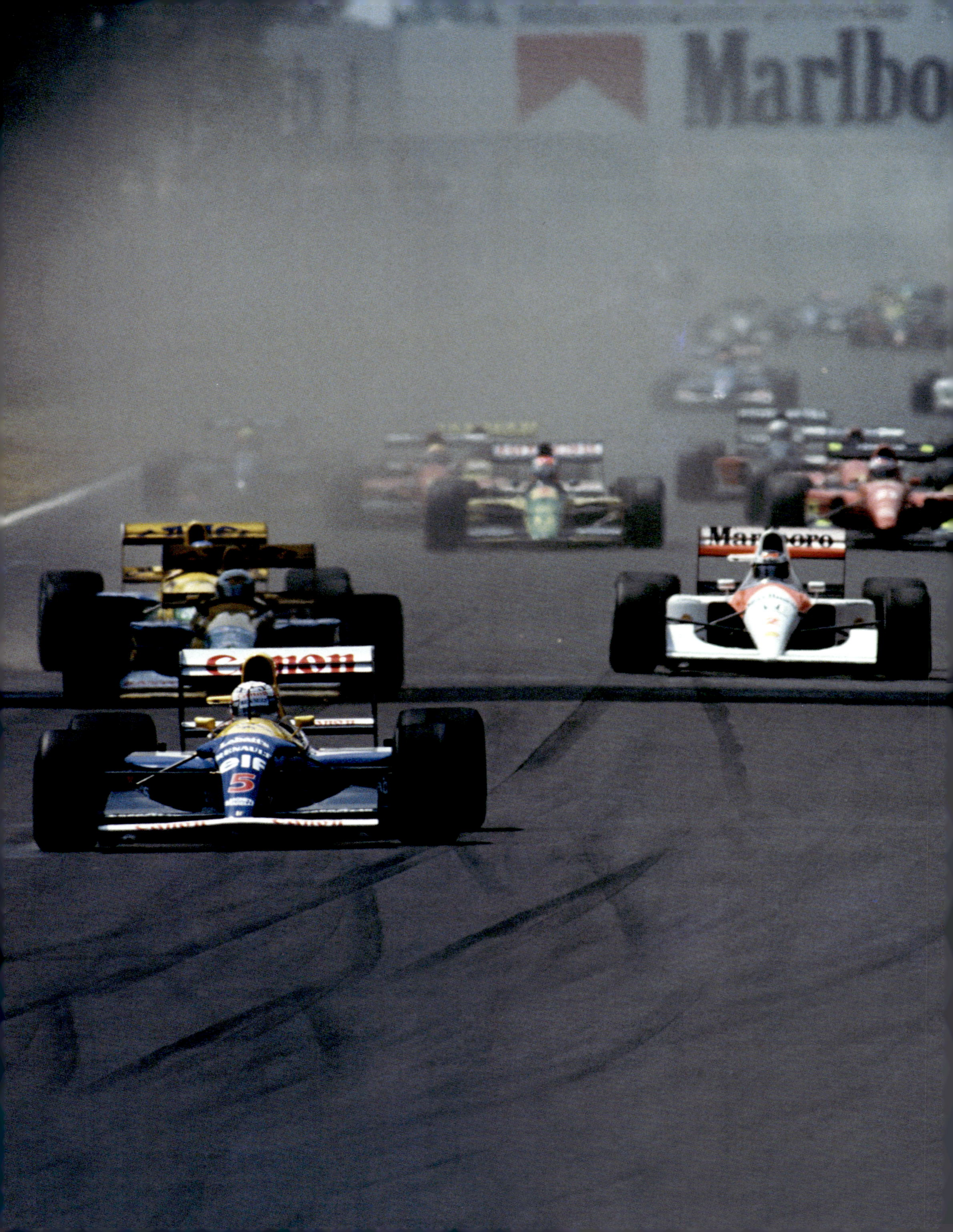
Marlbo
Canon
5

Chapter Three

The Williams FW14B in action

The FW14B opened its competition account with pole position, fastest lap and victory for Nigel Mansell at the first round of the 1992 World Championship in South Africa, with Riccardo Patrese finishing second to give the car a 1–2 on its debut. Mansell went on to win the first five races, with 1–2s for Williams at the first three rounds. At the end of the 16-race season, the record books credited the FW14B with ten wins, six 1–2 finishes, 15 pole positions and 11 fastest laps – a remarkable set of statistics.

OPPOSITE A common sight during the 1992 F1 season, as the two FW14Bs of Riccardo Patrese and Nigel Mansell lead away at the start of the Mexican Grand Prix. *(John Townsend)*

51

THE WILLIAMS FW14B IN ACTION

Pre-season testing

Williams held a four-day test at Barcelona early in December 1991 that determined whether or not the team ran active suspension for the 1992 season. There were two active cars and one passive car at the test. Nigel Mansell drove the active car for the first two days and Riccardo Patrese for the other two days. Damon Hill drove the passive car. The weather, along with a few technical hiccups, conspired to prevent the planned amount of running, but the team could see the potential of the active system and a decision was taken shortly after the test to race with it for 1992.

The first official run of what became the FW14B took place at an unprecedented seven-day test at Estoril at the end of February, where the team made a public announcement that the 1992 car would run with active suspension.

There was still a lot of work to do, especially to try to reduce the weight of the components, so the remaining winter test schedule was crucial. The good news was that the FW14B was effectively a refined FW14 fitted with active suspension, so, aside from the active system, all the car's other major components had already been raced and proved during 1991. The semi-automatic gearbox was carried over from the FW14, albeit with some revised components and an updated electronic control system. The Renault V10 engine was retained, again in updated form, with Renault moving from the RS3B specification used in the latter part of the 1991 season to the RS3C for the first race of 1992 (a further derivative, the RS4, arrived later in 1992).

Alongside the race programme, development continued relentlessly throughout the 1992 season. The test team continued to operate independently from the race team, with Hill, Mansell and Patrese sharing the driving duties during the year. At the races, meanwhile, Mansell had first call on a spare car, so two FW14Bs were effectively at his disposal for all rounds.

One significant change for 1992 was in tyre supply, for Pirelli withdrew from F1 at the end of 1991 to leave Goodyear as the sole supplier. Goodyear decided to stop making special qualifying tyres, so only race-spec tyres were available for qualifying from the start of 1992.

Whereas the FW14 had only run in a single test at Paul Ricard before the first race of the 1991 season, its successor went to the first round of the 1992 championship, in South Africa, with thousands of miles of testing and several grand prix distances under its belt, plus continuity in the driver line-up. Patrese was starting his 16th full season in F1 as the most experienced grand prix driver of all time, a record since surpassed by Michael Schumacher and Rubens Barrichello (the record holder at the time of writing).

The 1992 championship season

Ahead of the start of the season, Mansell was determined to give himself the best possible chance of championship victory, and to that end he set about making sure he was mentally and physically better prepared than ever before. He spent the winter at his new home in Florida, relaxing and working on his fitness. With a weight of 76kg, 2kg less than Patrese, at the beginning of the season, he was lighter than he had ever been in his F1 career.

Having suspected that the FW14B would have the edge over the competition, Mansell had come to the conclusion that his team-mate would be his main rival for the championship, and that any psychological advantage he could gain would aid his cause. In a 2002 interview in *Motor Sport* with Adam Cooper, Paul Fearnley

BELOW Patrick Head talks to Nigel Mansell during the first official run of the FW14B at a seven-day test at Estoril in February 1992. *(John Townsend)*

LEFT Damon Hill drove the FW14B extensively during testing, both pre-season and between championship rounds. He is seen here at Silverstone in April 1992. *(John Townsend)*

and David Malshar, looking back on the 1992 season, Adrian Newey recalled: "Nigel definitely outpsyched Riccardo, but I think he would have outdriven him in any case. The active car was suited to his style – aggressive, throw it in, have belief in it. You had to muscle it because it was generating so much downforce. In the high-speed corners, Nigel was much quicker; it didn't have power steering, which it should have done in hindsight, and Nigel has tremendous upper-body strength."

And so to the eagerly anticipated race debut of the car on which both Williams's and Mansell's championship hopes for 1992 rested – the FW14B.

Round 1 – South African Grand Prix, Kyalami

1 March 1992

For the first round in South Africa, two Thursday acclimatisation sessions were added to the programme to familiarise the drivers with the circuit, Kyalami having changed significantly since F1's previous visit in 1985. It was immediately clear that the FW14B gave Williams a significant advantage over its competitors. Mansell stamped his authority on proceedings right away and dominated every practice session.

There were early problems for Patrese, who found that his car was suffering from significant understeer, which he tried to solve, unsuccessfully, by adjusting the front wing to dial in additional front downforce. It transpired that the problem was due to the front ride height being too high, owing to a mechanic having misinterpreted the numerical codes used to set up the active system. Once the problem had been diagnosed, it was quickly solved, and the coding was changed to avoid future confusion.

At that time, qualifying comprised two one-hour sessions, the first held on the Friday, the second on the Saturday. A driver's overall fastest time, set in either session, determined his grid position. Mansell took pole by 0.741s over Ayrton Senna in his McLaren MP4/6B,

BELOW The tension is palpable as the Williams team watches the South African Grand Prix on a monitor in the pit garage. *(John Townsend)*

RIGHT A delighted Mansell celebrates victory at the South African Grand Prix, Patrese finishing second to provide a 1–2 for the FW14B on its debut. *(John Townsend)*

BELOW Mansell on his way to victory at the second round of the 1992 championship, in front of a packed crowd at the Autódromo Hermanos Rodríguez in Mexico City. *(John Townsend)*

with Gerhard Berger third in the second McLaren and Patrese fourth, 1.503s behind his team-mate – a substantial margin. That was a heavy first blow for Mansell in the intra-team psychological battle. Just to add to Mansell's impressive performance, he took pole in his spare car after spinning his race car during the final qualifying session.

There were a few minor electrical problems with the gearbox in Mansell's race car on Sunday morning. As the team could not identify the cause, a decision was taken to race the spare car, in which Mansell, continuing to assert his dominance, set fastest time in Sunday's warm-up session. Patrese felt that his FW14B was performing inconsistently during the warm-up, but the team was unable to identify any problem.

As the lights went out for the start of the race, Mansell made a slightly hesitant getaway, and the two McLarens were hot on his heels. Patrese made a stunning start, and carved his way through the McLarens to take second place behind his team-mate, while Mansell stormed away. 'Red 5' was 2.4s ahead of Patrese at the end of the first lap, 10s ahead by the end of lap 10.

Although Senna began to close the gap and pressure Patrese in the latter part of the race, it was obvious that the Williams was the quicker car, and that Senna would only be able to pass if Patrese had a problem. The two FW14Bs ran flawlessly, and finished a straightforward 1–2, Mansell 24.360s ahead of Patrese, and 34.675s ahead of third-placed Senna. Mansell also took fastest lap, two laps from the finish.

So far, so good!

Round 2 – Mexican Grand Prix, Mexico City (Autódromo Hermanos Rodríguez)
22 March 1992

The bumpy surface at the high-altitude and challenging Mexico City circuit proved to be a problem for many drivers during qualifying, not least Senna, who spun into the wall during Friday's qualifying session. It looked like a very nasty accident but fortunately the Brazilian escaped unscathed. Mansell started where he left off in South Africa by setting the fastest times in both the Friday morning practice session and in afternoon qualifying. Patrese was second in the morning, but third in qualifying behind a spectacular Michael Schumacher in the Benetton.

On Saturday morning, Patrese was fastest, ahead of Mansell, but the Englishman had a minor engine problem and the team decided to use his spare car for final qualifying. After losing time at the start of the session with more electrical gremlins, Mansell was unable to improve his qualifying time of Friday but nevertheless held on to pole, although Patrese, one of several drivers to improve, got within 0.016s. Schumacher and Brundle occupied the second row in the Benettons, with the McLarens on the third row, Berger ahead of Senna.

The two FW14Bs were again fastest in Sunday morning's warm-up session, but there was a brief scare for Mansell on the way to the grid as he encountered major oversteer, resulting in the team making changes to the car in its grid slot.

At the start, Mansell got away very rapidly, confirming after the race that he had used the car's traction-control system. Patrese followed his team-mate, and the two lead positions were set for the rest of the afternoon, Mansell again pulling away from Patrese to win by 12.971s. Schumacher finished third with Berger fourth, while Senna retired with transmission problems on lap 11.

It was another dominant performance for the FW14Bs.

Round 3 – Brazilian Grand Prix, São Paulo (Interlagos)
5 April 1992

At Interlagos, McLaren debuted its new car, the MP4/7A, hoping to be able to take the fight to Williams at Senna's home race, but to no avail. The FW14Bs were again the class of the field in the Friday morning session, and Mansell again dominated the afternoon qualifying session, his best lap a remarkable 1.888s quicker than Patrese's.

Mansell was unable to improve his time on Saturday, but Patrese managed to go quicker and reduce the deficit to his team-mate to 0.388s. Senna and Berger filled the second row in the new McLarens, both over two seconds behind Mansell. Towards the end of qualifying on Saturday, Mansell spun into the wall after

LEFT A second victory for Mansell, and another 1–2 for the FW14B, as team-mates Mansell and Patrese congratulate each other on the podium in Mexico. *(John Townsend)*

a close call with Senna, but both drivers considered it a genuine misunderstanding, and Mansell escaped without injury. The car was repaired for the race. In the race-morning warm-up, the FW14Bs were again quickest, Mansell ahead of Patrese.

Mansell made a poor start to the race, suffering from excessive wheelspin, and Patrese took the lead, Mansell following him into the first corner ahead of Schumacher and Senna. The order of the Williams drivers stayed that way but an intense battle developed, the gap between them never more than a second. Their dominance was such that they pulled away from the rest of the field, led by Senna, at the rate of two seconds a lap. Then Senna suddenly began to slow, several of his pursuers

BELOW Mansell celebrates victory in Brazil by waving the national flags of Britain and the host country on the slowing-down lap. *(John Townsend)*

passing him before he retired on lap 17 with electrical problems.

Mansell, still running second, stopped for tyres on lap 29 and then pushed very hard after rejoining. Patrese continued for two more laps, cutting through backmarkers, and then pitted. Although his stop was quicker than Mansell's, he rejoined 5.3s behind his team-mate.

As in Mexico, Mansell steadily pulled away from Patrese to win by a margin of 29.330s, the two Williams lapping the entire field. Schumacher was the other man on the podium.

After three races, Mansell had taken a hat-trick of poles and victories, and the only other driver to lead a race was Patrese! The team had also taken a hat-trick of 1–2s. A pattern was emerging...

Round 4 – Spanish Grand Prix, Barcelona (Catalunya)
3 May 1992

Spain was the next stop for the championship, and normal service was resumed. After a wet qualifying session on Saturday, the times from Friday stood, with Mansell again fastest, 1.005s ahead of Schumacher, followed by Senna, with Patrese fourth, 1.344s behind his dominant team-mate. Patrese had been unable to set up the car to his liking on Friday, and the rain prevented any progress on Saturday.

The rain continued for race day, and in the damp morning warm-up session Senna headed the times in his McLaren. On the face of it, it appeared that perhaps the FW14B's dominance was compromised in wet conditions. Despite easing briefly, the rain returned shortly before the cars were due to leave the grid for the parade lap, prompting all the front-runners to start on wet-weather tyres.

Mansell led away, Patrese instantly passed Senna and Schumacher to take second, and Jean Alesi, who had been fastest in the Saturday afternoon wet qualifying session, made a lightning start in his Ferrari to move from eighth on the grid to third place.

True to form, Mansell extended the gap to Patrese lap by lap, the two FW14Bs leaving the rest of the field in their wake. The treacherous conditions led to Patrese spinning out on lap 20 while attempting to pass a backmarker – the first Williams retirement of the season. After Alesi dropped back, having been tagged into a spin by Berger, Schumacher moved up to third. Senna had a couple of spins but recovered to finish the race in ninth position.

BELOW Red 5 prepares to leave the garage during qualifying for the Spanish Grand Prix. Mansell would again start from pole and take victory. *(John Townsend)*

The rain intensified for the final third of the race. As Mansell found the worsening conditions difficult, Schumacher began to close in and by lap 50 he was within five seconds of the FW14B. In response, Mansell changed his normal line through the corners in a quest for grip, and it had the desired effect as he won his fourth race in succession, finishing 23.914s ahead of the German. Alesi came home third, revelling in the wet conditions.

That made it four poles and four wins from four races for Mansell, and an FW14B had led every lap of the season so far…

Round 5 – San Marino Grand Prix, Imola
17 May 1992

When battle resumed at Imola, Mansell and Senna traded fastest times throughout the opening Friday practice session, the Englishman emerging on top by just 0.1s. His FW14B fitted with Renault's newer RS4 engine, Mansell once again dominated the first qualifying session, taking provisional pole 1.2s ahead of Senna, with Berger third and Schumacher fourth. After problems with his RS4 engine in the morning session, Patrese had to switch to the spare car for qualifying and ended up fifth fastest.

On Saturday morning, the Williams men were again 1–2 during the practice session, and their supremacy was maintained during final qualifying, despite an 'off' on to the grass for Red 5 on what was potentially Mansell's fastest run. Mansell's pole time was 1.053s better than second-placed Patrese's, while Senna lined up third and Berger fourth.

Both FW14Bs were fitted with RS3C engines for the race, and in the warm-up Mansell was – to nobody's surprise – fastest again, with Patrese fifth quickest.

As the race got underway, Mansell instantly opened up a gap to his team-mate, and repeated his normal routine by drawing away. The first two places remained unchanged to the chequered flag, Patrese unable to challenge Mansell, while Senna just could not find the pace to challenge the Williams pair.

So, after five races, Mansell's score was five poles, five wins and two fastest laps. No one else had ever won the first five races of a season.

The two Williams drivers, needless to say, dominated the points table. Mansell had the maximum score of 50 and Patrese was on 24, followed by Schumacher (Benetton) 17, Senna (McLaren) 8, Berger (McLaren) 8 and Alesi (Ferrari) 7.

Round 6 – Monaco Grand Prix, Monte Carlo
31 May 1992

Next came Monaco, where Senna had qualified in pole position for the previous four years, going on to take a hat-trick of victories, 1989–91, to add to his maiden win there in 1987. But even at Monaco Senna surely had no answer to the speed of the FW14B in 1992 – or did he?

On Thursday morning, Mansell was fastest once more, despite a brush with a barrier. He lapped 0.883s quicker than Senna, with Berger third from Schumacher and Patrese. In afternoon qualifying, Senna set the early pace, until Mansell went fastest with 20 minutes to go. It was an eventful session, with many spinners, including Mansell, who had a scare when he arrived backwards at the chicane! The session ended with Mansell on provisional pole from Senna and Patrese.

After the traditional Monaco Friday rest day, battle recommenced on Saturday morning with the two Williams drivers quickest, Mansell again ahead of Patrese, with Senna third. Mansell had a moment on his slowing-down lap, spinning and hitting the barriers, but fortunately there was no significant damage to driver or car. Then an intense final qualifying session saw the two Williams men trading fastest times, all the

ABOVE The FW14B showed the opposition a clean pair of heels once more at the San Marino Grand Prix on 17 May. Patrese, pictured here, again finished second behind team-mate Mansell to give the team its fourth 1–2 from five races. *(John Townsend)*

ABOVE Mansell tries to find a way past eventual winner Ayrton Senna during their epic battle for the lead in the closing stages of the Monaco Grand Prix. *(Williams)*

BELOW Winner Senna and third-placed Patrese offer an exhausted Mansell a helping hand after the podium ceremony at the Monaco Grand Prix. *(John Townsend)*

runners searching for gaps in the traffic, mindful of how important grid positions are at Monaco with so few passing opportunities during the race. Towards the end of the session, Mansell found the perfect moment and set a stunning time of 1m 19.495s, 0.8s faster than the best-ever lap of Monaco, and also 0.8s ahead of Patrese. Mansell's lap was all the more impressive for the fact that he set his time on a set of used tyres. The second row comprised Senna and a spectacular Alesi, with Berger and Schumacher on row three.

Patrese topped the times in the race-morning warm-up, with Mansell fifth after problems with traffic.

At the start, Mansell once again led away from pole, while Senna forced his way ahead of Patrese to steal second place. Mansell was in a class of his own, and pulled away easily from Senna to lead by 28 seconds at three-quarters distance, but seven laps from home Mansell informed the team by radio that he had suffered a puncture in the tunnel. He drove slowly back to the pits for new rubber, Senna relieving him of the lead as the FW14B left its pit box to rejoin. At the end of lap 72, with six laps to go, Senna led Mansell by 5.1s.

Now began Mansell's charge. Within two laps, he passed the only two cars, both backmarkers, between himself and Senna's McLaren. Driving on the absolute limit, he already had the gap below two seconds. On the following lap, Senna was held up as he waited to lap JJ Lehto's Dallara entering the chicane, and that allowed Mansell to close right up to the back of the McLaren. Both the leaders managed to pass the Dallara before the end of the lap, and were set for a titanic battle over the last three laps.

Mansell kept showing Senna his nose, feinting to the left and right at every opportunity, trying to prompt a mistake from the Brazilian. But Senna held his nerve, making his car as wide as possible around the confines of the street circuit – a major challenge bearing in mind that his tyres were well beyond their best. Both drivers drove absolutely flat out, but fairly, and there was nothing that Mansell could do to pass the McLaren. Senna powered across the line on the final lap to finish 0.215s ahead of the Williams.

Without the pit stop, Mansell would have

made it six wins in a row. As it was, Senna raised his Monaco tally to five wins, taking his fourth consecutive victory. Behind the battle for the lead, Patrese had a trouble-free race, and managed to fend off a late-race challenge from Schumacher to take the final podium position, nearly 32s behind the leaders.

Mansell's winning streak may have come to an end, but only Senna's determination had prevented him from using his clearly superior car to seize victory at the end of the race. The fact that the two cars did not make contact – with either each other or the barriers – was testament to the professionalism and skill of both drivers.

Round 7 – Canadian Grand Prix, Montréal (Circuit Gilles Villeneuve)
14 June 1992

In Montréal, Mansell failed to qualify on pole for the first time during the 1992 season, beaten into third place by Senna and Williams team-mate Patrese.

The Friday practice session, on a dusty track, saw Senna quickest ahead of Mansell and Patrese. When Senna took provisional pole on Saturday afternoon, with Patrese second from Berger and a disappointed Mansell, it looked as if McLaren might have made progress in its quest to catch Williams.

On Saturday morning, the weather took a turn for the worse, although by the end of the practice session the track had dried and Mansell was fastest, much happier with the car than he had been on Friday. After a chaotic afternoon qualifying session, peppered with incidents, the only change among the front-runners came from Mansell, who managed to better his Friday time to move up to third. The top three were very close: Senna qualified a fraction under a tenth ahead of Patrese, whose FW14B suffered leaks first of hydraulic fluid and then of engine oil, while Mansell was only seven hundredths adrift of his team-mate.

In the Sunday warm-up, Mansell was quickest by a mere 0.001s from Martin Brundle in the Benetton, both British drivers over a second ahead of Patrese and Schumacher, with Senna fifth.

Senna led away at the start, with Mansell making a lunge to slot his car in front of Patrese's for second place. It is notoriously difficult to overtake at the Canadian circuit, and although the FW14Bs were clearly capable of lapping faster than the leading McLaren, Senna did an excellent job of repeating his Monaco performance, avoiding mistakes and making his car as wide as possible. The Brazilian's defensive driving resulted in a train of cars building up behind him, headed by an increasingly frustrated Mansell.

Towards the end of lap 15, Mansell sensed what he thought was an opportunity to pass. He made a move down the inside of the McLaren to try to outbrake it into the chicane at the end of the straight preceding the start/finish straight. On the dirty side of the circuit, he found that he had little grip. The Williams bounced over the top of the chicane, its nose heavily damaged, then spun back on to the tarmac, coming to a stop in the middle of the track facing oncoming cars. Mansell's race was over, although he remained in his car for some time before assistance arrived.

In the confusion behind the incident, Patrese had to back off and was passed by Berger, the McLarens now running 1–2. However, Senna retired on lap 38, his McLaren struck with electrical problems. Berger now led from Patrese, but the second FW14B retired at two-thirds distance with gearbox problems, leaving Berger to win.

It was not a good weekend for Williams, but the damage to both the team's and Mansell's championship positions was minimal.

BELOW Mansell and his wife Rosanne enjoy the sunshine, while Mansell's Race Engineer David Brown tends to the set-up sheets and makes notes in between practice sessions for the Canadian Grand Prix at Montréal. *(John Townsend)*

ABOVE After passing Mansell, Patrese leads away at the start of the French Grand Prix. Patrese led until the race was stopped due to heavy rain, but, following the restart, the order was reversed when Patrese moved over to let his team-mate through.
(John Townsend)

Round 8 – French Grand Prix, Magny-Cours
5 July 1992

At Magny-Cours, normal service was resumed on Friday morning when Mansell was fastest, despite stopping at one point with a fuel-pump problem. Patrese, who suffered gearbox troubles, was in second spot, 0.35s ahead of Senna. Williams continued its regained form into the afternoon qualifying session, Mansell ending up 0.504s ahead of Patrese with Senna a distant third, 1.341s behind the Italian, and Berger fourth.

After overnight rain, Saturday practice started on a wet track, and there were several incidents, including a moment for Mansell when he slid off the track, although he still set the fastest time, ahead of Patrese. With the track drying for the afternoon qualifying session, most drivers improved on their Friday times, resulting in the familiar formation of Mansell, Patrese, Senna and Berger on the front two rows of the grid, Mansell 0.468s ahead of the second Williams, and 1.335s ahead of Senna.

The track was wet for the start of the race-morning warm-up, but began to dry as the session went on, and the FW14Bs were again fastest, Mansell from Patrese, with Alesi's Ferrari next up, and the Lotuses of Mika Häkkinen and Johnny Herbert ahead of the two McLarens.

On a dry track, Patrese passed Mansell to lead away, with Berger displacing Senna to take third. Further round the lap, at the hairpin, Schumacher attempted to pass Senna's McLaren but hit it, forcing Senna's immediate retirement. After four laps, Patrese was 1.5s ahead of his team-mate, and the two Williams were circulating almost two seconds per lap quicker than third-placed Berger. Meanwhile other incidents caused attrition in the midfield. After Berger retired on lap 11 with engine failure, the rain returned, and the conditions soon deteriorated to such an extent that the race was red-flagged.

As the rain eased, the grid reformed for the restart, with the result to be decided on aggregate times from the two halves of the race. Patrese once again took the lead but the two Williams jostled for position for most of the first lap, passing each other twice. Patrese still led Mansell across the line at the end of lap 20, at which point the Italian moved over and made an obvious gesture to relinquish the lead to the team leader. Despite the fact that the rain returned and all slick-shod cars had to stop again for wets, the two lead positions remained unchanged to the end of the race, giving Williams another 1–2. Mansell won by 46.4s from Patrese, with Brundle taking the final podium spot for Benetton.

So, at the halfway point of the season, Mansell led the championship with 66 points, with Patrese second on 34, Schumacher third on 26, and Senna fourth on 18. Mansell was clearly going to be difficult to beat...

Round 9 – British Grand Prix, Silverstone
12 July 1992

Mansell was already a hero before turning a wheel in front of the partisan home spectators at Silverstone. Almost everyone in the sell-out crowd made the trip to the Northamptonshire circuit for one reason only, to see their countryman continue his winning streak and repeat his dominant performance of the previous year, when he won by 42s from Berger on the newly reconfigured track.

The driver of Red 5 did not disappoint when the cars took to the track on Friday morning. An oil leak in his race car (running an RS4 engine with variable inlet trumpets for the first time) forced him to switch temporarily to the spare (with an RS3C), but soon Mansell was back in his race car to set fastest time, 1.1s ahead of Patrese and a full 2.48s ahead of Senna in third spot. This was impressive, but even the expectant crowd was astonished by Mansell's performance in the afternoon qualifying session.

With a time already comfortably good enough for pole, 1m 19.161s to Patrese's second-placed 1m 20.884s, the Englishman decided to take to the track again with four minutes of the session remaining, primarily to entertain his fans. He

BELOW Telemetry traces showing Nigel Mansell's stunning pole-position lap for the 1992 British Grand Prix. Paddy Lowe created this graphic and presented it to Nigel Mansell as a memento of his Silverstone performance. *(Paddy Lowe)*

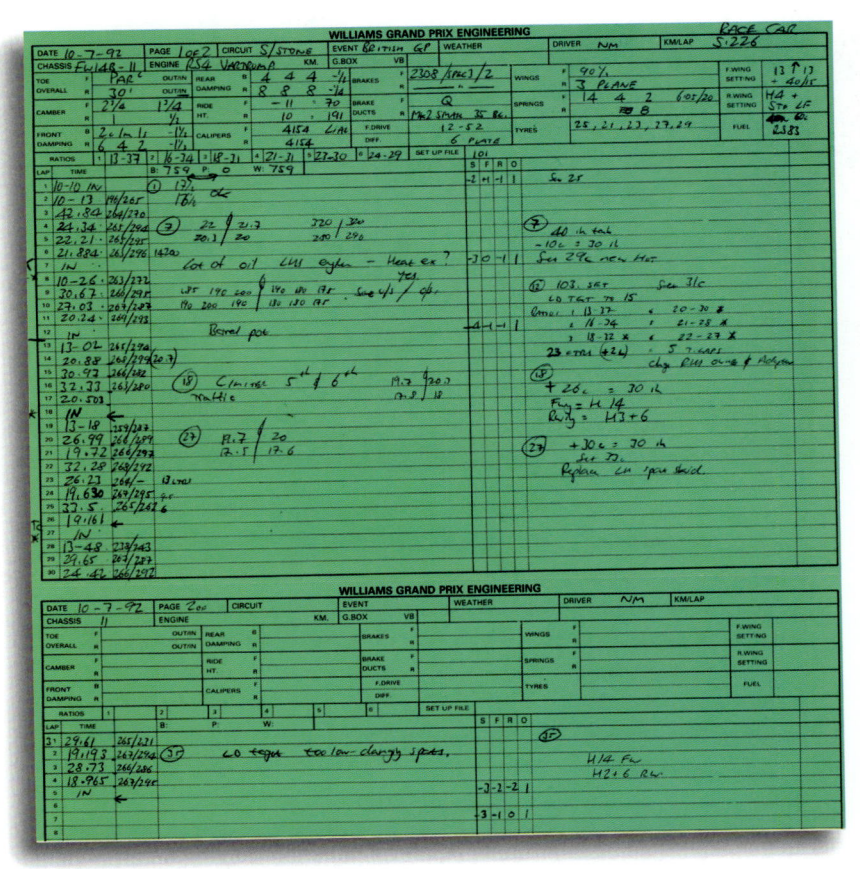

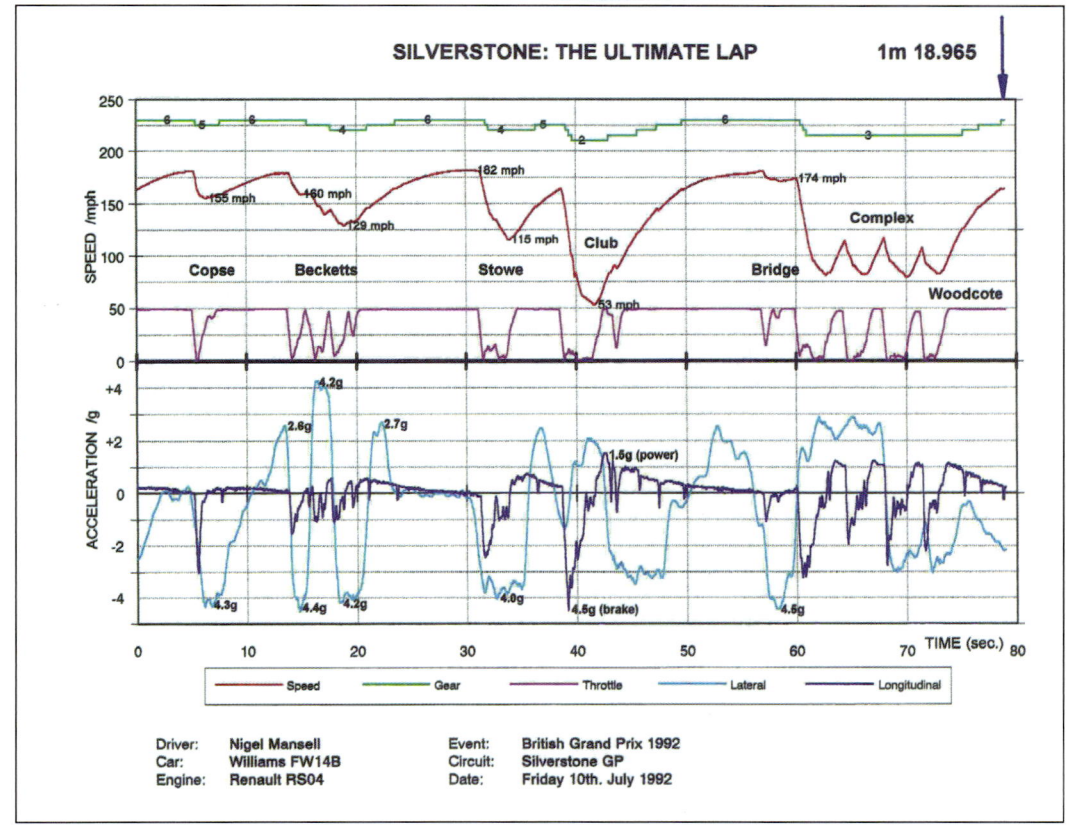

ABOVE The team's 'Green Sheet' for Nigel Mansell's car – FW14B/11 – at the Friday of the 1992 British Grand Prix meeting. Note the reference to 'RS4 Vartrump' in the 'Engine' box at the top of the sheet. In the left-hand column the times are given for each lap – 'IN' signifies the car pitting and the number immediately after 'IN' is the time the car returned to the track. See that Mansell went out for a final attempt at qualifying at 13.48, completing six laps, with the final lap his fastest, at 1m 18.965s, to cement a comfortable pole position. *(Williams Heritage Archive)*

ABOVE Home victory for Mansell at Silverstone resulted in a track invasion. Here, the FW14B negotiates the partisan fans between Vale and the entry to Club Corner.
(Steve Rendle)

stopped the clocks at an astonishing 1m 18.965s, taking provisional pole by an incredible margin of 1.919s over Patrese, 2.741s ahead of third-fastest Senna. The crowd justifiably expressed its appreciation. Patrese was incredulous, and marched to see Mansell after qualifying.

In a 2002 interview in *Motor Sport* with Adam Cooper, Paul Fearnley and David Malshar, Mansell's Race Engineer, David Brown, recounted: "The car was quite soft, and it used to move around a bit. Riccardo found it difficult at places like Copse Corner to put absolute faith in the car, whereas Nigel would just get on with it. He just had the confidence. Riccardo walked into the truck, came up to Nigel, looking very stern with his hands on his hips, and said, 'Stand up!' I thought, 'Oh my God, he's going to hit him!' Paddy Lowe was also present, and recalls: "Riccardo said, 'Let me feel the weight... the bo******!' – the greatest compliment I've ever heard one driver give another in 28 years!"

Everyone at the circuit knew they had witnessed something special. It was highly unlikely that anybody would be able to reduce the margin to Mansell the following day, but the weather meant that nobody had the opportunity to try, rain ensuring that the times from Friday stood. Mansell was again fastest in both the morning practice and afternoon qualifying sessions, ahead of Patrese, but the Italian was involved in a nasty incident towards the end of the morning session when Bertrand Gachot spun in the Venturi-Lamborghini at Vale. Patrese slowed under yellow flags as he approached the scene, but Erik Comas, in the Ligier-Renault, arrived at full speed and hit the back of the Williams hard, both cars striking the wall heavily. Patrese ran his spare car in the afternoon, as the team worked hard to build up a new race car for Sunday.

Silverstone was packed to bursting point for the race, with an estimated crowd of 120,000. Unsurprisingly, Mansell was quickest in the morning warm-up session, ahead of Patrese and Schumacher.

It seemed as if the whole of Britain was watching on Sunday afternoon, as Mansell suffered a little wheelspin off the line to allow Patrese to snatch the lead running into Copse. Red 5 tucked into Patrese's slipstream, and at Becketts took advantage of the tow to slingshot into the lead. Mansell pulled away immediately and led by a commanding 3.2s at the end of the first lap, and by 20s by lap 10. The home hero elected to make a precautionary tyre stop on lap 30, rejoining still with an 8s advantage over Patrese, who did not stop. Mansell retained his lead, unchallenged, for the rest of the race and finished a healthy 39.094s ahead of Patrese, having broken the lap record by an extraordinary 4s. Brundle finished third to add to the Britishness of the occasion.

The race will also be remembered for another reason. As Mansell crossed the line to win, ecstatically waving his fist in victory, a foolhardy spectator ran across the circuit behind him, with the following cars still racing at full speed. This precipitated track invasions around the circuit by large groups of spectators eager to congratulate their hero. The problem was that people were on the track while the race was still in progress, putting themselves and the drivers – some of whom were still racing for position – at huge risk.

The adulation of Mansell at Silverstone was almost a religious experience, and it perhaps illustrated both the best and worst aspects of British enthusiasm. It was not allowed to happen again.

Round 10 – German Grand Prix, Hockenheim
26 July 1992

During the Friday morning practice session at Hockenheim, Mansell carried on where he had left off at Silverstone, setting a time 2s clear of the McLarens of Senna and Berger, with Patrese fourth after his FW14B suffered from both hydraulic and electrical problems. In the afternoon, as expected, Mansell took provisional pole, 1.991s ahead of Senna, with Patrese third and Berger fourth.

The track was a lot quicker on Saturday, and during morning practice both FW14Bs were back on top once more, Mansell ahead of Patrese. In the final qualifying session, they again locked out the front row, Mansell on pole 0.350s ahead of Patrese, with the two McLarens third and fourth, Senna ahead of Berger.

In the Sunday morning warm-up, Mansell announced his intentions with fastest time, ahead of Berger and Patrese.

At the start, Mansell was slow to get away due to a software bug inadvertently introduced overnight during work on a revised clutch-control system, which curtailed the FW14B's acceleration. That allowed Patrese through, but Mansell made a pass under braking for the first chicane to take the lead and immediately opened up a gap. Behind Patrese, the two McLarens followed in grid order, Senna ahead of Berger. On lap 13, Mansell ran over a patch of dust thrown up by a backmarker and the Williams slid sideways. At the same time, a puncture warning light illuminated on the cockpit display so Mansell, believing he had a puncture, stopped for tyres on the following lap, rejoining in third place.

After stalking Senna closely for a few laps, Mansell attempted a pass at the newly built chicane before the Ostkurve, and in doing so missed the second half of the chicane completely, hitting a traffic cone and throwing up dust. Arguably, the Williams, which survived unscathed, gained an advantage by omitting part of the chicane, but no action was taken by the stewards. Mansell made short work of

ABOVE Patrese at speed during the German Grand Prix at Hockenheim. He was classified eighth after Senna closed the door when he tried a passing move on the final lap, forcing the FW14B to spin under braking. *(John Townsend)*

BELOW An interesting document – a set of notes from David Brown (Nigel Mansell's Race Engineer) to Dickie Stanford (Chief Mechanic) detailing points to watch for on the FW14Bs at the German Grand Prix. *(Williams Heritage Archive/John Colley)*

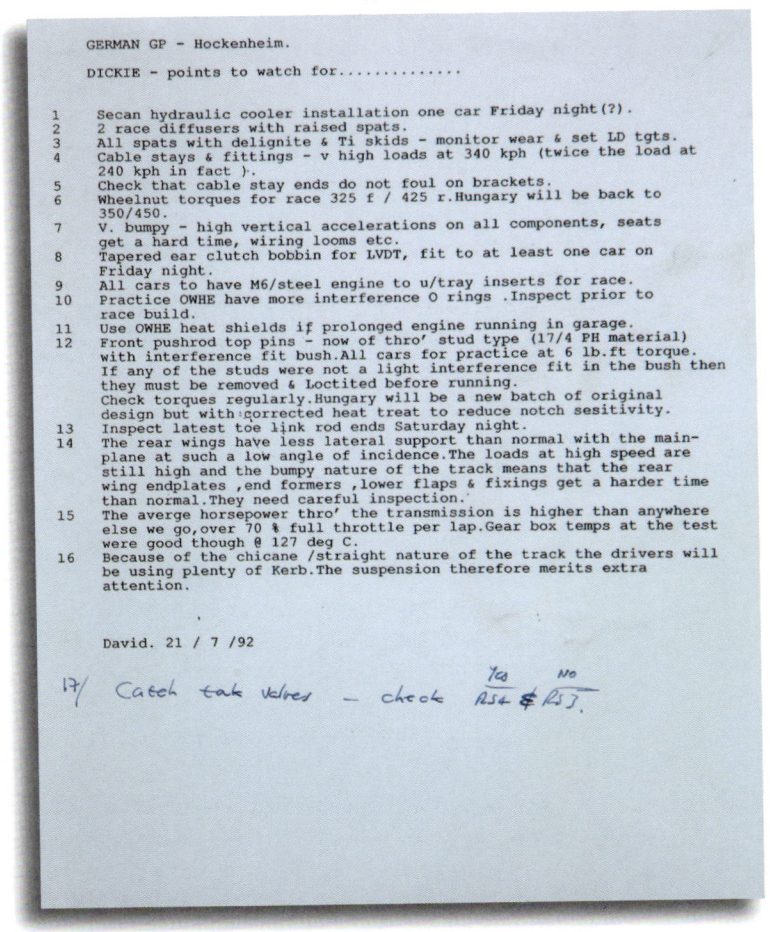

catching Senna again, passing him for second place on lap 19 on the run to the second chicane. When Patrese then stopped for tyres, Mansell was back in the lead.

Patrese rejoined in fourth place behind Schumacher's Benetton and soon put him under pressure, but the German was not keen to concede position at his home race. Eventually forced into a mistake, Schumacher slid and flat-spotted his tyres, allowing the FW14B to breeze past to pursue Senna. The Brazilian had elected to run one set of tyres for the entire race, and they were well past their best by the time Patrese caught him. For the following six laps, Senna managed to keep the Williams at bay, and on the final lap Patrese made a last-gasp attempt to pass the McLaren coming into the stadium section. In closing the door, Senna forced Patrese off line, causing him to spin out under braking. The Italian was able to resume and finished a lowly eighth.

Mansell duly took his eighth win from ten races, with Senna second and Schumacher third. As Senna was now out of the running for the championship, Patrese was the only driver with a mathematical chance of preventing Mansell from taking the drivers' title. Mansell's points tally was 86 to Patrese's 40, with 60 points still available. In the constructors' championship, Williams continued to lead McLaren, with 126 points to McLaren's 40.

Round 11 – Hungarian Grand Prix, Budapest (Hungaroring)
16 August 1992

As the F1 teams arrived in Hungary, all the odds were stacked in favour of Mansell becoming World Champion there. A ban on 'special-brew' fuels took effect at this race and it was thought that the FW14B's advantage might be reduced as Elf, fuel supplier to Williams-Renault, had made great strides in fuel technology during the season.

Prior to the Budapest race, rumours also began to surface that Alain Prost was in negotiation with Williams to drive for the team in 1993, a prospect that did not fill Mansell with enthusiasm as the French driver was unlikely to accept a job as his number two. With Williams now clearly the team to beat, Senna also had itchy feet and was keen to secure a seat there. Meanwhile, Patrese, the clear number two to Mansell, was eager to show his employer that he was worth retaining. There was a tense atmosphere ahead of practice and qualifying in Hungary.

Friday's practice session got off to a bad start for Mansell when he had a minor fire at the back of his race car as he was returning to the pits. His spare FW14B then suffered an electrical problem, which resulted in the car stopping on the pit straight. The team managed to get Mansell out again towards the end of the session, but he could not find the pace to catch the two McLarens. In the last minutes of the session, Patrese went almost a second quicker than second-placed Berger, with Senna third and Mansell fourth.

In the afternoon qualifying session, the bumpy track surface caught out a number of drivers, including Mansell, Senna and Berger, but all escaped their spins without damage. At the end of the session, Patrese sat on provisional pole, with Mansell second, Senna third and Schumacher fourth.

Saturday morning saw Patrese fastest in oppressive conditions. With grid positions particularly important in Hungary, due to the challenges of overtaking, the teams were very keen to make the most of the final qualifying session. Once again there were many spinners, and one of them, towards the end of the session, was Berger, who lost control while close behind team-mate Senna. Two following cars had to take avoiding action, which in turn pitched them into spins. Then the unfortunate Mansell arrived at full speed and clouted the barrier hard after spinning in avoidance. After a stoppage, the session briefly restarted, but few drivers improved their times from Friday. The front row was unchanged, Patrese on pole with Mansell and Senna respectively 0.167s and 0.804s behind him, and Schumacher fourth.

Mansell gave the outward signs of being relatively relaxed on race morning, despite the media pressure on him. After all, if he did not win the championship in Hungary, it was almost inconceivable that he would not score sufficient points in one of the five races to come. In the morning warm-up, the two McLarens were quickest, Senna ahead of Berger, with Mansell third and Patrese sixth. Ahead of the race, Patrese was disarmingly honest, saying: "I am not too worried about team orders. Today I am going for the win."

As the green light came on for the start of the race, Patrese made a clean getaway to take the lead, with Mansell challenging. As Patrese held his line, Mansell backed off, allowing both Senna and Berger to find their way around the Englishman before the first corner. Patrese instantly began to pull away from the two McLarens, which in turn held up Mansell, allowing fifth-placed Schumacher to close up to the rear of the Williams. For the next six laps, Senna, Berger, Mansell and Schumacher jostled for position, but there was no change until Mansell forced his car past Berger on lap 8. By now Patrese was already 12 seconds ahead of Senna. As Patrese continued to pull away, Mansell now had to find a way past the combative Brazilian. On lap 30, still stuck behind Senna, Mansell made a mistake and ran wide, enabling Berger to retake him. Four laps later, the Englishman muscled his way past Berger again and set about catching Senna.

Suddenly Patrese's advantage evaporated as he spun on the downhill section between Turns One and Two. After a push from the marshals, he rejoined in seventh place, but soon retired with an engine problem. As Senna, the new leader, began to open up a gap, Mansell now only needed to maintain position in second place in order to win the championship, and he settled for playing the long game. However, the drama was not yet over. On lap 61, the telemetry in the Williams pit suggested that Mansell had a puncture. The team called him in, and he rejoined in sixth place with new tyres all round.

If he wanted to take the championship in Hungary, Mansell now had a busy few laps in prospect. The order ahead of him was Senna, Berger, Schumacher, Brundle and Häkkinen. His sixth place soon became fifth as Schumacher's rear wing failed on lap 63, due to earlier contact with Brundle's sister car, causing the German's Benetton to pirouette several times. After Mansell easily passed Häkkinen's Lotus for fourth, he needed only one more place to seal the championship. The Williams rapidly closed on third-placed Brundle and passed

ABOVE With his FW14B looking in need of a valet, Mansell charges during a busy afternoon at the Hungarian Grand Prix. *(John Townsend)*

BELOW Mansell crosses the line to take second place in Hungary, earning him the 1992 Drivers' World Championship. *(Williams)*

the Benetton to put himself in the necessary championship-winning position.

Owing to a miscommunication behind the scenes, however, Patrick Head thought that Mansell had to finish second in order to win the championship in Hungary, and so he went on the radio to encourage the charging Williams driver to catch and pass Berger's McLaren. Mansell did just that, and then eased off to hold a comfortable second behind Senna, who was by now nearly a minute ahead. The Brazilian made a precautionary tyre stop towards the end of the race, but was still able to finish just over 40 seconds ahead.

After so many near misses, Nigel Mansell finally became World Champion. As for his team, Williams now had an almost unassailable lead in the constructors' championship, with 132 points to McLaren's 58.

Round 12 – Belgian Grand Prix, Spa-Francorchamps
30 August 1992

New World Champion Mansell showed no sign of easing off at the following race, at the classic Spa-Francorchamps circuit.

In Friday's morning practice session, Mansell was once again fastest, from Patrese and Senna, in a session shortened by a frightening accident for Erik Comas that completely destroyed his Ligier. Fortunately, the Frenchman escaped without injury. In the first qualifying session, Mansell was fastest, a huge 2.198s ahead of second-placed Senna, with Schumacher third and Patrese fourth. The Italian damaged the rear end of his FW14B when he spun into the wall at the exit to the revised Bus Stop chicane.

Friday night saw rain fall at the Ardennes circuit, and it soon became clear that the Friday qualifying times would settle the grid positions. In the Saturday morning practice session, Mansell had a brief spin, and Patrese did just a handful of laps. In the afternoon Mansell was quickest of all the drivers to venture out in the treacherous conditions – by 3.648s! – while Patrese decided to stay put.

In the race-day warm-up, Mansell was once again quickest, from Schumacher, Senna, Berger and Patrese. As rain returned after lunch, the race started on a damp track, although all the teams opted for slick tyres.

At the start, Senna took the lead from Mansell as the McLaren's traction-control system appeared to have the edge over the FW14B's software on this occasion, with Patrese third. Mansell followed close behind Senna on the opening lap, and on lap 2 took the lead. Patrese passed the Brazilian soon after, but by this stage rain was falling. Mansell and Patrese circulated in close formation, pulling a slight gap on Senna, until the end of lap 3, when Mansell pitted for wet tyres. That left Patrese leading by three seconds from Senna, Mansell rejoining in 14th position. Patrese stopped for wets on lap 6 but Senna stayed out, gambling that the track would dry.

After his stop, Patrese exited the pits just ahead of Mansell, but the Englishman passed his Italian team-mate before Eau Rouge. By now Schumacher, who, along with Benetton team-mate Brundle, had stopped for tyres shortly after Mansell, lay fifth and was in close pursuit of the Williams pair, while Alesi's Ferrari was second to Senna, with Mansell closing in. As Mansell made his move on Alesi at La Source, the Ferrari and Williams made contact, Alesi spinning out and Mansell slowing, which allowed Patrese to pass the sister FW14B for second place. Senna still led, with the order behind him now Patrese, Mansell, Schumacher and Brundle.

Mansell quickly repassed Patrese and set after Senna, his team-mate and Schumacher staying with him. On lap 11, Mansell passed Senna for the lead, Patrese following a lap later, with the two Benettons also soon passing the Brazilian, whose tyre gamble had most definitely not paid off. Mansell began to open up a gap to Patrese, but the Italian could not shake off Schumacher and Brundle.

On lap 30, Schumacher ran wide and, as Brundle went by, he observed that his team-mate's tyres were blistered. Shrewdly, Schumacher pitted for slicks. His early move proved to be a good call. Two laps later Patrese also stopped for slicks, rejoining behind Schumacher. Mansell, forced to wait an extra lap because his team-mate had pitted, finally made his switch three laps after Schumacher, and rejoined behind the German.

With seven laps to go, the order was Schumacher, Mansell, Patrese, with the two Williams closing on the leader. But the Renault

ABOVE **Patrese during the early stages of the Belgian Grand Prix, having pitted for wet tyres. The Italian finished third, behind Michael Schumacher and Mansell, after both FW14Bs were slowed by an ignition-coil problem.**
(John Townsend)

engine in Mansell's FW14B began to sound rough and he slipped back, and shortly afterwards Patrese's car started to suffer similarly. It transpired that both cars were slowed by problems with ignition coils, which removed any prospect of the Williams drivers challenging for victory. Despite the problems, Mansell and Patrese retained their second and third positions, the Italian just managing to hold off Brundle.

Schumacher duly took his first F1 victory, at a track that would bring him much success over the following years. Although the Williams drivers were frustrated that they had not been able to challenge for a win, second and third places were sufficient to give the team the Constructors' World Championship with four races to go.

Round 13 – Italian Grand Prix, Monza
13 September 1992

As the F1 teams arrived at Ferrari's home circuit of Monza for the Italian Grand Prix, there were numerous rumours circulating about Mansell's future with Williams. On the track, there was little sign of any change in the order, and on Friday morning Mansell was again fastest, continuing his form in the afternoon with provisional pole ahead of Senna, Alesi (the *tifosi*'s hero) and Patrese, whose FW14B ran out of fuel towards the end of the session.

It was notable that the FW14Bs did not seem to have their usual advantage, with Mansell only a relatively slender 0.236s ahead of Senna's McLaren. The Woking team's MP4/7A featured McLaren's active suspension system for the first time at a grand prix weekend. Both Williams drivers complained of a lack of power, which kept the Renault engineers busy trying to diagnose the cause of the problem.

Mansell was quickest on Saturday morning, and in final qualifying improved his Friday afternoon time to take his now customary pole position – his 11th in 13 races – with Senna second, Alesi third and Patrese fourth. The grid positions were relatively close compared with how the times looked in the early part of the season, with Mansell 0.601s ahead of Senna, and 0.801s ahead of fourth-placed Patrese.

In the Sunday morning warm-up, Mansell

67

THE WILLIAMS FW14B IN ACTION

again set the pace, with a time almost two seconds clear of Alesi, who was fractionally quicker than Patrese. After the warm-up, it became clear that all was not well between Mansell and his team when he held a press conference to announce his retirement from F1 (see panel opposite).

Mansell roared away at the start to lead, and immediately began to pull away, with Senna second, Alesi third and Patrese fourth. At the end of lap 1, Patrese passed Alesi for third, and the Italian, at his home grand prix, slowly caught Senna, passing the Brazilian on lap 14, by which time Mansell's advantage was nearly 11s. Then came unexpected drama.

Mansell, now 13s ahead, slowed suddenly on lap 20, allowing Patrese through to take the lead. Behind his team-mate, Mansell then maintained the gap at around 1s, with Senna a further 2s back, followed by Brundle's Benetton in fourth place. As further laps unfolded, it seemed that Mansell could close up on Patrese at will – on lap 27 he was only 0.5s behind – and then drop back. As there was no radio communication between Mansell and the pit crew, team personnel were as perplexed as everyone else!

When later interviewed, Mansell explained: "I let Riccardo by, and rode shotgun for him. Before the race he told me how much he wanted to win his home grand prix, and I was happy to help."

Mansell suddenly slowed again on lap 41, but this time there really was a problem. His FW14B was stuck in sixth gear, due to a hydraulic-pump drivebelt failure, and he retired to the pits. Remarkably, this was Mansell's first retirement of the season due to mechanical failure. Heartbreakingly for Patrese, his FW14B, with only five laps to go, suffered the same hydraulic-pump drivebelt problems, in his case causing the gearbox to become stuck in fourth gear and the active suspension to behave erratically.

Senna, who was 10s behind when Patrese struck trouble, inherited the lead, and in the closing laps Brundle, Schumacher and Berger also passed the ailing FW14B, Patrese limping home to finish fifth.

BELOW Senna closes on leader Patrese at the Italian's home race at Monza, as the FW14B slows with hydraulic-pump drivebelt failure. *(John Townsend)*

THE DRIVER MERRY-GO-ROUND

After the Hungarian Grand Prix, there was much speculation about who would be driving for Williams in 1993, with the team rumoured to have been talking to Alain Prost. In the meantime, it became public knowledge that Ayrton Senna had offered to drive for the team for free as it seemed likely that Williams would maintain its dominant form for 1993, and Riccardo Patrese was keen to keep his seat.

After much manoeuvring behind the scenes, both from the team and its star driver, Nigel Mansell called a press conference on the morning of the Italian Grand Prix at Monza to announce his retirement from F1. When the dust settled, it transpired that Mansell would leave F1 to move to the US and join the Newman-Haas IndyCar team, while Riccardo Patrese would also leave the team to move to Benetton, partnering Michael Schumacher.

Two weeks after Monza, on race morning at the Portuguese Grand Prix at Estoril, Williams made an official announcement that Prost would drive for the team in 1993. Damon Hill, the man who had done much of the development driving in the FW14B, would be promoted to the race team to partner the three-times World Champion. As Prost had a clause in his contract with Williams preventing Senna, his arch-rival, from joining the team, the Brazilian would remain at McLaren, but on a race-by-race contract.

Post-race in Portugal, Prost had his first run for Williams in a test session at Estoril with one of the FW14Bs.

Round 14 – Portuguese Grand Prix, Estoril

27 September 1992

Normal service was resumed at Estoril for the Portuguese Grand Prix, and on Friday morning the two FW14Bs were quickest, Mansell 0.314s ahead of Patrese, and a clear 1.6s faster than third-placed Berger's McLaren. Mansell's time was set despite a momentary hydraulic problem that resulted in a lively incident as the ride height dropped and the gearbox briefly faltered, causing Williams's latest World Champion to spin into the sand trap. The Williams pair again set the pace in the afternoon qualifying session, and at the end of the afternoon Mansell was on provisional pole 0.631s ahead of Patrese, and a healthy 2.076s ahead of Berger.

Saturday brought damp conditions for the morning practice session, and Mansell was again fastest as the track began to dry. The only front-runner to improve on his Friday time in the final qualifying session was Senna, who did a stunning lap to place himself third, behind Mansell and Patrese, with Berger fourth.

The race-day warm-up started in wet conditions, but the two FW14Bs were fastest nonetheless.

At the start of the race, the grid order remained unchanged for the leading four cars, Mansell employing his usual tactic of instantly opening up a lead. After 21 laps, he led by 10.5s from Patrese, with Berger now third, Senna having stopped for tyres and dropping to sixth. When Patrese pitted for tyres, there was a problem with the rear jack and he was delayed, rejoining fourth, but he immediately charged to catch up. When Mansell pitted, his lead was sufficient for him to rejoin without losing position.

On lap 30, with the front-runners all having pitted, the order was Mansell leading by 2.6s from Senna, with Berger third and Patrese fourth. On lap 43, Patrese was right on Berger's gearbox but failed to realise that the McLaren was slowing down and heading for the pitlane. He swerved but was unable to avoid hitting the rear of the McLaren, which launched the Williams skywards. The FW14B's rear wing and both right-hand corners were wiped off as the car hit the pit wall, and then slid along the wall for the entire length of the pit straight, scattering debris as it went. Patrese was clearly shaken, but fortunately clambered from the wrecked car unaided and escaped serious injury. Berger rejoined after his stop, his car undamaged, but several other cars went off as a result of the debris on the track.

After 45 laps, Mansell led by 12.6s from Senna, with Berger third, now over 50s behind the leading Williams. Mansell opened up the gap to over 30s before he and Senna began trading fastest laps prior to the Brazilian making another tyre stop, which dropped him behind team-mate Berger. At the finish, Mansell crossed the line to take victory, with Berger 37.5s behind and Senna a lap down. By taking his ninth victory of the year, Mansell set a new record for the number of wins in a season.

Round 15 – Japanese Grand Prix, Suzuka
25 October 1992

And so to the fast, sweeping Suzuka in Japan – Honda's home track and a circuit that was expected to play to the strengths of the FW14B – for the penultimate round of the championship. Honda had been working feverishly to improve the power of McLaren's V10 in a bid to close the gap to Williams, but after the Friday morning practice session it seemed that their efforts had been in vain, the two Williams again fastest. Despite heroic efforts from both Senna and Berger, their McLarens

ABOVE Mansell sits in the cockpit of his FW14B studying the timing monitor during qualifying for the Portuguese Grand Prix. He took pole and his ninth victory of the year to set a new record for the number of wins in a season.
(John Townsend)

BELOW Patrese on his way to a popular victory at the Japanese Grand Prix.
(John Townsend)

finished the session over a second behind Mansell. The qualifying session in the afternoon confirmed the status quo, with the FW14Bs occupying the front row, Mansell 0.859s ahead of Patrese, and 1.015s clear of Senna, Berger again fourth.

Saturday proved to be a complete wash-out, and Mansell was one of the few drivers to venture out in the morning, spinning harmlessly. Only six drivers – no front-runners among them – recorded times in the afternoon, before the session was abandoned due to low cloud, which would have prevented the medical helicopter from flying. The grid positions were therefore determined by Friday's times.

By Sunday morning the weather had cleared, and in the warm-up Patrese was fastest, from Mansell, who had a moment running over a kerb, seriously damaging the FW14B's undertray. Berger was third, Johnny Herbert fourth in the Lotus, and Senna fifth.

The race got underway with the leaders in grid order, Mansell opening a gap of three seconds over Patrese by the end of the first lap. Senna retired from third place on lap 3 with engine failure, so Berger moved up to pursue the two FW14Bs, which were running faultlessly. Approaching half distance, Mansell ran over some debris, damaging a sidepod. He pitted for tyres, but all seemed well, and he rejoined without losing the lead.

Suddenly, Red 5 slowed dramatically while exiting the chicane and Patrese sailed past. When Mansell's car then picked up pace, it became clear that this was a repeat of Monza, the Englishman again – in his theatrical way – helping Patrese in his points battle with Senna for second place in the drivers' championship. Mansell followed his team-mate closely until eight laps from the finish, when his engine blew, burning oil causing a fire at the back of the car. Patrese duly crossed the line to take his first victory of the season, 13.7s ahead of Berger, with Brundle occupying the final podium position.

Patrese's victory was popular within the Williams team, and was just reward for his loyal service to support Mansell's championship efforts over the year. The win put the Italian six points clear of Senna in the battle for second place in the drivers' championship.

LEFT Patrese celebrates a well-deserved win in Japan – his only visit to the top step of the podium in 1992. *(John Townsend)*

Round 16 – Australian Grand Prix, Adelaide
8 November 1992

As the 1992 season finale, the Australian Grand Prix was to be the racing swansong for the FW14B, at the end of a year in which the team had been rewarded for its faith in the active suspension technology – a significant element in the car's championship success – along with Renault's V10 engines and the excellent overall packaging of the car, complemented, of course, by the two drivers and the hard work of the entire team. It also appeared that Adelaide would be the last F1 race for Nigel Mansell and, it was rumoured, possibly Ayrton Senna too, as the Brazilian had become frustrated by McLaren's failure to challenge Williams, and had been ruled out of a seat at Williams for 1993 due to the signing of his nemesis, Alain Prost. The scene was set for a busy weekend.

On Friday morning, Senna was keen to make his mark, and set the early pace until Mansell went 0.6s quicker than the McLaren. Patrese had a spin and stalled the car, but was still third quickest. The first qualifying session saw a duel for pole between Mansell and Senna as they

72
WILLIAMS FW14B MANUAL

traded fastest times throughout the session. It was settled with Mansell on provisional pole, 0.470s ahead of Senna, while Patrese was third and Berger fourth.

Saturday was hot and dry, conditions that made it unlikely that anybody would improve on their Friday qualifying times. In the morning, Mansell was once again quickest, ahead of Senna. In the afternoon qualifying session, only the sluggish March cars were quicker than their Friday times, and so the grid was set. the The Williams mechanics were kept busy after Patrese's car developed an oil leak in the morning and Mansell's suffered a broken throttle linkage during the afternoon qualifying session, both drivers transferring to their spare cars.

With Honda about to depart F1, McLaren had been courting Renault for a supply of engines in 1993. In Adelaide on the Sunday Renault suggested that talks on that matter were at an end, so it looked likely that Senna would follow Mansell in leaving F1. Potentially, therefore, this was the final F1 race for both Mansell and Senna. With both drivers on the front row, fireworks were expected.

In the warm-up, the FW14Bs were quickest, but this time Patrese was ahead of Mansell, with Senna and Berger third and fourth. An engine change was carried out on the Englishman's car before the race.

At the start, Mansell led away from Senna, Patrese and Schumacher, who overtook Berger for fourth only to be repassed by him before the end of the second lap. Meanwhile, Mansell and Senna appeared to be on equal terms, battling furiously for the lead, Patrese dropping back. Although Mansell seemed to have the upper hand, leading by between one and two seconds, he could not open up the gap any further. On lap 19, Mansell was held up while lapping Nicola Larini's Ferrari, allowing Senna, who passed the Ferrari without trouble, to close right up on the Williams.

Coming into the final corner, Senna hit the rear of Mansell's car, putting both of them out of the race. Needless to say, it was a controversial incident and both drivers blamed each other. It was also a sad end to the season for the outgoing and incoming World Champions. Mansell's only consolation from the weekend was that he won himself another entry in the record books by taking his 14th pole position of the season.

Patrese now led the race by one second from Berger. Just before half distance, the McLaren stopped for tyres, rejoining without losing position. Berger was clearly quicker on the fresh tyres and began to catch Patrese, but on lap 51 the FW14B suddenly lost fuel pressure, causing the engine to stop. That left Berger to claim victory ahead of the Benettons of Schumacher and Brundle.

At the end of a dominant season, the FW14B had proved to be the most successful Williams design to date, taking the Constructors' World Championship and a 1–2 in the Drivers' World Championship, and breaking records along the way. Not bad for a car that was never intended to be!

OPPOSITE TOP Patrese holds off a challenge from Gerhard Berger in the McLaren during the Australian Grand Prix, prior to the Italian's retirement from the lead with low fuel pressure. *(John Townsend)*

OPPOSITE The Williams team assembled for an end-of-year photograph in Adelaide, marking the FW14B's swansong and the departure from the team of both Mansell and Patrese. *(John Townsend)*

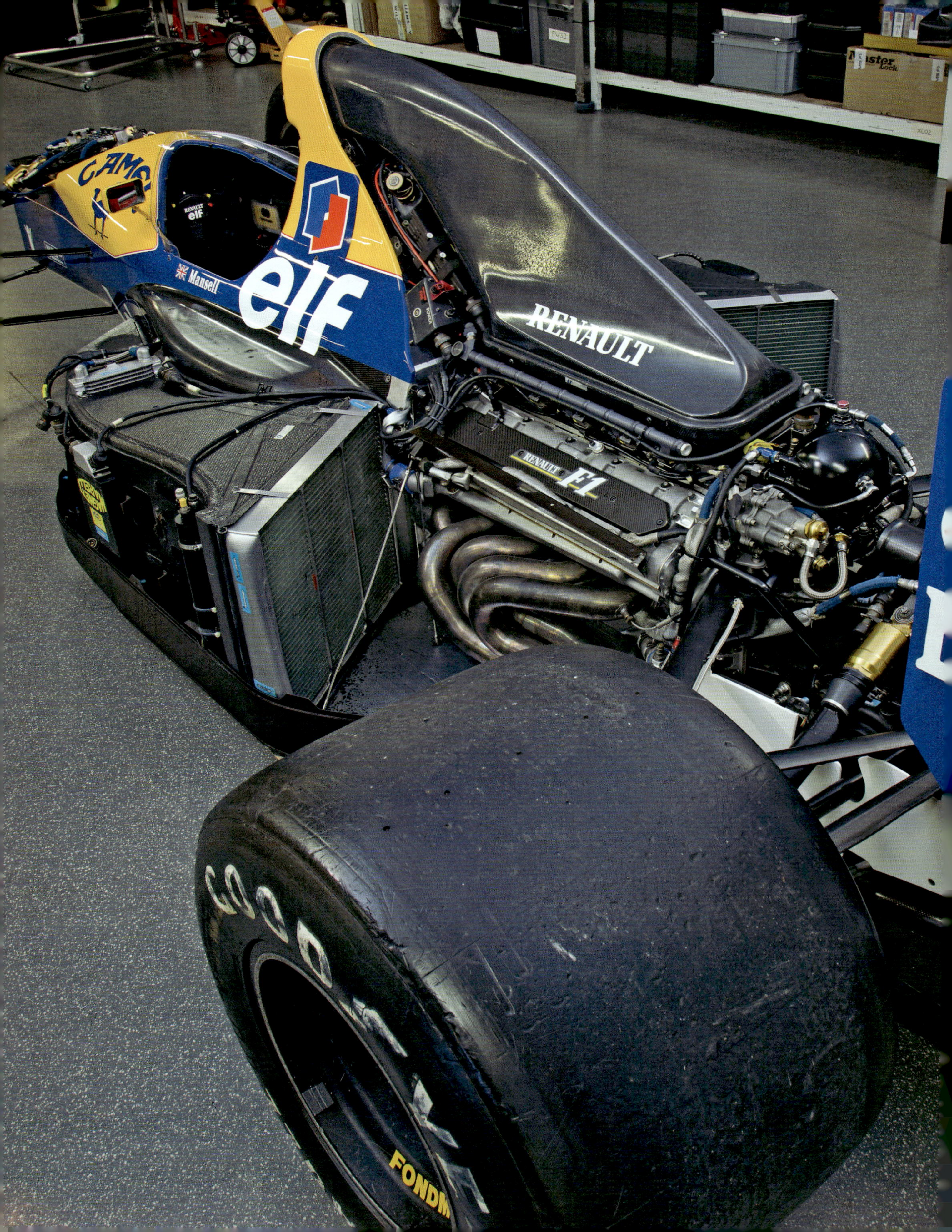
Mansell
elf
RENAULT
RENAULT F1

Chapter Four

Anatomy of the Williams FW14B

When the FW14B arrived in South Africa in March 1992 for its first race, it was the most technologically advanced car ever to compete in F1. The car's semi-automatic transmission had been proven in the previous season's FW14, while its active suspension system was the culmination of a project that had been running at Williams since 1984. The car was also pioneering in its use of electronic control systems and data logging and, impressively, all these systems were designed and developed in-house by the Williams engineering team.

OPPOSITE With bodywork removed, FW14B/11 sits in the Williams Heritage workshop. This car was used by Nigel Mansell to win the 1992 British, German and Portuguese Grands Prix. *(John Colley)*

ABOVE This superb cutaway illustration of a Renault RS4-engined FW14B was drawn by renowned illustrator Tony Matthews, with the cooperation of Williams, in 1992, but was never developed into full-colour, finished artwork. *(Tony Matthews)*

Introduction

When the FW14B made its race debut at the 1992 South African Grand Prix, it was immediately obvious that the car was significantly quicker than its rivals, and, as the season progressed, Williams, Renault and Elf worked together on an extensive test and development programme to maintain their advantage. Such was the success of this programme that the FW14B proved to be more than capable of staying ahead of the competition, and the introduction of the FW15, which was originally intended to be the team's 1992 challenger (see page 49), was postponed until 1993 when, in the hands of Alain Prost and Damon Hill, it emulated the success of its predecessor.

The fundamental configuration and many of the systems on the FW14B were carried over from the already proven FW14, which was a huge benefit to the reliability of the car during the 1992 season. Although the FW14B, like any F1 car of the era, was subject to a continual process of evolution throughout the season, the core components remained little changed, and perhaps the most significant upgrade during the year was the introduction of the Renault RS4 engine to supersede the RS3C. In terms of aerodynamics and major mechanical components, the car that finished the season was essentially very similar to the early-season version. The team saw no reason to expend resource and to risk reliability in order to make significant developments to a car that was already the class of the field.

Chassis

As in modern F1, carbon-fibre monocoques were *de rigueur* in the early 1990s, having first appeared in 1981 on the McLaren MP4/1. The FW14B's monocoque was changed very little from its FW14 predecessor – indeed the first two chassis, FW14B/06 and FW14B/07, were originally built as FW14 chassis in the second half of 1991, although they never ran with passive suspension, and only saw service as test cars equipped with active suspension. Both cars also appeared at various races as T-cars, but were never used in competition.

As with all Williams F1 car designs since

the 1985 FW10 (the team's first carbon-fibre chassis), and most F1 cars since, no separate bodywork was fitted to cover the monocoque itself, and the car's livery was applied directly to the outer surface of the tub, with a separate nose section, engine cover and sidepod panels attached to the monocoque.

The FW14B monocoque forms the 'safety cell' for the driver, and also houses the bladder-type fuel tank.

The monocoque has four bulkheads:

- Front bulkhead – on the forward face of which the steering rack and brake and clutch master cylinders are mounted. Also where the front nose/wing assembly attaches.
- Forward internal bulkhead – located forward of the cockpit opening, and cut away to enable the driver's legs and steering column to pass through.
- Rear internal bulkhead – forms the rear of the cockpit, to which the driver's seat is attached, and also forms the forward end of the fuel-tank bay.
- Rear bulkhead – to which the engine is bolted, and also forms the rear end of the fuel-tank bay.

The monocoque also incorporates both front and rear roll structures. The front roll structure is located in front of the cockpit opening, above the forward internal bulkhead, and the rear roll structure forms the highest point of the monocoque behind the driver's head (and incorporates the engine air intake).

The front suspension is mounted directly on metal brackets bonded into the monocoque structure during manufacture, and the Renault V10 engine is bolted directly to the rear bulkhead.

The monocoque was manufactured in-house at the Williams Grand Prix Engineering factory in Didcot, under the supervision of Brian O'Rourke, who joined the team in 1982. O'Rourke's experience proved invaluable to the team – he was instrumental in the design and manufacture of \s first composite monocoque, for the 1985 FW10 – and his expertise is still much in evidence today in his role as Chief Composites Engineer at Williams.

Talking about the 1992 season, O'Rourke recalls: "In 1992 we were at a transitional state in terms of how a monocoque was designed and built. Prior to the FW11 (pre-1986), design was an entirely manual process, meaning drawing boards and French curves – a laborious, time-consuming task. The reality was that we would issue a set of shapes as a starting point and the pattern-makers would do the rest for us. No designer in that era ever truly defined on paper what he ended up with.

"We began using a CAD [Computer Aided Design] system in September 1985, but its use was limited because our surfacing abilities were inadequate at the time (although I did the first Finite Element Analysis with it that year – CV joint cages). I recall doing the FW12 monocoque sections manually as well (late 1987), but did manage the nosebox via CAD; amazingly, it worked with little adjustment. The FW13 and FW14 [monocoques] were progressively defined using CAD, but the patterns were still manually cut (meaning that the result wasn't symmetrical).

"We began to encounter problems with the FW14 because the monocoque geometry was more complex than earlier cars, and it meant that the machined inserts within the

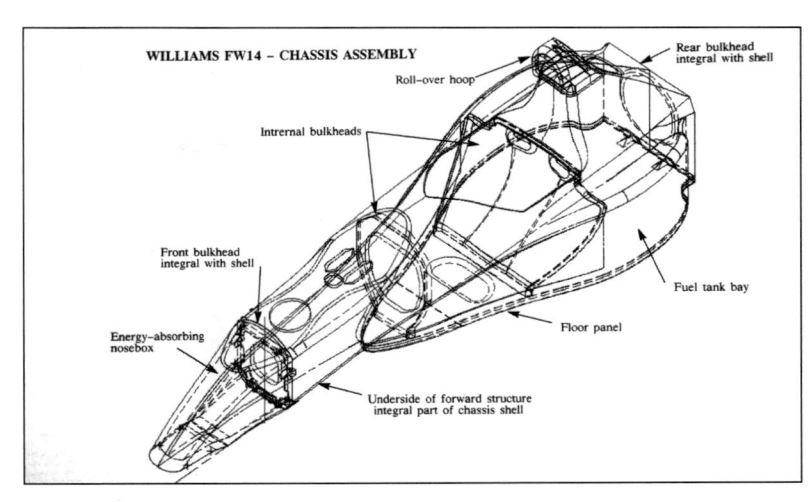

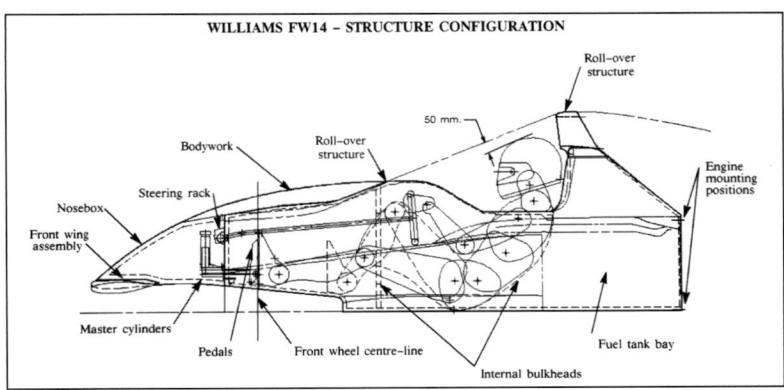

ABOVE Brian O'Rourke's drawings of the FW14 chassis structure from his document *Definition of Structure and report on Structural Testing*, dated March 1991. The FW14B chassis was almost identical to that of the FW14.
(Williams Heritage Archive/John Colley)

shell honeycomb were no longer fitting on flat surfaces. They were modelled properly in CAD and then machined from those files using CAM [Computer Aided Manufacturing], but the mating surfaces had been defined by manual working, and so fit became a real issue. This was recognised as being a major limitation for the future. Actually, it was while FW14B was racing in 1992 that we acquired our first five-axis router, which could be used to cut patterns for use in composite moulding from then on. The first tub where we used this was, therefore, FW15, built during the summer of '92. Thereafter, of course, progress was rapid, and everything that we do today is a progression of that work."

Detailed stress analysis and structural testing was carried out on the monocoque to ensure its structural integrity, and a test monocoque was subjected to FISA-defined 'push' load tests and impact tests under regulated loads.

O'Rourke explains the evolution of monocoque structural testing: "The very first test was imposed for 1985 – a single frontal impact – but, thereafter, others were added regularly. Static 'squeeze' tests appeared in 1988 and, for 1991, there were major changes in the form of a roll-hoop test, five squeeze tests and a tank-bay floor push, as well as an increase in crash speed. This constituted a major challenge at the time – and was all pretty nerve-wracking – but we carried them out without any problems. From then on there were many more additions to the point where, today, we have 19 different cases that must be demonstrated before we can even run the car. The FIA actually witness these tests for themselves and use their own equipment to measure the specified parameters."

Talking about the frontal impact test, O'Rourke continues: "In terms of the frontal-impact test, the nosebox, then as now, simply absorbed energy by means of controlled brittle fracture. Metallic structures absorb energy by means of 'plastic' deformation, forming lots of 'hinges' and exploiting the elongation-to-failure inherent to the material – 'crumpling' to put it crudely. Carbon-fibre/epoxy composites have no plastic behaviour and so will fracture in a brittle fashion. If you constrain the load direction to the plane of the material itself, however, you can manage the failure and cause it to progress from front to back. The big difference is that for a given mass of structure, you can absorb more than twice as much energy with the composite failure as a metal. Conversely, if the loading is 'out-of-plane' – such as bending in a wishbone – it is not so clever!"

RIGHT Again from Brian O'Rourke's March 1991 document, two photographs showing the general arrangement of the chassis lateral push-tests. *(Williams Heritage Archive/John Colley)*

FAR RIGHT 'Before' and 'after' photographs of the chassis frontal impact test (with nosebox in place) from Brian O'Rourke's document. *(Williams Heritage Archive/John Colley)*

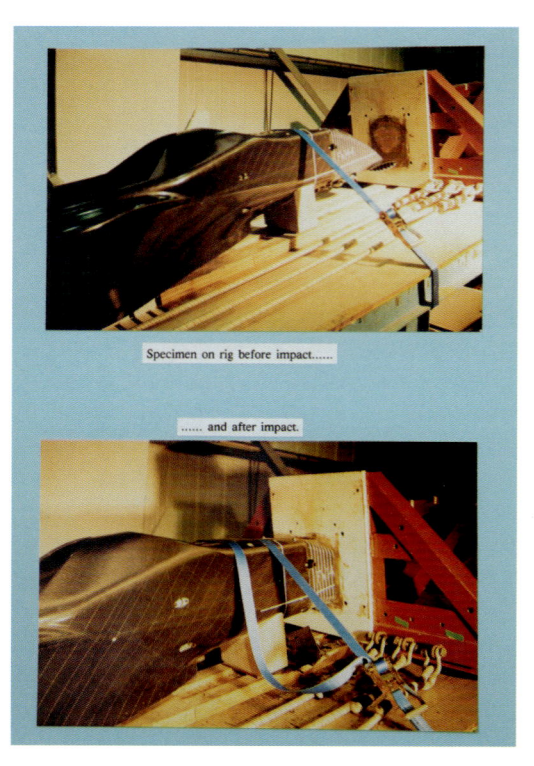

RIGHT **In this view of the front of the FW14B monocoque, with active-suspension hydraulic components in place, the additional fairings to accommodate the active-suspension struts can clearly be seen, as can the painted finish applied directly to the monocoque.** *(John Colley)*

Fuel tank

The bladder-type fuel tank, manufactured by ATL, is located behind the driver within the structure of the monocoque. The tank is manufactured from a Kevlar material, which is light but extremely flexible. The tank is designed to withstand a high-energy impact, and is also resistant to tearing and penetration to minimise the risk of fuel leakage in the event of an accident.

The fuel tank contains baffles to help to reduce fuel slosh inside the tank during acceleration, braking and cornering, and to help to ensure a constant supply of fuel to the engine. The tank also contains two electric fuel-lift pumps to ensure that the tank is scavenged of fuel, so that the car does not have to carry any more fuel than is absolutely necessary.

The filler is at the top of the tank, on the left-hand rear of the monococque, with the fuel tank vent connection on the right-hand side. When fuelling the tank, fuel is pumped in through the filler, with a vent tank connected to the vent to collect air and fuel vapour pushed out as the fuel enters the tank. As there was no refuelling during races in 1992, the fuel filler and vent are only accessible once the airbox/engine cover has been removed.

The only significant visual difference between the FW14 and FW14B chassis is the appearance of the fairings on the FW14B, on either side of the monocoque, to accommodate the active-suspension struts.

Bodywork

The FW14B's bodywork is all manufactured from carbon-fibre, and comprises:

■ A cover panel that fits over the suspension components at the front of the monocoque.
■ The nose/front wing assembly.
■ The airbox/engine cover.

LEFT **A view of the car with the front monocoque cover panel in place showing the fairings for the active-suspension struts.** *(John Colley)*

LEFT **With the engine cover and airbox removed, the fuel tank filler (1) and vent connection (2) can be clearly seen.** *(John Colley)*

LEFT **The Williams factory race bays during 1991, with FW14 monocoques being worked on. In the right-hand foreground of the photograph an ATL fuel cell can be seen resting on the floor.** *(Williams)*

LEFT To remove the front monocoque cover panel, the securing screws are removed...

CENTRE LEFT ... then the radio aerial must be unscrewed...

CENTRE RIGHT ... to allow the panel to be lifted off. *(John Colley)*

- The sidepod panels (one single panel on each side).
- A single small panel on each side, behind the sidepod panels and below the engine cover, which fits around the rear suspension and driveshaft.
- The rear wing assembly.
- The single-piece floor.

The front monocoque cover panel is removed to access the front suspension hydraulic components, or to remove the nose/front wing assembly. To remove the cover panel, its securing screws are removed, then the radio aerial has to be unscrewed to allow the panel to be lifted off. During testing, and throughout the 1992 season, the team cleverly used a black fabric cover to conceal the suspension hydraulic components from prying eyes! The cover was held in place over the suspension components with Velcro strips attached to the top of the monocoque, and could simply be pulled off for access to the components. The cars raced with this fabric cover in place under the monocoque cover panel.

The nose/front wing assembly is bolted to the front of the monocoque with four UNF bolts – two upper and two lower. The two upper bolts are only accessible once the cover panel has been removed from the front of the monocoque, so replacement of the nose during a race pitstop in the event of damage was not the quick procedure it is on today's F1 cars. The nose assembly incorporates a front crash structure, which is designed to dissipate energy in the event of a frontal impact (see page 78).

LEFT Throughout the 1992 season, a fabric cover was fitted under the front monocoque cover panel, to conceal the active-suspension hydraulic components from prying eyes. *(John Colley)*

FAR LEFT Chief Mechanic in 1992, and now General Manager of Williams Heritage, Dickie Stanford unscrews the lower nose/front wing assembly securing bolts...

LEFT ... followed by the upper bolts. *(John Colley)*

LEFT The ducts in the rear of the engine cover assist cooling and airflow around the back of the car. *(John Colley)*

The one-piece airbox/engine cover is secured by a series of bolts, and fits over the airbox, engine, transmission and rear suspension. Ducts at the rear of the cover assist airflow for cooling and also aid airflow to the lower plane of the rear wing and the diffuser.

The sidepod panels are a close fit over the sidepod ducts, which feed air to the radiators and also act as mounting points for various components, including electronic control units, the coolant header tank, etc. Towards the rear of each sidepod panel, a small cooling duct is secured by a series of screws. Cooling ducts of differing sizes – or a blanking plate – can be used, to suit various criteria, including the cooling requirements at specific circuits, the ambient temperature, and whether the car is

BELOW LEFT Dickie Stanford unscrews one of the airbox/engine cover securing bolts. *(John Colley)*

BELOW A view of the rear of the car with the airbox/engine cover removed. *(John Colley)*

81

ANATOMY OF THE WILLIAMS FW14B

RIGHT Unscrewing one of the sidepod panel securing bolts. *(John Colley)*

RIGHT A view of the right-hand sidepod panel removed, showing the air duct and heat-resistant foil covering on the inside face of the panel. *(John Colley)*

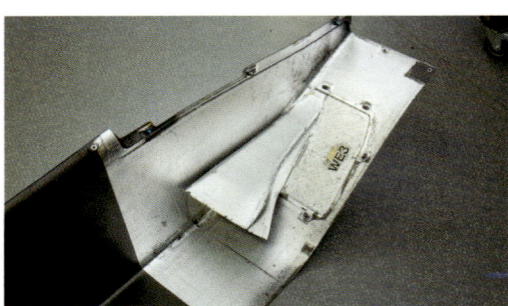

ABOVE Patrese at the Japanese Grand Prix, with blanking plates fitted to the sidepod air-duct locations. *(John Townsend)*

RIGHT The left-hand sidepod air duct on the Williams Grand Prix Collection's FW14B/11. *(John Colley)*

RIGHT The left-hand body panel to the rear of the sidepod in situ on FW14B/11. *(John Colley)*

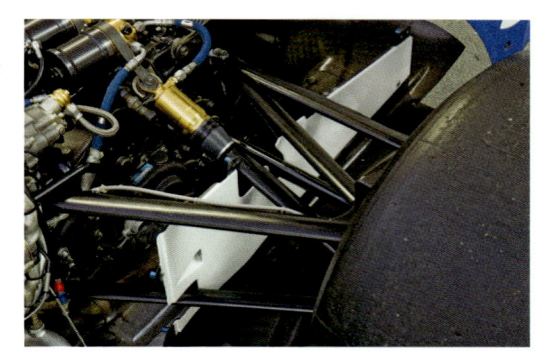

doing short runs in practice/qualifying conditions or a race distance.

The small body panels to the rear of the sidepods effectively fill the space between the engine cover, the rear of the sidepods and the floor, aiding airflow around the rear of the car.

Aerodynamics

The excellent aerodynamics of the FW14B contributed significantly to its success. Although the defining feature of the car was arguably its active suspension system, the main role of the active system was to provide a stable aerodynamic platform, and so the aerodynamic efficiency of the car was key to maximising the advantage offered by the suspension.

The FW14 had been developed using the wind tunnel at Southampton University, but during 1991 Williams Grand Prix Engineering invested heavily in its own half-scale rolling-road wind tunnel at its Didcot headquarters. This new wind tunnel was commissioned in time to develop the FW14B, and the aerodynamic team, led by Adrian Newey, put the new facility to good use to refine the new car.

During 1991, there was a significant number of aerodynamic developments for the FW14, but aerodynamic modifications to the FW14B during the 1992 season were minimal. The main changes involved altering the gurney flaps at the rear edges of the front wing, and varying the angle of the rear wing's upper elements (see pages 86–87).

The principal aerodynamic components on the car are:

- Front wing
- Floor/rear diffuser
- Rear wing

Brian O'Rourke recalls that there were far fewer aerodynamic changes to the FW14B during the 1992 season than had been the case with its predecessor, the FW14: "At one point on the FW14, we were up to a Mk.5 nosebox (although we only raced the short Mk.1 and the longer Mk.3), along with a Mk.5 front wing endplate, using a Mk.6 endplate footplate. That year we actually built 102 underbodies/diffusers, with just 14 people in our composites shop.

Part of the reason for that was the prevailing fashion to run the car very low and, basically, wear it away during the race.

"With the FW14B in '92, though, things calmed down, as the active-ride suspension made us better able to control the ride height. On the aero front, generally, the configuration was more stable that year."

Front wing

The front wing is the car's most important aerodynamic component, as it affects the airflow over every other part of the car in its wake. The FW14B front wing has two elements – the lower main element, and an upper element that has gurney flaps attached to its rear edges.

The endplates extend rearwards and curl inwards to form horizontal extensions, or 'footplates', which continue under the suspension behind the rear edges of the tyres. These footplates were designed to draw the outer edges of the wing planes down, closer to the track, thus generating increased downforce – an early form of the flexible front wing concept that would cause much controversy two decades later. Originally, these footplates were untethered to allow maximum flex, but FISA later insisted that the team added bracing wires (one on each side) to reduce the flex.

Brian O'Rourke recalls: "Front-wing endplates were becoming very sophisticated during this era, and had sprouted 'footplates' that extended a long way rearwards. Of course, it was only a matter of time before teams started to let them rub on the ground, using titanium strips to control wear. FISA wanted to limit this, and so made us stiffen the wings to prevent it happening. We wanted to retain the footplate, however, so the cable stays were really just there to prevent it bending downwards and making contact with the ground. One thing you can do with composite materials, however, is build a wing structure that is stiff in a bending sense, but flexible in torsion, so allowing you to have the wing twist under load and so become more effective. This was explored as well, so there was a worry that the footplate would get near to the ground as the wing rotated. Hence the cable is connected to the rear edge."

TOP Note the large gurney flaps fitted to the back edges of the front wing upper element to increase front downforce on Patrese's car at Monaco. *(John Townsend)*

ABOVE Contrast the Monaco front wing set-up with that used on the FW14Bs for the Italian Grand Prix at high-speed Monza, where no gurney flaps were fitted. *(John Townsend)*

LEFT The nose/front wing assembly removed from FW14B/11 with the gurney flaps clearly visible. *(John Colley)*

LEFT A rear view of FW14B/11's nose/front wing assembly, showing the rear of the nosebox, the gurney flaps, and the right-hand endplate 'footplate' with its bracing wire. *(John Colley)*

RIGHT The front of the floor/diffuser assembly extends forwards ahead of the sidepods, just behind the back of the front wheels. *(John Colley)*

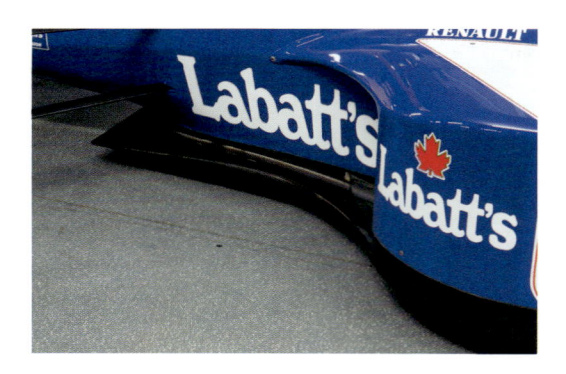

ABOVE A lip at the top edge of the floor forms the bottom edge of the sidepod. Note the silver heat-reflecting material on the inner face of the floor around the engine and exhaust manifolds. *(John Colley)*

LEFT The floor is supported by bracing wires and struts at various points. In this view, two bracing struts (arrowed) can be seen attached to the rear upper-wishbone mounting bracket on the gearbox casing. *(Author)*

BELOW A view of the rear of the diffuser on FW14B/11. Note the carbon struts (arrowed) securing the floor/diffuser assembly to the rear-wing endplates. *(John Colley)*

Floor/rear diffuser

The floor/rear diffuser assembly forms a single component that is attached to the underside of the car, running from under the nose, just behind the line of the rear of the front wheels, to the rear tip of the diffuser behind the rear wing. A lip at the top edge of the floor, around the profile of the sidepods, forms the bottom edge of the sidepod and the lower locating face for the sidepod panel.

Removing the floor/rear diffuser is a major operation due to the number of ancillary components connected to it, and the fact that it is supported at various points by bracing wires and struts connected to the engine, gearbox, rear-wing endplates, and so on.

At the rear of the car, the two exhaust tailpipes feed into fabricated metal shrouds bolted into the surface of the diffuser. These shrouds direct the exhaust plumes under the rear of the diffuser, helping to increase the velocity of the air under the car, in turn lowering the air pressure and increasing downforce. One helpful effect of this 'blown diffuser' from the driver's point of view was a significant increase in rear downforce under 'on-throttle' conditions, which was particularly beneficial at low speeds, when traction was at a premium, but also made a considerable difference to grip in high-speed corners. This was a trait that Nigel Mansell found easier to deal with than Riccardo Patrese, as Paddy Lowe noted in an interview with *Autosport* in 2014: "It required a lot of confidence from the driver. The combination of Nigel's balls and that '92 car was unbeatable because he trusted the downforce would be there when he hit the throttle." This system was an early form of 'exhaust blowing' – a concept

LEFT The rear-wing assembly on FW14B/11, with a medium- and high-downforce, three-upper-element set-up. *(John Colley)*

ABOVE A view with the rear bodywork removed, showing the metal exhaust shroud fitted to the diffuser into which the left-hand exhaust tailpipe feeds. *(John Colley)*

that, in refined form, would make controversial headlines in F1 some 20 years later.

Whereas on today's F1 cars the floor is a major area of development, with numerous evolutions often introduced during a season, only minimal changes were made to the FW14B's floor and diffuser during 1992. The main changes carried out were to the vertical fences (strakes) at the rear of the diffuser, to which circuit-specific detail changes were made.

Rear wing

The rear wing is mounted on two vertical carbon supports bolted to the sides of the gearbox. The two brackets are bonded to the lower mainplane of the rear wing. Simple, flat endplates connect the upper wing elements to the lower elements.

ABOVE The rear-wing assembly carbon supports are bolted to the gearbox. *(John Colley)*

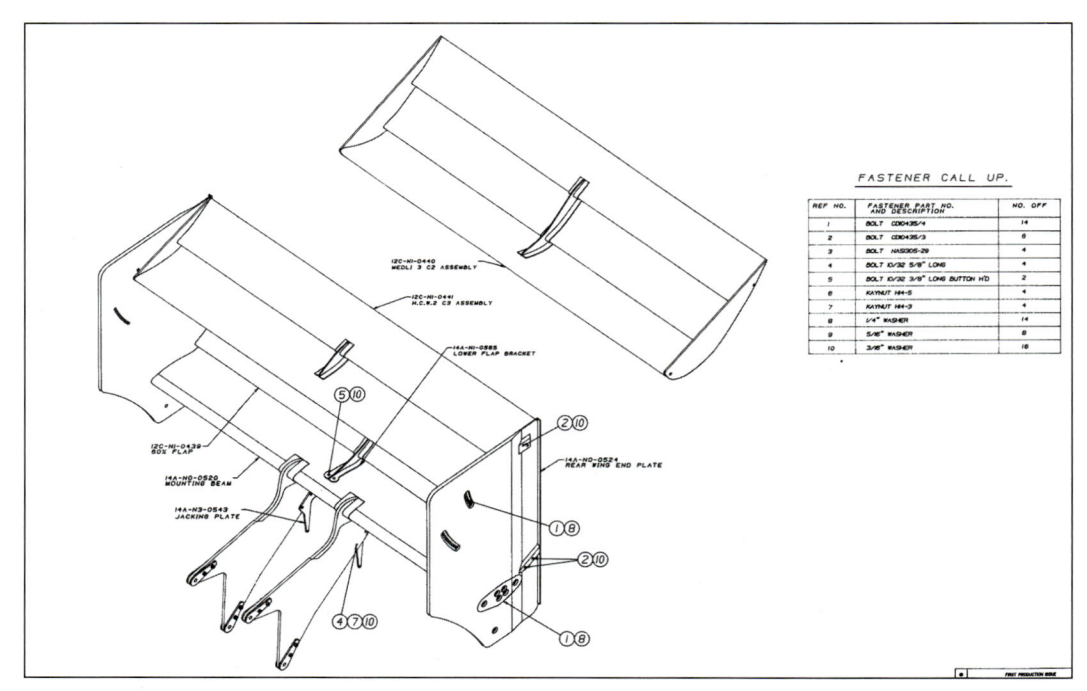

LEFT An engineering drawing for the FW14/14B rear-wing assembly, showing the two- and three-element upper-element assembly options. *(Williams Heritage Archive)*

85

ANATOMY OF THE WILLIAMS FW14B

RIGHT An engineering drawing for the rear-wing endplates, showing the fixings and adjustment bolts for the upper and lower elements. *(Williams Heritage Archive)*

BELOW Patrese's FW14B at the Hungarian Grand Prix, with a high-downforce three-element upper rear wing set-up. *(John Townsend)*

BOTTOM Mansell at the Belgian Grand Prix with a low-downforce two-element upper rear wing set-up. *(John Townsend)*

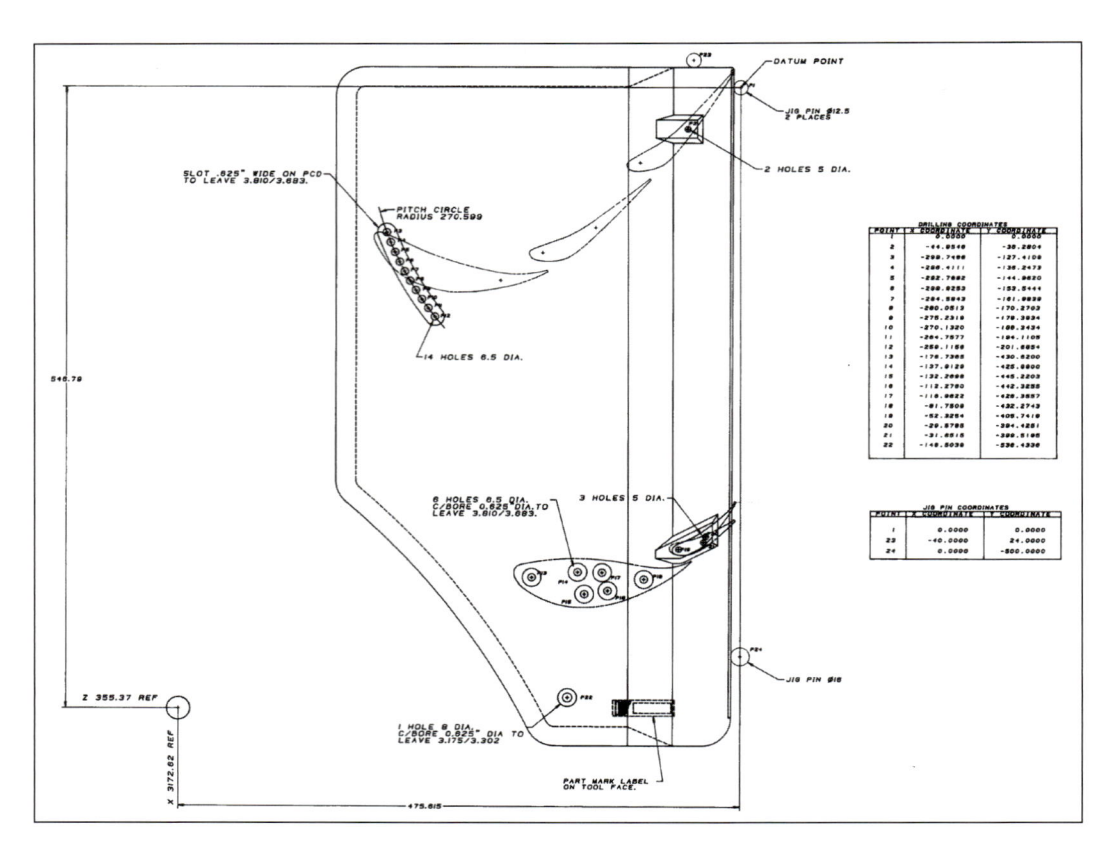

The lower wing comprises a mainplane and an upper flap. Neither the mainplane nor the upper flap is adjustable, but alternative upper flaps can be fitted to adjust downforce.

During 1992, either two or three upper wing elements were used, depending on the circuit and downforce requirements. At most medium and high-downforce circuits, a three-element upper assembly was used, with a plain black

BELOW Unscrewing the rear-wing upper-element left-hand adjustment bolt. *(John Colley)*

'PUSH-TO-PASS' BUTTON

To aid overtaking, the FW14B features an innovative system that was unique in 1992, and made possible by the active suspension system.

By pressing a button on the steering wheel, the driver can send a command, via the VCM (Vehicle Control and Monitor module), to the suspension actuators to temporarily lower the rear ride height and raise the front ride height by an optimum amount to reduce the downforce provided by the front and rear wings, and stall the rear diffuser. This reduces drag, thus effectively increasing top speed, without adversely affecting the car's handling. In many ways, this concept was an early equivalent of the modern DRS (Drag Reduction System), although the DRS used today stalls the rear wing rather than the diffuser.

This novel idea could be used to good effect to aid overtaking on straights.

---

carbon lower mainplane, while at high-downforce circuits – namely Imola, Hockenheim, Spa and Monza – a two-element upper assembly was used. Both of these upper wing assemblies were the work of Williams aerodynamicist Egbhal Hamidy, and first appeared on the FW12C in 1989. The upper elements are part of a single bonded assembly, and the angle (incidence) of the whole assembly can be adjusted by rotating the assembly around the top rear fixings, and altering the position of the lower end within an arc of fixing holes.

Suspension

One of the most significant features of the FW14B is its active suspension system. The components of the active suspension system simply fulfil the role of conventional springs, dampers and anti-roll bars, and the layout of the double-wishbone suspension is conventional, having been carried over from the FW14. The suspension is pushrod-activated, with Williams-built hydro-pneumatic active-suspension actuators taking the place of conventional spring/damper units.

Front suspension

The front suspension comprises fabricated uprights (with shrink-fit hub bearings), upper and lower steel wishbones, with pushrod-operated hydro-pneumatic active-suspension actuators, a damper-valve block, and a single remote disc-spring pack (located in the cockpit behind the driver's seat).

The inner ends of the wishbones are bolted to brackets bonded to the monocoque. Brian O'Rourke explains: "In the case of the forward pick-ups, we moulded a recess into the front bulkhead, behind which were large machined-aluminium inserts in the honeycomb. These were drilled and tapped to accept bolts but, to make the connection double-shear, a plate was bolted to the bulkhead inboard of this, and had a decent lug at its outboard end aligned with the end of the wishbone rod. A bolt then passed through this lug, the rod end and into the solid insert. At the rear positions, each had a honeycomb insert backed up by a bulkhead, and an external fork-end (clevice) bracket was bolted all the way through these. The rear rod

ABOVE An FW14 being worked on in the garage at the 1991 Portuguese Grand Prix. The front suspension bellcranks and longitudinally mounted spring/damper units can be seen on top of the monocoque, making an interesting comparison with the active front suspension layout on the FW14B. *(John Townsend)*

LEFT An overall view of the FW14B left-hand front suspension. The black rubber sleeve at the top of the pushrod, visible below the active-suspension strut fairing, is a packer used for transport and storage only, to limit the movement of the suspension, and is removed when running the car. The packer appears in many of the photographs in this manual. *(John Colley)*

RIGHT The front upper wishbone rear mounting bracket is bonded to the monocoque. *(John Colley)*

RIGHT A view of two front upright/hub assemblies – on the left, a 'naked' left-hand upright, and on the right a right-hand upright with brake disc fitted. *(John Colley)*

RIGHT A front camber plate in position on the car. The left-hand side of the car is shown, with the front towards the top of the photograph. *(John Colley)*

RIGHT A front left-hand camber plate showing the camber-angle marking – 2¾° in this case. *(John Colley)*

ends then fitted into the clevices and bolted through vertically."

On each side of the car, the fabricated upright connects to the upper wishbone and steering track rod via a camber plate that bolts to the top of the upright. To adjust front camber angle, the camber plates (one on each side of the car) are changed. Each camber plate is marked with the relevant camber angle. The camber often differed from the left to the right of the car, depending on the specific circuit set-up. FW14B/11 currently has a 2¾° front camber plate fitted on the left, and a 2° plate on the right.

The lower end of the upright is connected to the lower wishbone via a through-bolt.

The top end of the pushrod is connected directly to the lower end of the active-suspension actuator, with the lower end of the pushrod attached to the outer end of the lower wishbone via a rose joint. The upper end of the active-suspension actuator is attached to a stud on the top of the monocoque via a rose joint.

The brake caliper is mounted to two studs at the rear of the upright, the upper stud on the camber plate, the lower stud on the upright itself. The brake fluid hose runs through the forward leg of the lower wishbone.

Rear suspension

The rear suspension comprises fabricated uprights (with shrink-fit hub bearings), and steel upper arms and lower wishbones, with

BELOW The left-hand front active-suspension actuator, showing the upper attachment to the stud on the monocoque, and the pushrod attachment at the lower end of the actuator. In this photograph, the packing spacer has been removed from the actuator. *(John Colley)*

pushrod-operated, hydro-pneumatic active-suspension actuators and remote left- and right-hand disc-spring packs (incorporating damper valves) located longitudinally on the top of the gearbox.

The inner ends of the upper suspension arm and the lower wishbone are bolted to brackets attached to the gearbox casing.

On each side of the car, the fabricated upright connects to the forward upper suspension arm via two studs in the suspension arm. The two studs pass through a metal block and two spacer washers, one on each stud. The spacer washers can be changed to adjust the rear camber angle. The metal block attaches to the forward end of the upright via a through-bolt. The lower end of the upright is connected to the lower wishbone via a though-bolt.

The rear leg of the upper suspension arm connects to the rear of the upright via a rose joint. This rose joint is screwed into a rear toe-angle adjuster sleeve, which is itself screwed into the end of the suspension arm. The rose joint is connected to the upright via a through-bolt. The adjuster sleeve and rose joint are locked in position with two locknuts. Once the two locknuts have been slackened, the adjuster sleeve can be turned to adjust the toe angle.

The top end of the pushrod is connected directly to the lower end of the active-suspension actuator, while the lower end of the pushrod is attached to the outer end of the lower wishbone via a rose joint. The upper end of the suspension actuator is attached to a stud on the gearbox casing via a rose joint.

The brake caliper is attached to two studs at the front of the upright. The brake fluid hose is clipped to the forward leg of the upper suspension arm.

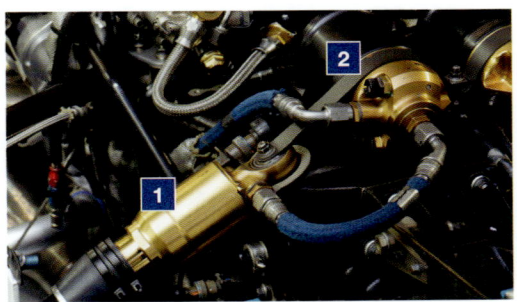

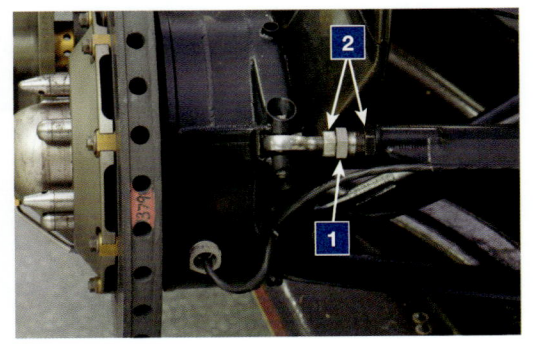

LEFT An overall view of the FW14B left-hand rear suspension, showing the three-leg upper arm, lower wishbone and pushrod. Behind the pushrod, the driveshaft is visible. *(John Colley)*

LEFT A view of the left-hand rear suspension hydraulic actuator (1) and the disc-spring pack/damper valve assembly (2). At the bottom end of the actuator note the packing spacer, which would be removed for running. *(John Colley)*

LEFT The right-hand rear-suspension lower-wishbone rear mounting bracket (arrowed) on the gearbox casing. *(John Colley)*

FAR LEFT Rear camber-angle adjustment spacer washers (arrowed) – right-hand side of car shown. *(John Colley)*

LEFT Rear wheel toe-angle adjuster sleeve (1) and locknuts (2) – left-hand side of car shown. *(John Colley)*

ABOVE Front active-suspension hydraulic system components, showing: (1) Fluid filters; (2) Hydraulic valve block; (3) Moog valves; (4) Front damper valve assembly; (5) Front suspension actuators. *(John Colley)*

The FW14B active-ride system

The origins and development of the Williams active-ride system are described in Chapter 2, but in the final form used on the FW14B the system was quite different from the version first raced during 1987–88 on the FW11B and FW12. Although the basic principles of the systems were similar, the most significant difference was in the control system.

The FW14B active suspension system comprises the following components:

- Hydraulic pump – mounted on the gearbox on the RS3C engine, or within the vee of the engine (at the gearbox end) on the RS4 engine.
- Front hydraulic actuators (struts) – one left and one right, mounted on the top of the monocoque and connected to the pushrods.
- Front spring pack – single pack located under the driver's seat back on the right-hand side of the cockpit.
- Rear hydraulic actuators (struts) – one left and one right, mounted on top of the gearbox and connected to the pushrods.
- Rear spring packs – one left and one right, mounted longitudinally on top of the gearbox.
- Rear damper valve assemblies – one left and one right, incorporated in the housings for the rear spring packs.
- Front damper valve assembly – fitted ahead of the hydraulic valve block on the top of the monocoque at the front of the car.
- Hydraulic actuator (strut) position sensors – incorporated inside the hydraulic actuators.

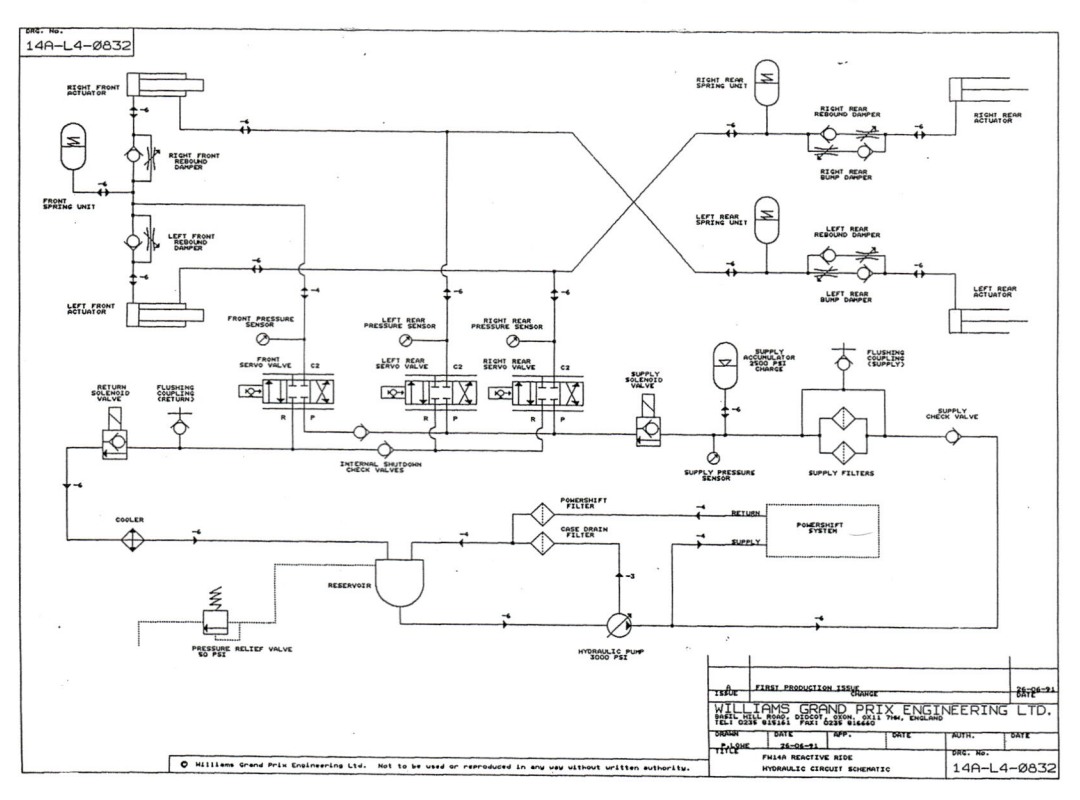

RIGHT A layout drawing titled 'FW14A Reactive Ride Hydraulic Circuit Schematic' drawn by Paddy Lowe in June 1991, showing the layout of the system that would be used on the FW14B. *(Williams Heritage Archive)*

- Hydraulic fluid accumulator – mounted behind the dashboard bulkhead, in the cockpit.
- Hydraulic fluid reservoir – mounted on top of the gearbox, behind the airbox.
- Hydraulic valve block – mounted at the front of the car on top of the monocoque.
- Three Moog hydraulic servo valves – for the front, left-rear and right-rear hydraulic circuits, mounted in the valve block on top of the monocoque.
- Three pressure sensors – for the front, left-rear and right-rear hydraulic circuits (located in the hydraulic valve block).
- Accelerometers – mounted on the floor of the cockpit, under the driver's seat.
- Supply and return solenoid valves.
- Supply pressure sensor.
- Fluid supply filters – incorporated at the rear of the hydraulic valve block.
- System flushing supply and return couplings.
- Supply and internal shut-down check valves.
- Hydraulic fluid cooler – located at the top of the left-hand sidepod.
- Hydraulic fluid expansion tank – mounted in the left-hand sidepod.
- System pressure relief valve.
- Gearbox powershift and case-drain filters (not part of suspension system, but sharing the active-suspension hydraulic circuit).
- Gearbox powershift system (as above).

Hydraulic fluid

The hydraulic fluid used in the system is aerospace-spec Shell AeroShell mineral-based hydraulic fuild, and the system capacity is approximately 1.5 litres. The system runs at a pressure of 3,000psi (about 207 bar). The hydraulic fluid is changed before the start of each day's running, and a flushing, refilling and bleeding procedure is carried out, using a special rig known within the team as the 'washing machine'.

Hydraulic pump

The hydraulic pump used on the FW14B is a variable swash-plate pump manufactured by Vickers (now Eaton Limited), and was originally designed for use in aircraft hydraulic systems.

In the early days of the active system, the development of the hydraulic pump proved challenging. One of the most significant problems was cavitation inside the pump, which caused air bubbles to form in the hydraulic fluid. Chris Dietrich, who worked on the development of the active system, recalls: "There was a story from Vickers about that, because basically the swash plates couldn't cope with the vibration, so you got cavitation. Simon [Wells] went back to Vickers and said we'd had this problem – we saw a drop in the pressure when the engine went through a resonance – and they said: 'Oh yes, we had something similar on a Jaguar [aircraft], or something – yes, we saw that same issue.' So we said: 'What happened?' They said: 'Oh, we don't know, the pilot bailed out!'"

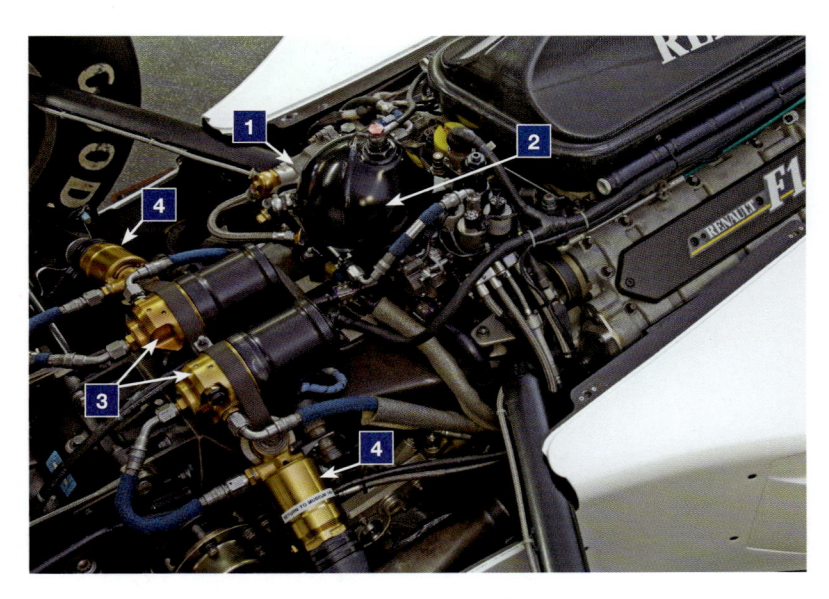

Part of the problem with the pump in the early days was that an F1 car runs under a uniquely challenging set of operating conditions, even compared with a jet aircraft, as Dave Lang explains.

"Usually on an aircraft the pump comes up to speed and stays at that speed. Its life in a civil airliner was several thousand hours, and when it was used in a fighter application it was probably OK for less than half its 'civilian' lifespan. By the time we'd had a pump for about an hour and a half, we were already reaching its limits! The original 022 pump that we used on the FW14 was updated to an 011 pump for the FW14B, which I think may have been used on a training aircraft and possibly also on a missile! It was an off-the-shelf component and we were using it in an environment it had never been designed for, so we had to do a lot of development work with Vickers to get it to last on the car.

ABOVE Rear active-suspension hydraulic system components, showing: (1) Hydraulic pump; (2) Hydraulic fluid reservoir; (3) Rear spring packs; (4) Rear suspension actuators. *(John Colley)*

RIGHT The hydraulic pump (arrowed) on FW14B/11, fitted with an RS3C engine.
(Steve Rendle)

"We had problems with the shaft seal that required work, and we did loads of development work with Vickers on the internals of the pump. They were happy for us to make things for them to put in the pump, and then for us to try it. Quite often we'd take a pump assembly down to Havant [the Hampshire base of Vickers Hydraulics], change a few bits and pieces while we were actually testing up at Silverstone, put it in the car, try it, and take it back down to them to have a look at overnight, maybe make some more changes and bring it back for the following day."

The hydraulic-pump installation on an FW14B fitted with the RS3C engine features a pump mounted on the top of the gearbox casing and driven via a step-up gearbox drive from a gear mounted on the rear of the left-hand cylinder bank inlet camshaft. This mounting arrangement requires the pump mounting to be shimmed to allow for the tolerances between the engine and gearbox mountings. Each time the engine and gearbox are separated, the pump shimming has to be checked using a specially made jigging tool. One of the knock-on effects of this is the increased time required for an engine or gearbox change – in 1992 a typical RS3C engine change took around an hour and a half.

When the car is fitted with an RS4 engine, the hydraulic pump is mounted within the vee of the engine, and is belt-driven from the rear (gearbox end) of the right-hand cylinder bank inlet camshaft.

Before running the pump, the hydraulic system has to be pressurised to a minimum pre-charge pressure (by connecting a nitrogen bottle to the hydraulic-system fluid expansion tank) in order to prevent cavitation.

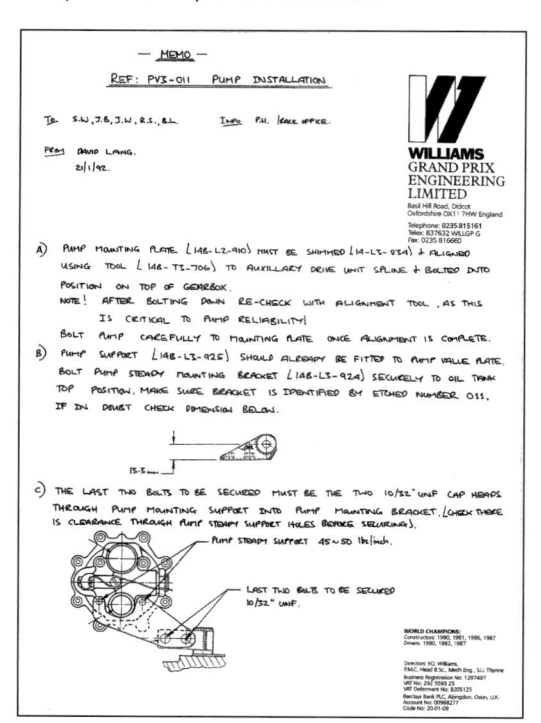

BELOW An engineering drawing, from Dave Lang, showing the step-up gearbox drive for the hydraulic pump on the RS3C engine.
(Williams Heritage Archive/John Colley)

BELOW RIGHT A memo from Dave Lang, dated January 1992, detailing the recommended fitting and shimming details for the hydraulic pump fitted to the RS3C engine. *(Williams Heritage Archive)*

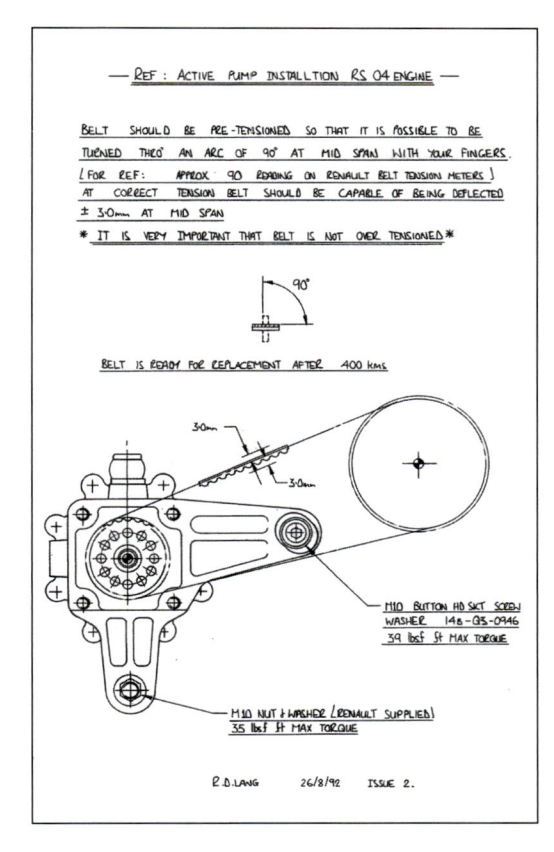

ABOVE Recommendations concerning the belt-driven hydraulic pump installation for the RS4 engine. *(Williams Heritage Archive)*

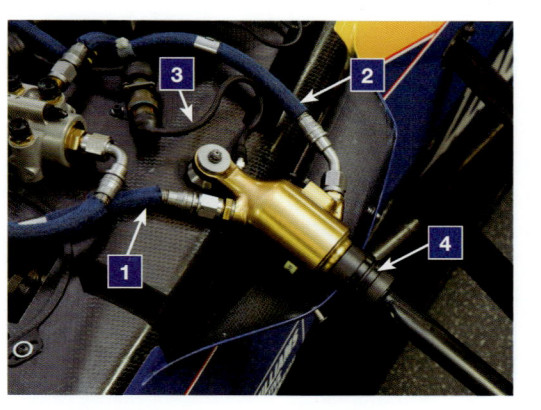

Suspension actuators (struts)

The suspension actuators are used to control the ride height at each corner of the car. Each actuator incorporates a built-in position potentiometer, developed in conjunction with Williams by Penny & Giles, who had previously worked in the aviation industry.

The front suspension actuators are mounted on the monocoque. The upper end of each actuator is secured to a stud bonded to the monocoque, while the lower end connects to the upper end of the pushrod.

The rear actuators are mounted on the top of the gearbox casing. The upper end of each actuator is secured to a stud on the gearbox casing, while the lower end connects to the upper end of the pushrod.

LEFT The front left-hand suspension actuator showing: (1) Hose connecting to damper valve; (2) Hose connecting to opposite (rear right-hand) suspension actuator; (3) Actuator position potentiometer wiring; (4) Rubber packer fitted for transport and storage. *(John Colley)*

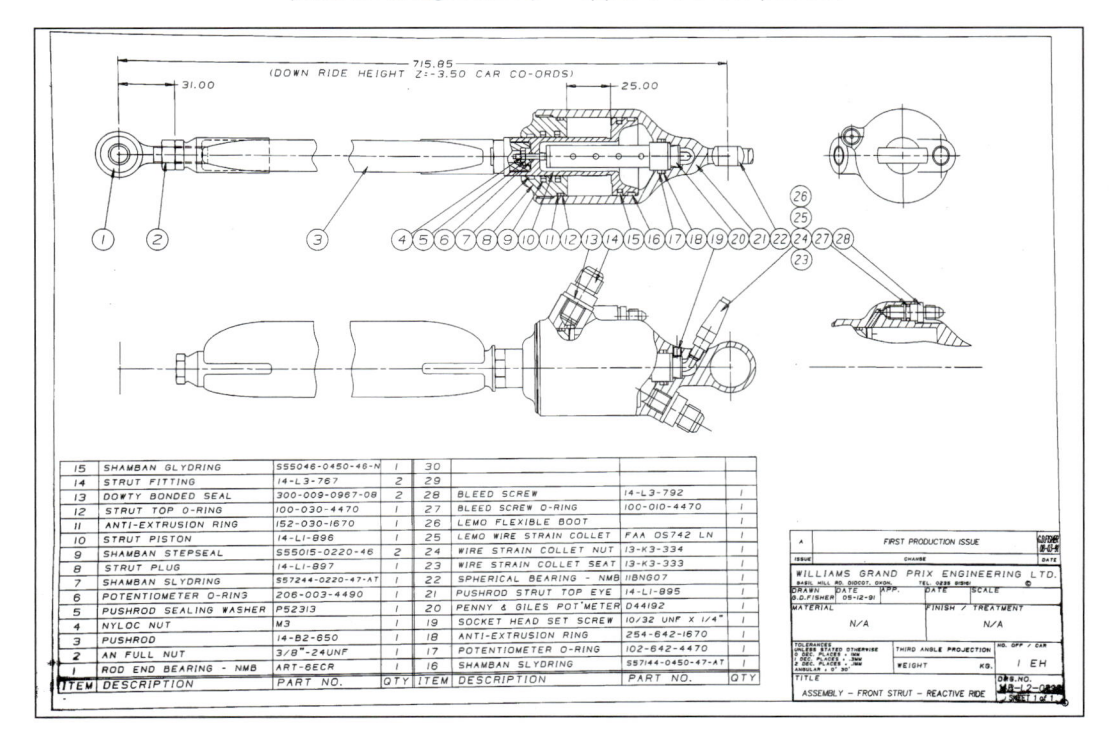

LEFT An engineering drawing by Gavin Fisher, dated December 1991, showing the construction of the front hydraulic suspension actuator and its connection to the pushrod. *(Williams Heritage Archive/John Colley)*

RIGHT A view of the rear right-hand suspension actuator. The rubber packer at the lower end of the actuator is fitted for transport and storage. *(Steve Rendle)*

BELOW An engineering drawing, again by Gavin Fisher, showing the front spring pack components. *(Williams Heritage Archive)*

ITEM	DESCRIPTION	PART NO.	QTY
9	END PLUG	14-L3-919	1
8	MAIN BODY	14-L2-920/20	1
7	DISC SPRINGS	∅70X∅40.5X5.0	20
6	SPRING CAP	14-L2-784	1
5	RETAINING CLIP	14-L3-918	1
4	PISTON	14-L2-917/1	1
3	SHAMBAN SLYDRING	SS7144-0635-47-AT	2
2	SHAMBAN STEPSEAL	SS5018-0635-46	1
1	TOP CAP	14-L2-922	1

RIGHT A close-up view of the left-hand rear spring pack, showing the damper valve bump (1) and rebound (2) adjuster screws. *(Steve Rendle)*

RIGHT A view of the rear spring pack components showing the casing (1), spring pack (2) and spring cap (3). *(John Colley)*

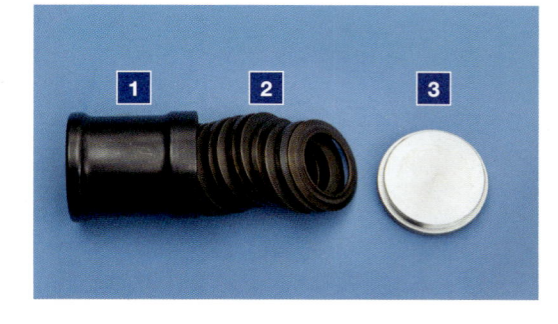

Front spring pack

The front spring pack is located behind the driver's seat back on the right-hand side of the cockpit. Fluid is routed from the front damper valve assembly through a hose running along the right-hand side of the monocoque to the spring pack. The disc springs inside the spring pack resist the fluid pressure.

Rear spring packs

The two rear spring packs are located side-by-side on top of the gearbox casing, between the two rear suspension actuators.

Fluid is routed from each suspension actuator to the relevant spring pack, and the disc springs inside the spring-pack housing resist the fluid pressure.

Damper valves

The front damper valve assembly is mounted remotely, ahead of the valve block on the top of the monocoque, and contains adjuster screws to enable adjustment of the bump and rebound damping for the left- and right-hand sides of the car. The rear damper valves are integral with the rear spring packs mounted on top of the gearbox casing.

Dave Lang explains the operation of the damper valves: "We had little damper valves with a shim either side of them, and then also across these damper valves we had little needle cartridge valves that we could tune as well, so we could control the fluid flow and bypass the shim pack. In effect we still had low-speed damping and high-speed damping – the shims in the damper valves were for bumps and kerbs, etc, but then for the low-

BELOW A view of the cockpit with the seat removed, showing the location of the front spring pack (arrowed). *(John Colley)*

speed the fluid just went through a bypass needle valve – more or less the same as a conventional damper."

Hydraulic fluid accumulator

The hydraulic fluid accumulator is located behind the dashboard bulkhead, in the cockpit, above the steering column.

The accumulator holds a reserve of hydraulic fluid at system pressure (3,000psi), which can be released according to the demands of the system. The accumulator also acts as an anti-surge device and pulse damper.

Hydraulic fluid reservoir

The hydraulic fluid reservoir is located at the rear of the engine, on top of the gearbox casing. The reservoir contains fluid at the pump pre-charge pressure, rather than full system pressure.

Before the car's engine is started, the hydraulic system is pressurised to a pre-charge pressure, using nitrogen applied at the hydraulic fluid reservoir expansion tank located in the sidepod.

Hydraulic valve block

The hydraulic valve block houses the three Moog valves, the two hydraulic system filters, the pressure sensors for the front and rear hydraulic circuits, and the safety solenoids.

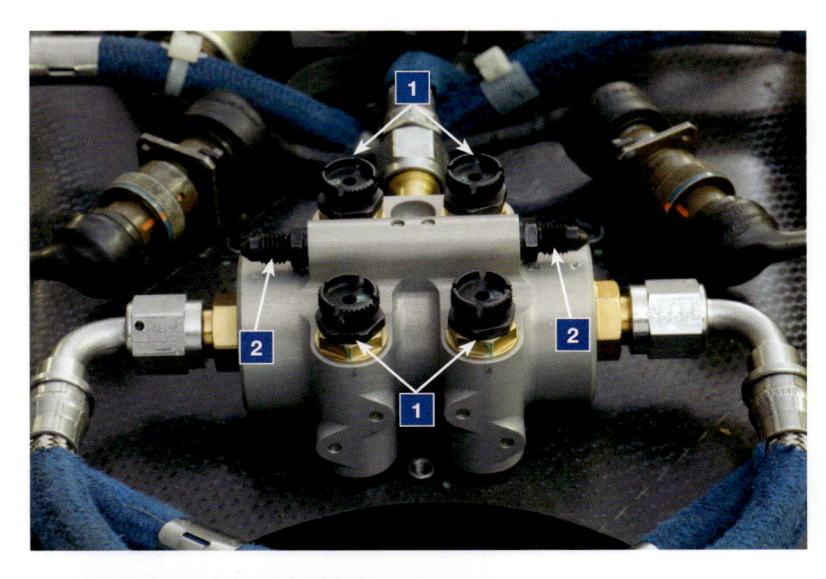

ABOVE The damper valve assembly, mounted ahead of the hydraulic valve block, showing the bump and rebound damping adjustment screws (1) and bleed screws (2). *(John Colley)*

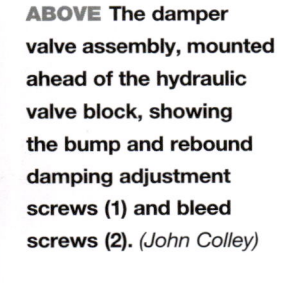

LEFT The hydraulic fluid reservoir (arrowed) mounted on top of the gearbox. *(John Colley)*

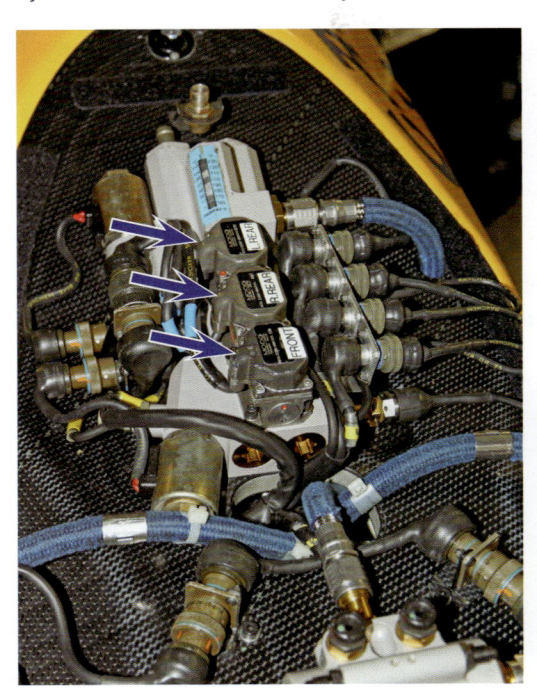

FAR LEFT The hydraulic valve block assembly in situ on FW14B/11. Note the Moog valves (arrowed). *(Steve Rendle)*

LEFT A view of the hydraulic valve block, along with its engineering drawing. The valve block shown has blanking plugs fitted to the fluid ports. *(John Colley)*

LEFT The active-suspension system accelerometers viewed with the driver's seat removed. *(John Colley)*

95
ANATOMY OF THE WILLIAMS FW14B

RIGHT The locations of the hydraulic fluid filters (arrowed) fitted to the rear of the hydraulic valve block. *(Steve Rendle)*

FAR RIGHT The hydraulic fluid cooler location on the top of the left-hand sidepod. The duct from the sidepod feeds cooling air across the fins of the cooler. *(John Colley)*

RIGHT A photograph taken by the engineering team, showing the hydraulic fluid cooler from the car used by Mansell for the Italian Grand Prix. Note the heavy contamination picked up in the cooler fins during the race. *(Williams Heritage Archive/John Colley)*

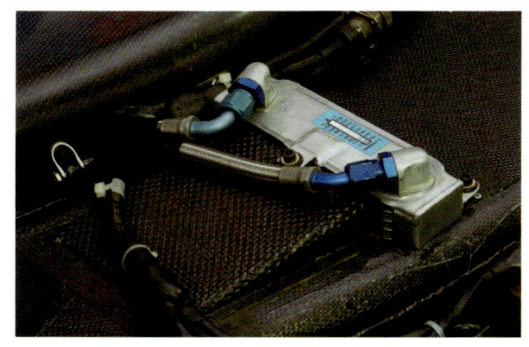

Accelerometers
The accelerometers are mounted under the driver's seat on the floor of the cockpit.

Fluid filters
The hydraulic system is fitted with two fluid filters, located in housings at the rear of the hydraulic valve block. These filters are fitted in series – the hydraulic fluid passing through both filters. Two filters are used purely to provide adequate filtration, while keeping the components compact.

The filters are disposable, and in 1992 were renewed for each event, with one pair of filters used for the complete race weekend.

Hydraulic fluid cooler
A small hydraulic fluid cooler is located on the top of the left-hand sidepod. A duct at the front

---

HYDRAULIC SYSTEM MAINTENANCE

During 1992, before an FW14B was run at the start of a day on-track, a flushing-pack device christened the 'washing machine' by the Williams engineers was used to circulate fluid through the hydraulic system to flush, filter and bleed the system. In the early days of active suspension development, contamination of the fluid caused many problems, and it was necessary to observe scrupulous cleanliness, and to filter the fluid to a considerable degree.

To connect the flushing pack, the top plate, containing the Moog valves, was removed from the hydraulic valve block, and a blanking plate was fitted in its place with integral hose connections for the flushing pack. The top plate and Moog valve assembly was refitted once the flushing/filtering/bleeding procedure was complete.

Dave Lang explains the use of the flushing pack: "The whole car used to be connected up to the flushing pack, which was like a power unit that we used to circulate all the fluid through. While the car was in the garage [when the flushing pack was connected], we were circulating fluid all through the system, because we learned that we had to filter the fluid down to 3 to 5 microns (aircraft-specification filtering). When we first built the car, we didn't put the Moog valves on – they went on last – so we circulated fluid for around 20 minutes, and there was a big filter in the flushing pack. The hydraulic system on the car has inbuilt filters anyway, but the Moog valves and the filters wouldn't be fitted until the car had been run on a flushing sequence. We took the Moog valves and the filters off the valve block and fitted a blanking plate to the top of the valve block for flushing. The first flush was done without the Moog valves and filters fitted, then once they were fitted there were other sequences carried out during the course of the weekend."

of the cooler feeds air from the sidepod opening to the cooler fins.

Hydraulic fluid expansion tank

The hydraulic fluid expansion tank is located towards the rear of the left-hand sidepod. The tank allows for expansion of fluid in the system as the fluid heats up during a race. An internal tube runs to the bottom of the tank, so that the fluid can be picked up and returned to the main system when it cools.

Steering

The FW14B is fitted with manual steering (power-assisted steering was used for the first time on a Williams on the 1994 FW16) by means of a conventional rack-and-pinion steering rack mounted via two metal clamp brackets on the front bulkhead of the monocoque. The rack is adjustable for preload (driver feel) by turning an adjuster screw using a square key, in similar fashion to a road-car steering rack.

Each track rod is secured to the end of the steering rack via a balljoint and a threaded adjuster stud that screws into the end of the track rod.

Front-wheel toe angle is adjusted by slackening a locknut on each adjuster stud and turning the stud on each side of the car.

The single-piece tubular-steel steering column is supported in the cockpit by an aluminium bracket that is bolted to a metal insert in the monocoque forward internal bulkhead, ahead of which is a carbon/epoxy honeycomb sandwich. The column runs in a bush fitted to the support bracket, and is connected to the steering rack via a universal joint and clamp bolt.

Steering wheel

Details of the steering wheel are provided on page 124.

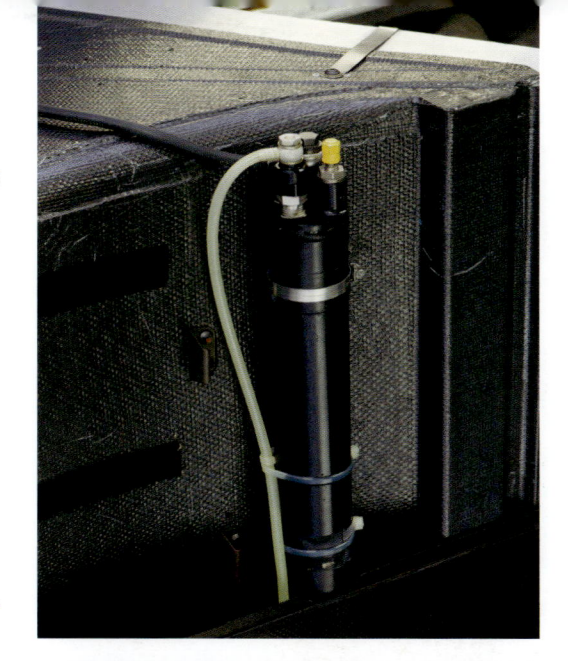

LEFT The hydraulic fluid expansion tank, located in the left-hand sidepod. *(John Colley)*

BELOW The steering rack mounted on the monocoque front bulkhead, showing the rack mounting clamps (1), the rack (2), the rack adjuster screw (3) and the track-rod ends (4). *(John Colley)*

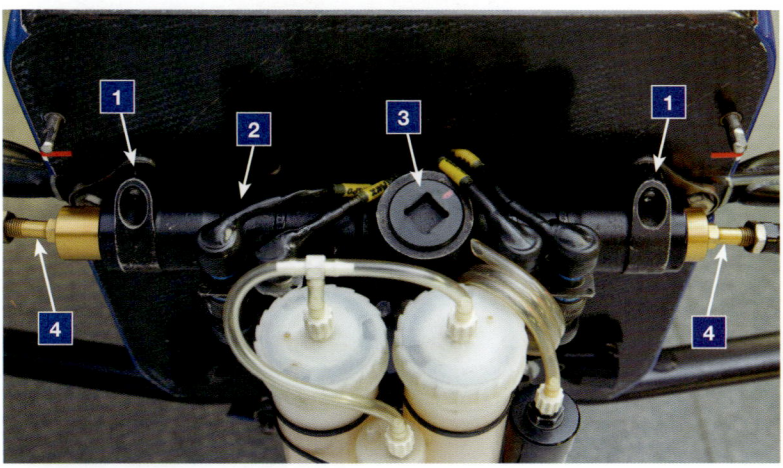

LEFT The steering-rack internal components, showing the pinion (1), the rack (2), a track-rod end (3), sleeve (4 – slides over track-rod end and screws on to rack), shim (5) and spacer (6). *(John Colley)*

FAR LEFT Slackening the track-rod-end locknut while counterholding the flats on the track rod, to adjust the front toe angle. *(John Colley)*

LEFT The steering column is supported by an aluminium bracket (arrowed) . *(John Colley)*

97

ANATOMY OF THE WILLIAMS FW14B

RIGHT The brake and clutch master cylinders are mounted on the monocoque front bulkhead – the two brake master cylinders are on the left of the photograph, and the clutch master cylinder on the right. *(John Colley)*

RIGHT The left-hand front brake components. Note the trailing brake caliper, and the ventilation holes drilled in the circumference of the carbon disc. *(John Colley)*

RIGHT The left-hand rear brake components. Note the leading caliper and the pad-locating plate (arrowed). *(John Colley)*

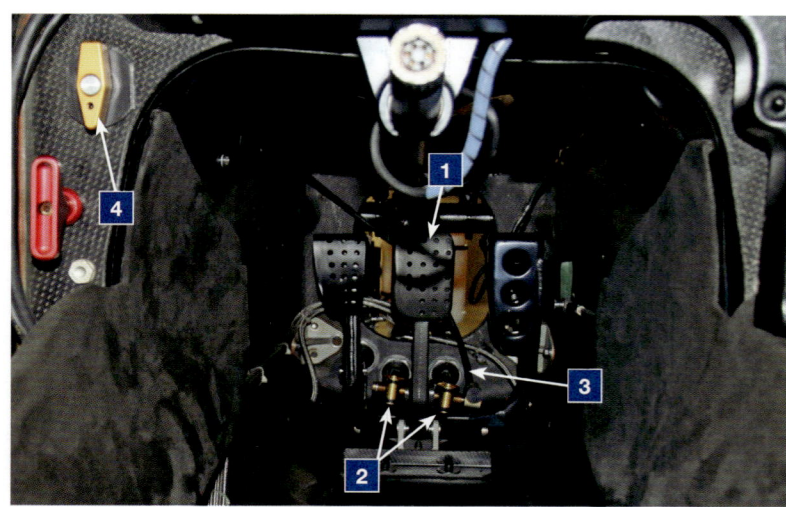

Brakes

A conventional twin-circuit hydraulic braking system is used on the FW14B. It has been reported in the media that the FW14B ran with an anti-lock-braking system (ABS), but this is incorrect. Although the team was developing ABS during 1992, it was not fitted to a race car until it appeared on the FW15C in 1993.

The hydraulic system is split into front and rear circuits, and separate Girling master cylinders and fluid reservoirs are used for the front and rear circuits. The master cylinders and fluid reservoirs are mounted on the monocoque front bulkhead, with the reservoirs mounted directly on the top of the master cylinders. A small breather bottle is connected via a hose to the top of the two fluid reservoirs. The breather bottle is secured to the main fluid reservoirs using cable ties.

Carbon/carbon (ie, carbon discs and carbon pads) ventilated disc brakes are used all round. Both Carbon Industrie and Hitco discs and pads were used at various points during 1992, with alloy calipers from AP Racing. Each disc is ventilated with radial holes drilled into the rim around the circumference of the disc.

Six-piston alloy calipers are used front and rear, three pistons acting on each pad. Each caliper has two bleed nipples – one for each set of three pistons – to allow both sides of the caliper to be bled. The pads simply slide into the caliper, and are located by small metal plates screwed to the edge of the caliper. Each caliper is secured to upper and lower studs on the upright using nuts. An external metal pipe at the bottom of each caliper carries fluid between the two caliper halves.

The alloy brake pedal pivots at its lower end, and is connected to each of the two master cylinders via a separate pushrod. A mechanical brake-bias adjustment system is fitted. A lever on the left-hand side of the cockpit is connected via bevel gears and a rotating cable to the brake master cylinder balance bar at the

LEFT A view inside the cockpit showing the brake pedal (1), master cylinder pushrod connections (2), brake-bias adjuster cable (3) and brake-bias adjuster lever (4). *(Steve Rendle)*

pedal. By turning the bias lever, the driver can adjust the front-to-rear brake bias.

All the flexible brake fluid lines are manufactured from Aeroquip metal-braided, reinforced rubber hosing of aerospace quality. The only rigid brake pipe used on the car is one that runs from front to rear through the cockpit and fuel cell housing.

Brake cooling ducts are fitted at the front and rear of the car. The ducts are manufactured from carbon, and when racing the duct specification could be altered to suit the specific cooling requirements at each circuit. At some tracks, tape was applied to the ducts to reduce the cooling effect in order to keep the brake temperature within optimum limits. The tape could be pulled off at a pitstop if necessary.

Engine

Engine development

The Renault engines used in the FW14B were evolutions of Renault's first V10 F1 engine, the 3.5-litre RS1, which was developed to meet the new F1 regulations introduced for 1989 that stipulated 3.5-litre normally aspirated engines.

The following paragraphs briefly describe the evolution of Renault's V10 engine, from the RS1 (used in the Williams FW12C during 1989) to the RS4 (used in the FW14B for the latter part of the 1992 season).

The RS1 (type EF30) first ran on the test bench on 22 January 1988, just 12 months after its design was started (see panel on pages 102–103). Developed by a small team at Renault Sport, the design of the RS1, with a specific 67-degree vee angle, was relatively conservative in other areas, and its layout and many of its features were derived from Renault's previous V6 1.5-litre turbo engines.

The camshafts and the oil, coolant and fuel pumps were driven by a toothed belt, and the engine featured magnesium castings for the lower crankcase, camshaft carriers, cam covers and oil pump bodies. In spite of these carry-overs from previous Renault designs, the RS1 included two significant innovations. First, an integral pneumatic valve-operating system was incorporated in the design; although pneumatic valve operation had been developed and used on the 1.5-litre turbo V6, that system, in contrast, comprised add-on parts, allowing the option of reverting to mechanical valve springs. Second, the engine featured 'coil-over-plug' ignition, with one coil per cylinder, and no distributor. Initially, the design team also included variable valve timing for both the inlet and exhaust camshafts, but after initial testing this system was shelved due to performance concerns and the additional weight and size of the necessary components.

The RS1 was initially tested in an FW12B mule (the FW12 raced with a Judd V8 engine) during the autumn of 1988, before powering the FW12C for the 1989 season. In 1989, the only other V10 engine to appear in F1 was the Honda unit used by McLaren. Other F1 engine manufacturers opted for V8 (Ford, Yamaha and Judd) or V12 (Ferrari and Lamborghini) configurations, a situation that continued into 1990 with the exception of the unsuccessful

ABOVE The front brake caliper hose runs through the lower suspension wishbone. *(John Colley)*

BELOW The evolution of Renault's V10 3.5-litre F1 engines can be seen here, progressing through RS1 (top left), RS2 (bottom left), RS3 (top right) and RS4 (bottom right). The RS3C and RS4 were both used in the FW14B. *(Renault Sport/DPPI)*

ABOVE For the first track test of a Renault-powered Williams, at Paul Ricard in October 1988, Patrese drove an FW12 mule fitted with an RS1 engine. Patrick Head can be seen on the left, behind the car, with Bernard Dudot on the far right. *(Renault Sport)*

Subaru flat-12 used in the Coloni, and the Life W-12 used in an eponymous chassis.

In spite of the design compromises, the RS1 performed well, Riccardo Patrese taking pole position and fastest lap for the engine's debut race at the 1989 Brazilian Grand Prix. The RS1's first race victory was achieved at the 1989 Canadian Grand Prix with Thierry Boutsen, who won again at the final round in Australia.

The RS2 (type EF40) engine, introduced for 1990, was a major step forward from the RS1. The most significant change was a move to gear-driven camshafts and pumps, with several aims:

- To improve the accuracy of the valve timing, particularly at high revs.
- To increase the stiffness at the forward face of the engine, thereby increasing the stiffness of the engine-to-chassis mounting.
- Decreases in the engine's overall length (by 48mm) and height (by 15mm), resulting in reduced weight and a correspondingly lower centre of gravity.

The other significant improvement for the RS2 was better integration of the oil and water systems, taking into account the requirements of the Williams (FW13B) chassis. These improvements included:

- A 'crossover' water system, whereby the cooling passages, before entering the cylinder heads, crossed over from the left-hand to the right-hand side and vice versa.
- A direct connection between the oil pump and the oil tank, mounted in the gearbox casing.
- Oil scavenge pumps and ducts integrated directly into the cylinder head.
- An oil gallery integrated into the timing-gear casing.
- Improved oil scavenging of the lower crankcase.
- Cylinder head redesigned to improve the inlet characteristics.
- Lower crankcase and timing case cast from aluminium (using an 'investment casting' process – a process in which a wax pattern is used to enable the casting of complex shapes), which enabled the integration of several ducts that had previously been external (pipework) to the engine.

The FW13B scored two wins with the RS2 engine, and five fastest laps.

The RS3 (type EF45) engine was another step forwards. Whereas the modifications introduced for the RS2 concentrated on improving integration of the engine with the chassis, the revisions made for the RS3 were mainly internal and aimed at improving performance. The changes included:

- Revised bore and stroke, to 93.0mm x 51.5mm.
- A modified cylinder head, incorporating revised inlet tracts, new combustion chambers, integral camshaft bearings and an integral coolant outlet.
- Modified camshaft drive, with revised roller bearings and gear hubs to improve stiffness.
- Modifications to the oil scavenging of the lower crankcase (using a reed-valve system).

RIGHT A view of the rear of an RS3 engine. The clutch and alternator drive (from the right-hand cylinder bank inlet camshaft) are clearly visible at the rear of the engine, with the left-hand oil (black) and water (grey) pumps fitted back-to-back at the lower left of the photograph. *(Renault Sport/DPPI)*

- A reduction in overall engine height of 14mm.
- An all-new, smaller and lighter Magneti-Marelli ECU, with significantly improved processing power.

The RS3 was introduced in the all-new FW14 at the beginning of 1991, and during the season Renault implemented an extensive development programme. In parallel, the team's fuel partner, Elf, worked with Renault on extracting more power from the exotic blends of fuel in use at the time, an avenue of development that was closed during 1992 with the introduction of new FISA regulations stipulating the use of 'pump fuel'.

At the Portuguese Grand Prix in September 1991, the upgraded RS3B was introduced. Featuring modifications to the combustion chambers, aimed at improving power, this version was only used a few times towards the end of the season.

For 1992, the Renault Sport staff numbers increased to around 140, as Renault was now supplying engines to Ligier as well as Williams. The deal with Ligier was as a 'customer' team, and Renault sub-contracted the assembly and preparation of Ligier's engines to Mecachrome, a company with which Renault had been involved since 1979. Williams, whose contract with Renault extended until the end of 1993, did not pay for its engines, whereas Ligier did. Contractually, Williams had priority on any new developments, as the two partners had been working together since 1989.

Although Renault was working on the development of the RS3's successor, the RS4, for the 1992 season, it was decided that it would be sensible to minimise risk – owing to the introduction of active suspension – by continuing with a new evolution of the well-proven RS3 engine, the RS3C, at least for the early part of the season. The RS3C featured revised combustion chambers, giving an increased compression ratio, which improved power. It transpired that the RS3C was used in the FW14B for the first ten rounds of the championship, winning a total of eight races, including the first five rounds.

Remarkably, in addition to a total of 15 wins, 14 pole positions and 16 fastest laps, the various evolutions of the RS3 engine achieved a 100 per cent reliability record in the 26 grands prix – 16 in 1991 (FW14) and ten in 1992 (FW14B) – in which they were used by Williams.

The RS4 (type EF50) engine included major revisions to the engine architecture, and incorporated the following modifications:

- Revised bore and stroke to 96.0mm x 48.3mm.
- A new cylinder head, incorporating valves actuated by finger followers instead of tappets, and new combustion chambers.
- Throttle control via butterfly valves instead of throttle slides.
- An aluminium camshaft cover, with integral coolant outlets.
- Relocation of the alternator to the timing-gear end of the engine, with belt drive taken from the left-hand cylinder-bank inlet camshaft.
- A revised hydraulic-pump drive, by means of a toothed belt from the right-hand cylinder bank inlet camshaft, at the gearbox end of the engine.
- A fuel-tank-mounted fuel pump, driven by an intermediate shaft running between the engine and chassis (the intermediate shaft runs inside the splined shaft of the gear driving the oil and coolant pumps on the left-hand side of the engine).
- Later in the season, Renault developed a pneumatically controlled variable inlet-trumpet system that was first used during a race weekend on Mansell's qualifying RS4 engine at the British Grand Prix.

ABOVE A view of the front of an RS3 engine. The canister-type oil filter can be seen within the vee, and the right-hand oil (black) and water (grey) pumps can be seen at the lower forward end of the crankcase. The pressure gauge visible in front of the oil filter is used to monitor the pressure in the pneumatic valve system. *(Renault Sport/DPPI)*

THE STORY BEHIND RENAULT'S DECISION TO BUILD A V10 ENGINE

Renault first entered F1 in 1977, building its own car – the RS01 – powered by the first F1 engine to feature an exhaust-driven turbocharger, the V6 1.5-litre Renault-Gordini EF1. The company ran its own 'works' team until 1985, when a decision was taken to continue in F1 purely as an engine supplier.

Renault's first customer team was Lotus, who used the Renault V6 from 1983, and by 1986 Renault was also supplying engines to Ligier and Tyrrell.

At the end of the 1986 season, Renault withdrew from F1, but the company retained a small technical team whose brief was to keep watch on developing F1 engine technology. Subsequently, the team was tasked with proposing the most suitable technical solution for an engine to meet the new F1 technical regulations due to be introduced in 1989, when turbocharged engines were to be outlawed in favour of 3.5-litre normally aspirated units.

The first, and most fundamental, question to address was whether to opt for a V8, V10 or V12 configuration. In order to determine the best option, the team began a comparative study of these three options, considering size/weight versus estimated performance.

The team collated data for the size/weight options taking into account overall engine dimensions, installation in the chassis, the layout and housing of ancillary systems, and the knowledge gained by the engineers and teams who had used Renault engines in the past, including Gérard Ducarouge (who worked with Renault engines at Lotus) and Gérard Larrousse (team principal of the Renault works F1 team from 1977 to 1984).

To evaluate potential performance, the team looked at the design of combustion chambers and inlet and exhaust tracts, and then built mock-ups in order to evaluate the various options on a flow-bench. The engineers also used Renault-developed software to analyse parameters such as power, torque, maximum engine speed, fuel consumption, and the external forces and torques produced by the engine.

After a three-month study, the engineers concluded that:

■ The extra power produced by a V12 would not compensate for handicaps such as larger dimensions, increased weight, higher fuel consumption and higher aerodynamic drag (due to the required cooling radiator size).
■ The power deficit of a V8 would be too big, even taking into account the packaging advantages of smaller dimensions, lower weight, reduced fuel consumption and lower drag (smaller radiators).

RIGHT A photograph taken in May 1988 showing the technical team at Renault Sport tasked with keeping a watching brief on developing F1 engine technology. Back row, from left: Jean-François Robin, Paul Pasquier, Jean-Philippe Mercier, Bernard Dudot, Michel Royer, Alex Kermorvan, Jean-Pierre Menrath, Patrick Babonnaud, Philippe Chasselut, Michel Palfroy, Philippe Coblence. Front row, from left: Gérard Malivin, Jean-Paul Fargues, Gilles Hauty, Patrice Pelletier, Georges Corbeau, Guy Thibault. *(Philippe Coblence/Renault Sport)*

ABOVE Renault Sport Technical Director Bernard Dudot with an RS3 engine. *(John Townsend)*

■ A V10 engine with a narrow vee angle was the best compromise.

And so, in January 1987, the team decided to pursue a design study for a V10. This choice was thought to be the least simple engineering option, and was met with mixed reactions by Renault's technical partners. A 'double five-cylinder' engine raised questions about vibration, acoustics and balance, with no data from any previous V10 engine designs available for reference. However, with the rapidly developing progress in the use of computer software for engineering simulation, the team was confident that it could tackle the challenges.

Later in 1987, Renault's arch-rival engine manufacturer, Honda, revealed that its solution for the 1989 regulations was also a V10. Although the Renault engineers were already confident that they had made the correct choice, the fact that Honda, who had dominated F1 during 1987 and 1988, had chosen a similar configuration allayed any fears amongst Renault's partners, and boosted Renault's motivation to proceed with development of its V10.

The Renault Sport team was headed by Technical Director Bernard Dudot, who was also responsible for developing Renault's pioneering 1.5-litre turbocharged V6 F1 engine, which debuted in the works Renault RS01 at the 1977 British Grand Prix.

First tested in an FW14B at Estoril in February 1992, the higher-revving and more powerful RS4 was introduced for qualifying at the Spanish Grand Prix. It was then used for qualifying for the subsequent six races before making its race debut at the Hungarian Grand Prix.

In a 1992 interview with F1 journalist Alan Henry, Renault Sport's Jean-Jacques His said of the RS4: "At just under the 140kg mark, the weight of the RS4 is the same as the RS3C and it is slightly more compact. Performance-wise, there is a significant difference between the two engines and, for a given level of fuel consumption, the RS4 is more powerful and produces more torque."

However, the introduction of the RS4 for the Hungarian race coincided with the hastily implemented changes to the fuel regulations,

LEFT A view of the RS4 used for the official presentation of the engine, showing it in its original version. Note the two fuel rails, one either side of the airbox, beneath the inlet trumpets. This arrangement was changed after initial dynamometer testing (see page 110). Note also the oil filter, above the oil pump on the side of the engine nearest the camera. *(Philippe Coblence/Renault Sport)*

BELOW Technicians assemble an RS3 engine in the workshop at Viry-Châtillon. *(Renault Sport/DPPI)*

103

ANATOMY OF THE WILLIAMS FW14B

which required the teams to abandon the use of exotic fuel blends and to adopt the use of 'pump fuel' (see panel on page 111). This posed challenges for both Renault and Elf, as engine and fuel development had been running in parallel up to this point.

A rare valve failure on Patrese's race engine led to his retirement in Hungary, and both cars had problems at Spa with broken connections between several of the ignition coils and spark plugs. Despite the various challenges, the RS4 was still able to power the FW14B to wins in Portugal and Japan.

In the early 1990s, there was no restriction on the number of engines that a team could use during a season, and in 1992 Renault supplied a total of 50 brand-new engines to Williams, plus a number of rebuilt units.

RENAULT SPORT'S DYNAMOMETER

During the 1992 season, the Renault engine facility at Viry-Châtillon worked relentlessly on improving its V10 engine. No fewer than six dynamometers there were allocated to V10 engine development, but one ('No. 4') was specially modified to enable the running of an engine coupled to a gearbox (a manual five-speed), driveshafts and brakes, to allow simulation of the conditions found at various race circuits. Renault Sport had originally devised this dynamometer configuration for development of the 2.0-litre V6 turbo engine used in the Renault Alpine A442B that won Le Mans in 1978.

The advantage of this dynamometer was that it allowed the engineers to dynamically load the engine in order to replicate the load and speed conditions encountered when driving a car on a circuit. When used for endurance testing, the test cycle used was always the same, replicating the most severe track conditions encountered during the season – Monza in the case of 1992. The rig was also used to investigate problems, as it allowed the exact conditions encountered on-track leading up to a problem to be simulated. With the advent of improved data logging and computing power, this dynamometer rig was later automated so that it was able to exactly replicate running to match recorded data, allowing simulation of any track in any conditions.

In 1992, for dynamometer 'No. 4', the engine/transmission unit, along with the necessary ancillary equipment, was housed in a sound-insulated chamber with an observation window. The engine could be 'driven' from outside the chamber by an engineer sitting in a racing seat, complete with pedals and a manual gearlever. The engineer could simulate reasonably closely the throttle, gear and brake inputs that an F1 driver would apply at a specific circuit. Despite the sound-insulation, the noise of an engine operating under simulated race conditions was apparently impressive to behold, and could be heard throughout the Renault Sport factory!

The test rig was set up to allow the engineers to collect valuable data to aid engine development and reliability, and testing ranged from brief test runs to full race-distance simulations and endurance testing. All this 'test-driving' required a skilled 'driver' who understood exactly what was happening to the engine from an engineering perspective. The point of endurance testing was to take the specific component being tested close to breaking point without destroying the whole engine – a scenario that would result in very little useful data!

All this hard work on engine development resulted in a remarkable reliability record during 1992, and only two retirements during the year could be attributed directly to the failure of engine components – Patrese's in Hungary and Mansell's in Japan.

BELOW A V10 engine under test on the Renault Sport dynamometer at Viry-Châtillon. *(Renault Sport/DPPI)*

Crankcase

The two-piece aluminium-alloy crankcase is split around the crankshaft centre line, and each casting was produced in a separate factory. The lower crankcase casting was produced at the Ciral foundry in Evron, west France, and the upper crankcase was produced at the Messier foundry in Arudy, south-west France. Messier still specialises today in producing complex castings in magnesium and aluminium alloys for the engineering and aerospace industries. The castings were then sent to Renault Sport partner Mecachrome's facility for machining before continuing their journey to the Renault Sport facility at Viry-Châtillon, south of Paris, where the Williams engines were assembled and prepared.

The cylinder bores are cast into the upper crankcase, and are fitted with 'wet' steel cylinder liners, with an internal Nikasil coating to reduce wear and friction as the pistons move inside them.

The lower crankcase casting, which is integral with the sump, is bolted to the upper casting. The crankshaft main bearing caps are integral with the lower crankcase casting.

Crankshaft

The crankshaft is machined from a single forged-steel cylindrical blank. As with all Renault V10 F1 engines, the crankshaft runs in six main bearings. Copper/lead bearing shells are used for both the main bearing and big-end bearing shells.

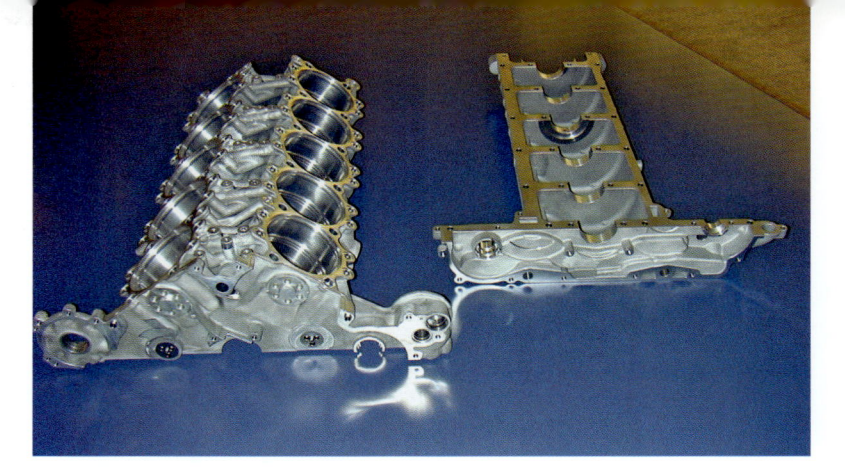

Connecting rods

Forged titanium connecting rods are used, and two connecting rods (one for each side of the engine vee) run on each crankshaft pin.

Pistons

The pistons are forged from aluminium/silicon alloy, and each piston has two rings – one compression ring and one oil-control ring. The pistons have recesses in their crowns to accommodate the valves. The pistons are extremely shallow, which helps to reduce friction and weight, and hence inertia forces, so enabling higher revs. The shallow pistons also

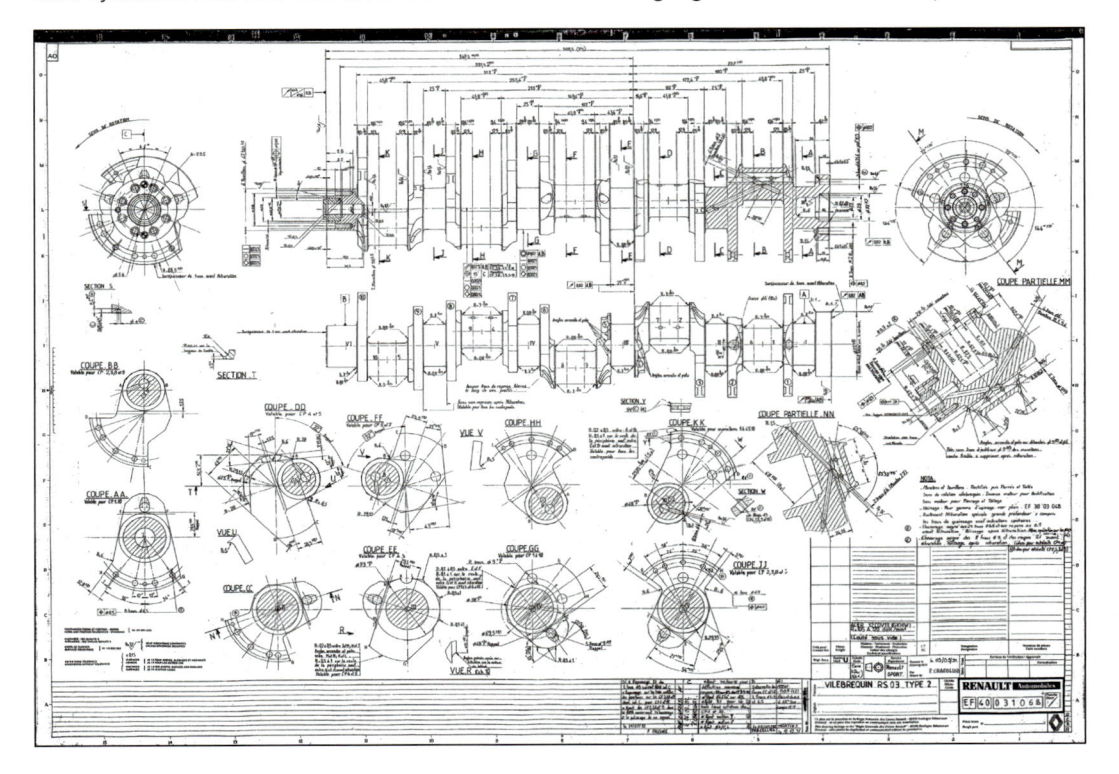

ABOVE The machined castings for the upper and lower halves of the crankcase. *(Renault Sport/DPPI)*

LEFT An engineering drawing, dated September 1991, for the RS3 engine crankshaft. *(Renault Sport)*

ANATOMY OF THE WILLIAMS FW14B

RIGHT A view of the crown of a used RS3 engine piston, showing the pockets for the valves.
(Philippe Coblence)

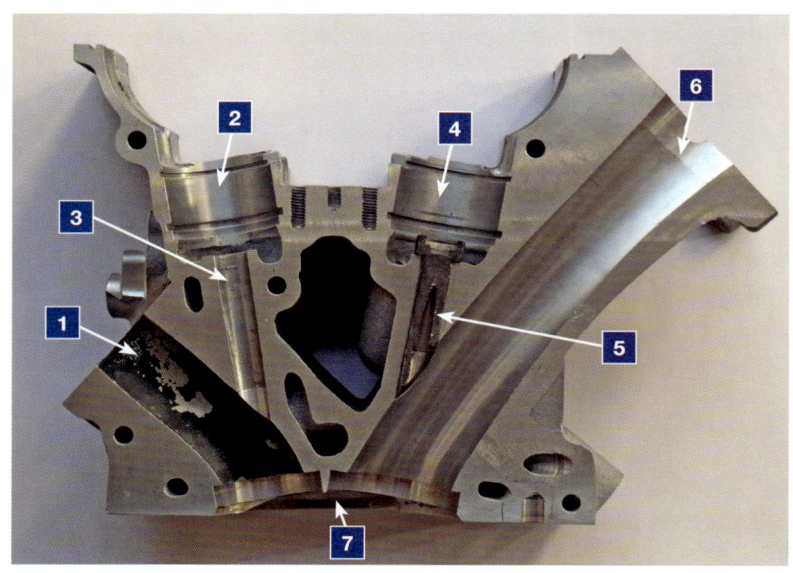

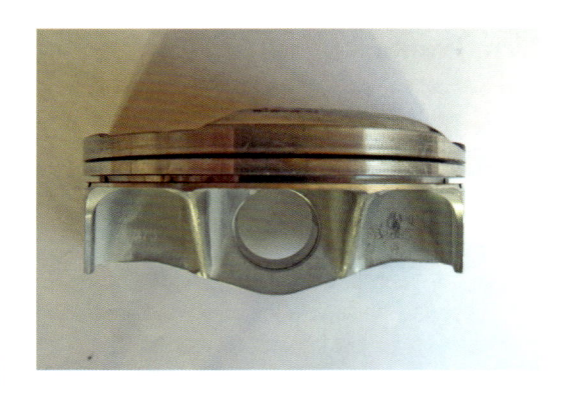

ABOVE This side view of a piston shows the extremely narrow piston skirt, with just sufficient metal to include a single oil-control and single compression ring. The depth of the valve pockets is also clearly visible. *(Philippe Coblence)*

contribute to keeping the overall height of the engine low, in turn lowering the centre of gravity.

Cylinder heads

The cylinder heads (a separate head for each cylinder bank) are cast from aluminium alloy. Rather than a single-piece cylinder-head gasket, a separate metallic ring gasket is fitted for each cylinder between the cylinder head and upper crankcase.

The lower camshaft bearing halves are

ABOVE A sectioned cylinder head showing: (1) Exhaust tract; (2) Exhaust valve pneumatic piston bore; (3) Exhaust valve bore; (4) Inlet valve pneumatic piston bore; (5) Inlet valve bore; (6) Inlet tract; (7) Combustion chamber.
(Philippe Coblence)

RIGHT An engineering drawing, dated December 1990, showing the RS3 engine right-hand cylinder head.
(Renault Sport)

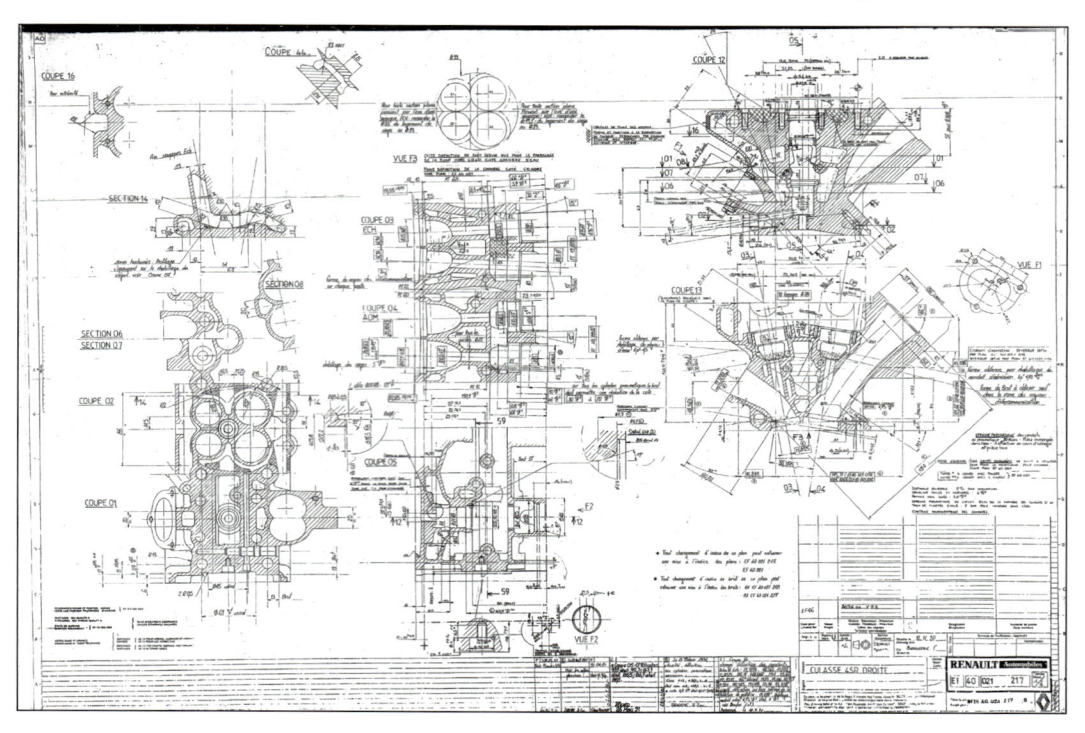

RIGHT Renault technicians about to fit the right-hand cylinder head to an RS4 engine. The wide-angle lens has distorted the perspective, but the left-hand cylinder head is already in place (nearest the camera), and the throttle butterflies can be seen at the tops of the inlet tracts. The pistons are visible at various positions in the bores in the right-hand crankcase (nearest the technicians). *(Renault Sport/DPPI)*

PNEUMATIC VALVE MECHANISM

Renault's pneumatic valve system (christened 'Distribution Pneumatique' by Renault) first appeared in 1986 on the 1.5-litre turbocharged EF15 engine used by the Renault works team, Lotus and Ligier. The principle of operation is as follows.

The metal coil springs that close the valves on an engine with conventional valve gear are replaced by a metal piston acting in an air chamber. When a valve opens, the camshaft cam lobe pushes down on the valve to lift it off its seat in the cylinder head in the normal way, but, in place of the valve spring, a piston acting in an air chamber resists the movement of the valve. As the camshaft pushes the valve down, the air in the chamber resists the movement (air is compressible), pushing the valve closed as the cam continues to rotate.

The seals in the system are vital to avoid leaks and to prevent oil from entering the air chamber. If oil leaks into the air chamber, there is a risk that it could cause the piston to lock (oil is incompressible), which in turn could lead to catastrophic engine failure.

The system is a low-loss type (a small quantity of air is lost during normal operation), and so a reserve air supply is provided via a remote reservoir. The reservoir is located at the left-hand rear of the cockpit, under the driver's seat. Two sizes of reservoir were used – a smaller version for practice and qualifying, and a larger version for races. A sensor constantly monitors the pressure in the reservoir, and if the pressure drops below a predetermined level a warning is flagged up via telemetry.

A pressure gauge is fitted to the rear of the monocoque, below the airbox, to enable the air pressure in the pneumatic valve system to be monitored. Before the engine is started, the system must be pressurised to a minimum of 100 bar, although the actual system runs at a pressure of around 20 bar.

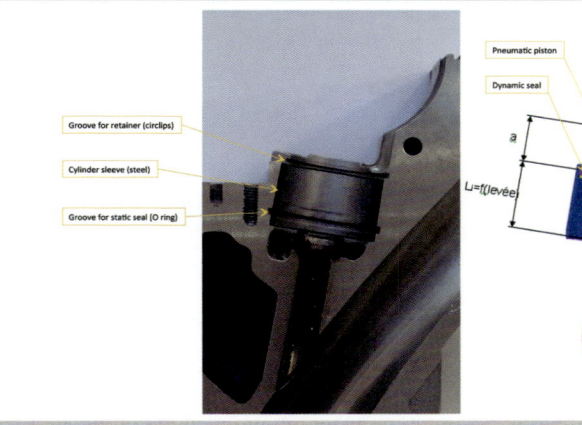

ABOVE A graphic originated by Philippe Coblence showing the details of the pneumatic valve mechanism. *(Philippe Coblence)*

FAR LEFT The reserve air bottle for the pneumatic valve system, viewed with the driver's seat removed. *(Tony Matthews)*

LEFT A pressure gauge (arrowed) allows the pneumatic valve system air pressure to be monitored. *(Steve Rendle)*

RIGHT Valves, stored in foam blocks, ready for fitting to an engine. Note the waisted stems to reduce weight. *(Renault Sport/DPPI)*

integrated into the cylinder head (no separate bearing shells are used). The upper camshaft bearing halves are integral with the camshaft cover, which is bolted to the top of the cylinder head.

Valves

The inlet valves are made from titanium, the exhaust valves from steel. The valves run in bronze (copper/beryllium alloy) guides pressed into the cylinder heads. The inlet and exhaust valve sizes are as follows:

	Inlet	Exhaust
RS3C	38.4mm	32.0mm
RS4	39.6mm	33.0mm

The pneumatic valve pistons fit between the ends of the valve stems and the tappet (RS3C) or finger follower (RS4), in the position occupied by the valve spring in a conventional system (see panel on previous page).

Camshafts

Separate hollow steel exhaust and inlet camshafts are fitted for each cylinder bank – four camshafts in all. The exhaust camshafts are fitted on the outboard sides of the cylinder heads, while the inlet camshafts are fitted on the inboard sides – ie, facing each other across the engine vee.

The camshafts activate the valves via solid tappets on the RS3C engine, and via finger followers on the RS4 engine.

Camshaft drive

The camshafts are gear-driven from the crankshaft via a series of gears at the front of the engine (the monocoque end when mounted in the car). The drive components are lubricated via a pressurised oil feed delivered through drillings in the block and cylinder head.

Lubrication system

Two mechanical oil pumps are fitted, one on each side of the crankcase, both driven by shafts. The shafts are driven from the timing gears at the front of the engine and also drive the coolant pumps, which are fitted back-to-

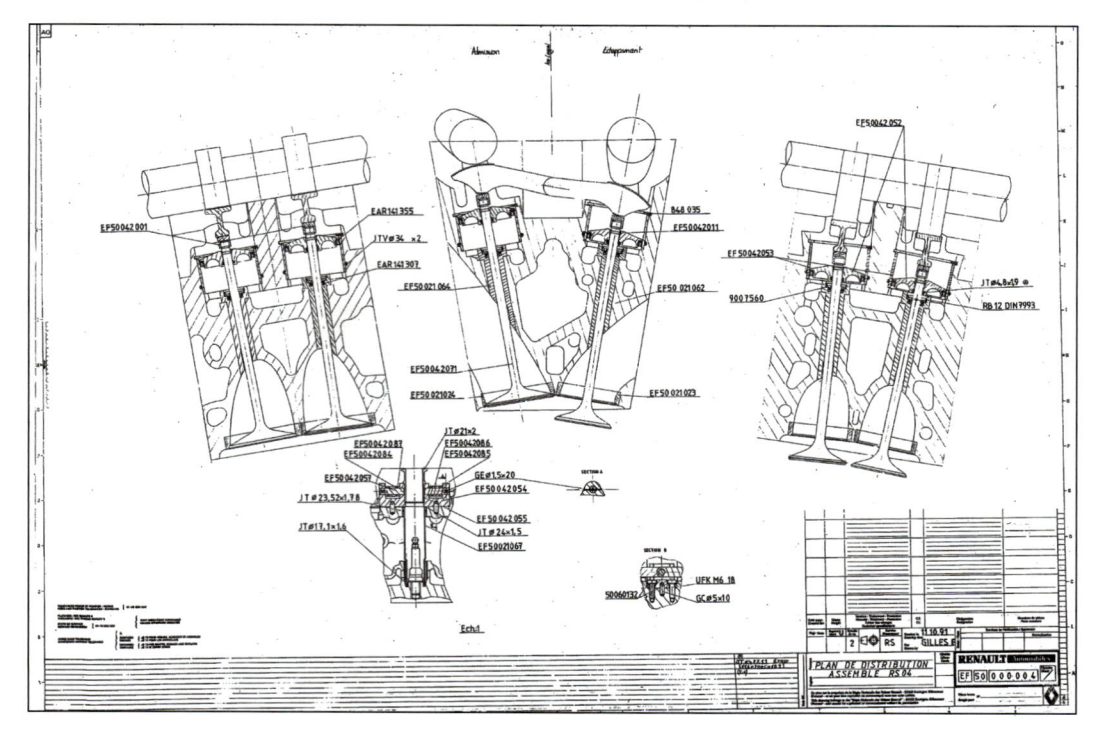

RIGHT An engineering drawing showing the camshafts and finger-follower valve-operating mechanism for the RS4 engine. *(Renault Sport)*

back with the oil pumps. The oil pressure pump is on the left-hand side of the engine, and the crankcase oil scavenge pump is on the right. Both are gear-type pumps.

Two cylinder-head scavenge pumps are fitted, one for each head. The cylinder-head scavenge pumps were added for the RS1 engine after the first track tests at Paul Ricard in 1988, and were integrated into the cylinder head from the RS2 engine onwards. The pumps are located at the gearbox end of the engine, and act primarily when the car is under positive acceleration. Under braking, the oil is effectively scavenged through the timing-gear casing by the deceleration forces through an oil gallery running to the crankcase scavenge pump. The head scavenge pumps are lobe-type pumps, with the inner rotor of each pump driven directly from the end of the relevant exhaust camshaft.

On the RS3C engine, a screw-on cartridge-type oil filter is fitted within the cylinder vee, at the monocoque end of the engine. The filter screws on to a flange on the top of the crankcase. On the RS4 engine, a similar cartridge-type oil filter is fitted, but it is located horizontally, above the oil pump on the left-hand side of the crankcase (see photo on page 103). The filter was moved to this location to make space for the alternator within the engine vee.

The engine oil tank is an integral part of the gearbox casing, and is machined into the alloy casing. The engine oil level can be checked using a dipstick inserted into the oil tank. The oil capacity of the RS3C and RS4 engines is around seven litres.

Two (oil-to-water) engine oil coolers are fitted, one for each cylinder bank, and they are located either side of the engine, mounted longitudinally between the crankcase and the exhaust manifold.

Cooling system

A sealed, pressurised cooling system is used, and the header tank is located at the rear of the right-hand sidepod.

The engine is fitted with two coolant pumps – one on each side of the crankcase, fitted back-to-back with the oil pumps, as described previously (see photographs on pages 100 and 101).

LEFT A Renault technician checks the clearances for the right-hand oil pump/coolant pump drivegear on an RS4 engine. The locations of the camshaft drivegears (not yet fitted) can be clearly seen. The camshafts and cam covers are not fitted in this view. *(Renault Sport/DPPI)*

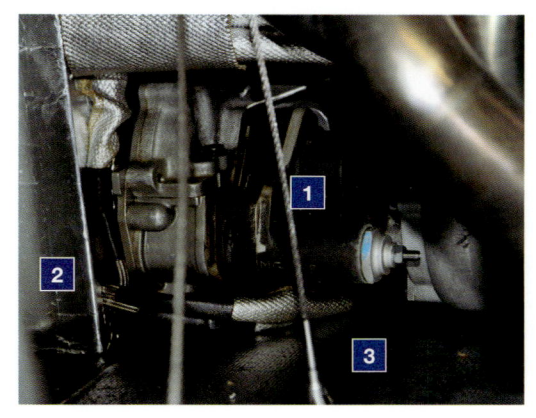

LEFT The left-hand (pressure) oil pump (1) on an RS3C engine; (2) is the monocoque rear bulkhead, and (3) is the car's floor. *(Steve Rendle)*

BELOW The left-hand oil cooler (arrowed) located behind the exhaust manifold. *(John Colley)*

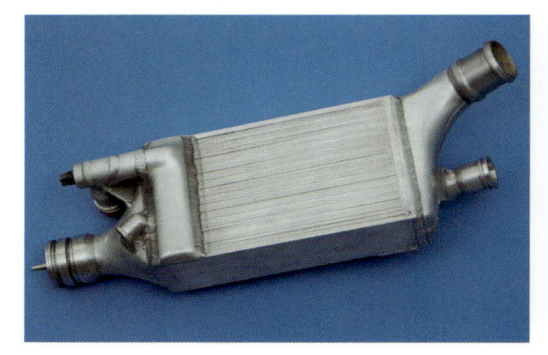

BOTTOM An oil cooler removed from the car showing the impressive fabrication details. *(John Colley)*

BELOW The cooling system header tank, located at the rear of the right-hand sidepod. *(Steve Rendle)*

RIGHT Left-hand coolant radiator (arrowed) located in the sidepod. *(John Colley)*

Two coolant radiators are fitted, one on each side of the car, housed in the sidepods.

Fuel system

Two or three electric fuel-lift pumps are fitted inside the fuel tank to scavenge fuel from the tank, ensuring that as much fuel as possible is picked up as the level in the tank drops. The number of pumps fitted during the 1992 season was dependent on the characteristics of the individual tracks. The larger lift pump is located towards the rear of the tank, and can be fitted on either side of the tank, depending on the circuit. The lift pumps send fuel to a lightly pressurised 'collector' tank within the main tank, which feeds the pressure pump.

On the RS3C engine, the mechanical fuel-pressure pump, which raises the fuel pressure to around 10 bar (145psi), is mounted on the timing-gear casing, and is driven directly from the end of the left-hand cylinder bank inlet camshaft.

On the RS4 engine, the mechanical fuel-pressure pump is located inside the collector tank, and is driven by a shaft fitted between the engine and the chassis. The fuel pump driveshaft is driven from the splined shaft that drives the oil and water pumps on the left-hand side of the crankcase (the splined end of the fuel pump shaft fits inside the oil/water pump driveshaft). The fuel-pump driveshaft is splined at both ends to allow for any minor misalignment/movement/vibration between the engine and gearbox.

Fuel is injected into the engine inlet tracts by a single fuel injector per cylinder. On the RS3C engine, the fuel injectors are located in the magnesium throttle-slide housings, just above the throttle slides and below the aluminium inlet trumpets, with a separate fuel rail for each set of injectors. Initially, the same arrangement was used for the RS4 engine, but Philippe Coblence, head of the Renault Sport drawing office in 1992, recalls: "This was changed rapidly after the first test-bench runs, when we realised that fuel vaporisation was not good with the injectors so close to the throttle butterflies [which replaced throttle slides on the RS4]. It was much better having the injectors above the inlet trumpets, fitted to a single fuel rail above the trumpets."

Air is fed to the engine from the intake in the engine cover, above the driver's head, via a carbon airbox to the inlet trumpets. The aluminium inlet trumpets are attached to the magnesium throttle housing on the engine, and sit inside a carbon tray into which the airbox fits. An air filter element and gauze screen can be fitted to the tray to prevent debris and contamination from entering the engine.

Throttling is via throttle slides on the RS3C engine, and via throttle butterflies on the RS4 engine.

A mechanical throttle cable is used, but later during the 1992 season a 'throttle blipper' system was fitted, using a hydraulic actuator to operate the throttle mechanism on the

BELOW The airbox (1), fuel rail (2) and fuel injectors (3) on the RS3C engine currently fitted to FW14B/11. *(Steve Rendle)*

RIGHT The airbox feeds air from the intake above the driver's head to the engine. *(John Colley)*

ABOVE The inlet trumpets on the RS3C engine fitted to FW14B/11, with the throttle slides (in their magnesium housing) below the trumpets clearly visible. Note also the injector nozzles visible above the throttle slides. *(John Colley)*

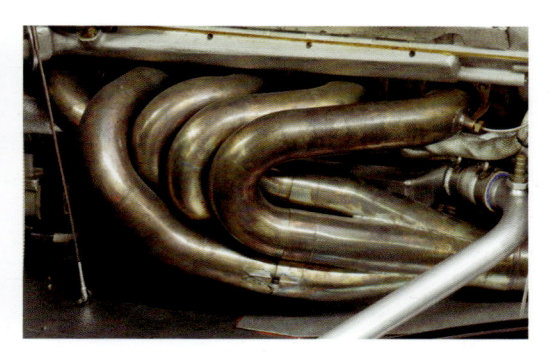

LEFT A close-up view of the left-hand exhaust manifold on FW14B/11. Each branch bolts to the cylinder head via a flange welded to the end of the pipe. *(John Colley)*

engine. This enabled the throttle to be blipped automatically, via the VCM (Vehicle Control and Monitor module), allowing fully automatic downchanges through the gears without the driver needing to use the throttle pedal. Even with the throttle blipper, the throttle pedal was still connected to the engine via a cable.

Exhaust system

A single five-into-one exhaust manifold is fitted for each cylinder bank. The manifolds are fabricated from Inconel alloy, and feed directly into fabricated metal shrouds bolted to the diffuser, thus providing an 'exhaust-blown' diffuser to improve rear downforce.

Ignition system

A distributorless, coil-over-plug ignition system is used, with a single spark plug per cylinder. Each spark plug is fed HT voltage by an individual coil fitted directly over the plug. The ignition system is controlled by the Magneti-Marelli engine ECU. After problems for both FW14Bs at the Belgian Grand Prix, due to the coils detaching from the spark plugs (attributed partly to vibration), the components were modified to improve reliability. The spark plugs were supplied by Champion.

Engine management system

The Magneti-Marelli engine management system controls both the fuel and ignition systems, and the engine ECU has a number of ignition and fuelling maps stored in its memory. Suitable maps

FUELLING CONTROVERSY

Exotic fuels became an area of significant development in the 1990s, and competition between fuel companies – particularly Elf (Williams), Shell (McLaren) and Agip (Ferrari) – became intense, with the use of additives and power-boosting chemical blends unrestricted. Some observers at the time estimated that, at the height of this 'fuel war', the use of high-octane 'special' fuels could lead to an increase in engine power of up to 60bhp.

Elf made significant progress in 1991 with Williams-Renault, only for Shell to respond with major improvements for McLaren-Honda. Elf worked extensively with Renault over the winter to develop the fuel for 1992, and the fuel war continued throughout the season.

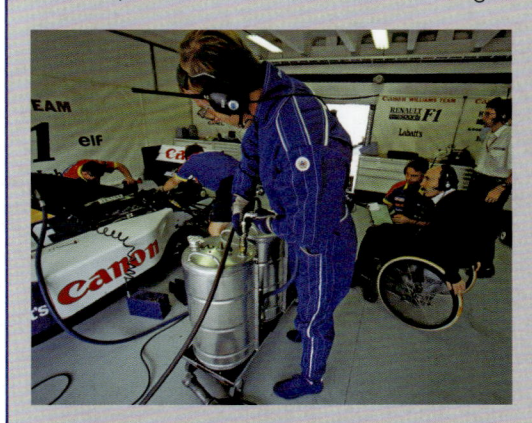

LEFT Nigel Mansell's car connected to the refuelling rig at the Hungarian Grand Prix. *(Getty Images)*

In an effort to reduce the risks associated with the ever-more exotic fuels, FISA decided to introduce regulations stipulating that only constituents found in commercially available 'pump fuel' could be used in F1. However, as in recent years, this change to the regulations was perceived by some as an attempt to rein in the dominance of Williams-Renault, as some people believed that Renault and Elf had made greater gains through fuel development than other engine/fuel partners.

Controversially, FISA gave the teams only six days' notice of the implementation of the new rule, which took effect from the Hungarian Grand Prix on 16 August. This gave the engine manufacturers major headaches as they were forced to recalibrate fuel and ignition systems to allow the engines to run using the new fuel.

RIGHT A view of the Magneti-Marelli engine management ECU, mounted on the rear of the fuel-cell housing/roll structure on the monocoque. The airbox has been removed in this photograph.
(John Colley)

are selected to optimise engine performance and reliability according to signals received from various sensors. The engine ECU also controls the ignition cutting for the traction control system (see page 121), according to signals received from the VCM (Vehicle Control and Monitor module).

Renault Sport worked closely with Magneti-Marelli throughout the development of the engine and its control systems. The two companies had a long history of cooperation, to the extent that Magneti-Marelli wrote the engine-control software.

Transmission

The FW14B's transmission comprises a conventional clutch, a semi-automatic gearbox with integral differential, and hollow steel driveshafts.

Clutch

The multi-plate AP clutch unit is bolted to a plate attached to the engine crankshaft, and is hydraulically operated, via a master cylinder bolted to the monocoque front bulkhead.

The clutch is driver-controlled via the clutch pedal. In parallel with the foot clutch, a Moog valve-operated concentric release cylinder is fitted to the clutch mechanism, so that the clutch can be operated electronically by the VCM (Vehicle Control and Monitor module) in conjunction with the semi-automatic gearbox. Initially, it was necessary to disengage the clutch for gearshifts, but later in the development process gearchanges were clutchless. Although the clutch could be controlled electronically, this was never used for 'launch control' at the start of a race – despite what was suggested in some contemporary press reports. Electronic 'launch control' was used for the first time on a Williams in 2001, on the FW23.

Gearbox

The semi-automatic, six-speed transverse gearbox used in the FW14B was an evolution of the TG3 (Transverse Gearbox 3) unit used in the FW14. The gearbox design was overseen by Patrick Head, and was his own interpretation of the concept that had been used by Ferrari since 1989, with an electro-hydraulic gearchange mechanism. A development gearbox was first tested on a purpose-built test rig during 1990, and many hours of testing were completed before the gearbox was first run on-track in an FW13B chassis. The gearbox performed impressively when first track-tested.

The goal behind the design of the gearbox was to improve lap times by reducing the time taken to change gear. At a circuit such as Monaco, which involves around 3,000 gearchanges during a race, the FW14B's semi-automatic gearbox saved 0.2–0.3s per lap, a significant advantage over a race distance when compared with a manual gearbox.

After evaluating the development work carried out during 1990, Patrick Head decided that the semi-automatic gearbox should be incorporated in the 1991 FW14 from the start of the season. To suit the packaging of the FW14, it was decided to reduce the overall length of the gearbox by 50mm, which entailed a major redesign, and arguably compromised reliability. Gearbox gremlins caused several retirements during 1991, particularly in the early part of the year, but reliability improved from mid-season, and from the Mexican Grand Prix onwards the FW14 won seven of the 11 remaining races.

With the semi-automatic gearbox proven in the FW14, and the reliability problems ironed out, the unit was retained as the FW14 metamorphosed into the FW14B.

RIGHT The compact multi-plate AP clutch fitted to an RS3 engine.
(Renault Sport/DPPI)

The gearbox components (gear clusters, differential and associated components) are housed in a magnesium-alloy housing, bolted directly to the rear of the engine in conventional F1 fashion. The gearbox is a fully stressed component, carrying the rear suspension pick-up points and the mounting for the rear wing. As such, the complete gearbox/rear suspension/brake/driveshaft/rear-wing assembly can be removed from the car as a unit. The gearbox casing incorporates the engine oil tank, and also the engine breather tank – both of which are machined into the casing.

Gearchanges are implemented using a solenoid, which controls the hydraulic pressure fed to the gearchange-barrel actuator, which moves the gearchange barrel. The VCM (Vehicle Control and Monitor module) sends a signal to the solenoid which, via the actuator, moves the gearchange barrel as necessary to select the appropriate gear.

On the FW14, the gearbox hydraulic fluid is pressurised by a small gear-type pump, driven from the engine's left-hand inlet camshaft. On the FW14B, the gearbox hydraulic system takes its fluid from the active-suspension hydraulic system.

A hydraulic valve block mounted next to the hydraulic fluid accumulator on the top of the gearbox distributes fluid from the main hydraulic system (supplying both the active suspension system and the gearbox system) to the gearbox control system (known as 'powershift' by Williams). The valve block was designed by Mark Loasby, who was working as a Development Engineer at Williams in 1992.

One significant change made from the FW14 was that a pressure-reduction function was added to the hydraulic valve block – necessary because the main hydraulic-system pressure rose from 1,500psi (about 103 bar) to 3,000psi (about 207 bar) with the adoption of active suspension. The transmission hydraulic-system operating pressure remained at 1,500psi, as the solenoid valve used to operate the gearchange barrel could not cope with higher pressures. When the FW15 was developed for 1993, the solenoid valve was replaced with a Moog valve, which allowed the adoption of a constant 3,000psi pressure throughout the hydraulic system.

The gearchange-barrel actuator is located on the right-hand side of the gearbox. The actuator incorporates a hollow, internally splined 'neutral' shaft. By inserting a special splined key into this shaft, the mechanics can ensure that the gearbox is in neutral before engaging the electric starter to start the engine. Beneath the gearbox barrel actuator is another hollow splined shaft into which the starter shaft is inserted to start the engine. The starter has a right-angled shaft, which must be engaged with the hollow shaft in the gearbox.

Starting the engine is a tricky operation that requires practice, as the splined key has to be engaged with the gearbox actuator shaft to ensure that the gearbox is in neutral before the starter shaft is engaged with the gearbox, from the rear of the car, behind the rear wing. If the engine stalls, the process has to be repeated, the mechanic having to reach under the back of the car to knock the gearbox into neutral using the splined key before re-engaging the starter – a challenging operation with a hot engine and with hot exhaust gases waiting to assault the mechanic as soon as the engine fires.

Opposite the gearchange-barrel actuator is one of the most critical components on the gearbox – the gearchange-barrel potentiometer. This sensor provides a signal to the control system corresponding to the gearbox zero (neutral) position. This datum position is vital to ensure the safe operation of the gearbox. If

LEFT The gearchange-barrel potentiometer (arrowed) mounted on the left-hand side of the gearbox casing is one of the most critical components on the gearbox. *(John Colley)*

LEFT A view of the gearchange-barrel potentiometer, showing the cooling hose running to the duct in the rear body panel. *(John Colley)*

RIGHT The gearbox-barrel actuator (1), 'neutral' shaft (2) and starter shaft (3). *(John Colley)*

RIGHT The hydraulic valve block (arrowed) mounted on top of the gearbox distributes fluid to the gearbox control system. *(John Colley)*

RIGHT The gearbox oil cooler (arrowed) is located on the rear-wing mounting. *(John Colley)*

RIGHT The gearbox oil filter slotted cover (arrowed). *(John Colley)*

the sensor provides an inaccurate signal, the result is likely to be catastrophic gearbox failure due to the internals being forced into mesh without optimum synchronisation – noisy and embarrassing on a road car, but potentially a gearbox-destroying scenario for an F1 car. The sensor is fitted low on the left-hand side of the gearbox, close to the exhaust, and is fed with cool air via a hose from a small cooling duct in the left-hand rear body panel.

The gearbox lubricating oil is cooled via an oil-to-air cooler located on the rear-wing mounting. Ducts in the rear of the engine cover feed air to the cooler. Before running the car, the gearbox casing is warmed using heaters, but there is no requirement to warm the gearbox oil separately.

A disposable gearbox oil filter is fitted in the gearbox casing below the right-hand driveshaft. The filter is removed by engaging a tool with the slotted cover.

The gearbox control software is built into the VCM (see page 117). Wheel-speed sensors fitted at all four wheels supply signals to the VCM. The front wheel sensors provide a signal indicating a reference speed in order to block gearbox downshifts that would otherwise cause engine damage through overspeeding (over-revving). These sensors also provide control signals for the traction-control system, as well as allowing the VCM to compute the distance travelled by the car, and hence its position on the track.

Later in the 1992 season, the gearbox control system was developed to a point where it was capable of automatic downchanges. This worked by dividing the relevant circuit into segments, with a target gear programmed into the system for each corner. The driver simply had to pull the shift paddle once, and the system automatically changed down through the gears to achieve the correct target gear as the speed reduced prior to corner entry. This system was used in conjunction with the hydraulic 'throttle blipper', developed by Renault, which allowed automatic blipping of the throttle for gear downchanges (see pages 110–111).

Steve Wise, who developed the software for the semi-automatic gearbox, explains the evolution of the gearbox software: "The very first thing we did was an autoshift system that just tried to do all the basics. The first time we ran it, we introduced a block, so that if the driver pulled for a downshift, the software looked at the front wheel speed and decided what the engine speed would be after the shift, and if it was going to be too high, it just ignored it. We thought we'd gone out to speed up the gearshift by 100 milliseconds or something like that, but actually by far the biggest advantage we found in those early days was that we never blew up engines any more, because we didn't overspeed them. So that was the first intervention, if you like, that the driver didn't have to worry about. He could just pull the gearshift, and it wouldn't do anything if it was going to blow the engine up.

"Fairly soon afterwards, we thought, well, we can do automatic upshifts, because we know the best engine speed to do an upshift. Doing an upshift automatically was very straightforward, because we just sent a 'cut' command to the engine controller, then we did our sequence of moving the gears, and moving the dogs around. The driver could stay full on the gas, because we just cut the ignition.

"During a gearshift, we would send data over the serial link, called CAN [Controller Area Network], which is still in use today. This was effectively a command for the engine ECU to cut cylinders, or in some way change the operation of the engine, during the gearshift.

"To do automatic downshifts, you need full control of the throttles, and that's the reason why that came in a little later, but from my side it was very easy to write the software. One implementation of it was, we said to the driver: 'Well, why don't we write the software so that you do the number of gearshifts that you want for the next corner, and then when you come on the brakes, the computer will do it for you, and you don't have to worry about it.' So if he was in sixth gear, and he knew he wanted to be in third, somewhere down the straight he'd do three downshifts on the paddle, but nothing would happen. He'd get to the corner, and at the right speed, the system would just change down through three gears.

"We then started to automate it a bit more, and again from our point of view it was fairly easy to pre-program it for a lap. You knew how far round the lap you were because you knew the distance from the speed sensor and you had a marker every lap. The system was circuit dependent, and eventually we'd program which target gear to go down to for each corner round the lap. That was quite a lot harder, because then you've got to cope with things like the failure of a lap marker, and you don't want to mess up your sequence of gears round the lap if that happens, so quite a lot of extra thought went into that. The driver told us which gear he would like to use for a particular corner, so in some cases the two cars were set up differently."

Driveshafts

Hollow steel driveshafts are fitted, with tripod joints at each end.

Wheels

The forged magnesium-alloy, four-spoke wheels used on the FW14B were manufactured by Italian specialist wheel-manufacturing company Fondmetal. In 1992 the regulations stipulated a wheel diameter of 13 inches (330mm), with maximum rim widths of 11.4 inches (290mm) for the fronts and 16.3 inches (414mm) for the rears.

Each wheel is secured by a single nut, which screws on to threads on the end of the stub axle. The nuts securing the left-hand wheels are colour-coded grey, and have a conventional thread, while the nuts securing the right-hand wheels are colour-coded blue, and have a left-hand thread (to reduce the risk of them loosening under the rotational forces of the wheel). Unlike today's F1 cars, there is no locking mechanism to retain the wheel nuts.

LEFT An FW14B Fondmetal wheel, fitted with an original Goodyear Eagle F1 tyre. *(John Colley)*

LEFT Left-hand (grey) and right-hand (blue) wheel nuts. *(John Colley)*

RIGHT The rear wheels locate on lugs on the hub.
(John Colley)

The rear (driven) wheels locate on lugs on the hub to provide positive location under the very high torque acting through the tyres. There are no locating lugs for the front wheels.

Tyres

During 1992, and indeed for all its race-winning seasons up until 1992, Williams's tyre supplier was Goodyear. Pirelli had been supplying several teams up until the end of 1991, but pulled out of F1 at the end of that season, leaving Goodyear as the sole tyre supplier for all the teams.

As one of Goodyear's contracted teams, as opposed to being a customer team, Williams was a major player in Goodyear's tyre-testing programme. In an interview with F1 journalist Alan Henry in 1992, Goodyear's International Director of Racing, Leo Mehl, estimated that Williams had carried out 40 per cent of Goodyear's F1 tyre testing over the previous few years.

Although there was no restriction on tyre testing in the early 1990s, during 1992 Goodyear carried out less tyre testing than in previous seasons. With the requirement to supply all the teams and no competition from a rival supplier, reduced testing helped Goodyear to control costs and ease the strain on its production facilities. A single compound of slick tyre was used for each race during 1992.

Another area of cost reduction was Goodyear's decision to cease supply of special qualifying tyres. From the start of the season, the cars qualified on race tyres, with 30 cars taking part in a one-hour qualifying session on Friday afternoon, followed by a second hour session on Saturday afternoon. Each driver's fastest overall time was taken to decide his position on the 26-car grid.

Typical tyre pressures used on the FW14B were 18psi front and 20psi rear.

Although no tyre-pressure sensors were fitted on the FW14B (these were not introduced until much later), following a testing accident for Riccardo Patrese at Imola, and Mansell's puncture at the Monaco Grand Prix, the team developed a Puncture Detection System (PDS – see page 121) that looked for changes in the mean ride height at each corner of the car, and warned the driver of any anomalies via a warning light on the dashboard.

Electronics

The 1990s saw significant developments in electronic systems in F1, with ever-more complex engine management systems, telemetry and, on the FW14B, electronic gearbox control and active suspension control.

Electrical system

The FW14B is fitted with a 12-volt electrical system that can be isolated using a master toggle switch located in a 'power box' attached to the rear left-hand side of the monocoque, on the roll structure below the airbox. Before any electrical circuits on the car can be operated, the car must be 'switched on' using the power switch. This switch can be operated with the bodywork fitted by inserting a screwdriver through a small hole in the engine cover to flick the switch. The slave battery used in the pitlane and garage to supply power to the car is plugged into a connector on the power box,

RIGHT The 'power box' (1) located on the left-hand side of the car, showing the power switch (2) and the slave-battery connector (3).
(John Colley)

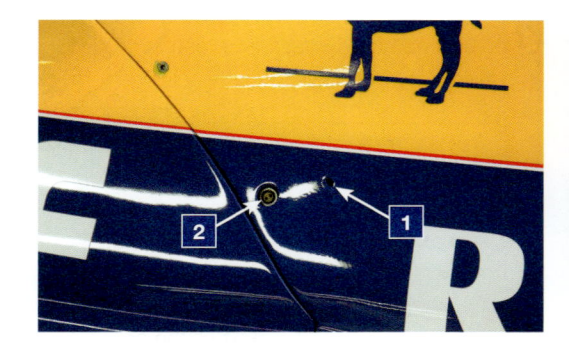

ABOVE The electrical master switch can be accessed by mechanics through the hole (1) in the engine cover. The slave-battery connector (2) is also visible. *(John Colley)*

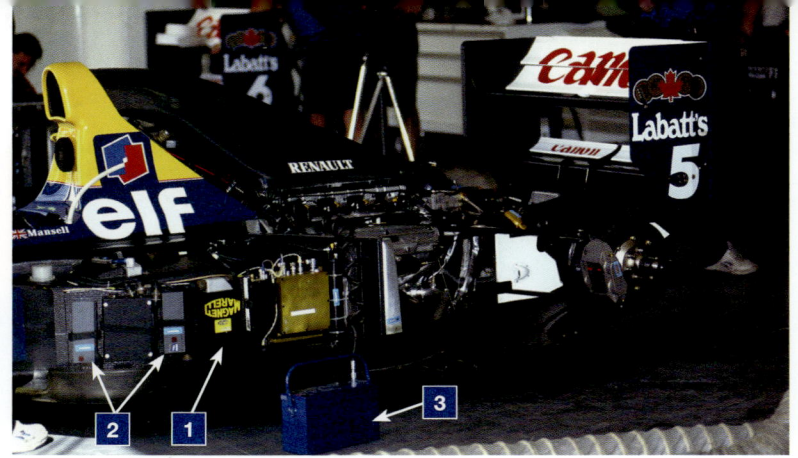

ABOVE Mansell's FW14B in the pit garage at the season-opening South African Grand Prix showing the voltage regulator (1) and batteries (2) in the left-hand sidepod. The slave battery (3) can be seen next to the car. The other units fitted in the sidepod are data loggers/test units used during testing and practice. *(Schlegelmilch/Getty Images)*

and this connector is also accessible with the engine cover fitted. The master switch can also be operated via the pull ring on the right-hand side of the engine cover. Linked to the switch via a cable, the pull ring also operates the fire extinguisher.

The lead-acid battery is located in the left-hand sidepod, ahead of the voltage regulator, and secured by Velcro tabs and locating straps. The battery is charged by a belt-driven alternator, located within the engine vee. On the RS3C engine, the alternator is driven from a pulley fitted to the right-hand cylinder bank inlet camshaft, at the gearbox end of the engine, whereas on the RS4 engine the alternator drive is taken from a pulley fitted to the left-hand cylinder bank inlet camshaft, at the timing-gear end of the engine.

At races where the average engine speed was low, alternator output was not sufficient to be sure of keeping a single battery charged, so two batteries were fitted.

As a consistent baseline voltage is critical for the correct operation of the electronic systems, a Magneti-Marelli voltage regulator is fitted, located in the left-hand sidepod. There was a known issue with the alternator used on the FW14 and FW14B: with a certain combination of high gear and low engine revs, the alternator's voltage output could drop below the minimum threshold necessary to maintain a stable electrical supply to the car's electronic systems, and very occasionally the engine could stall. This was the reason for Nigel Mansell's retirement on the final lap of the 1991 Canadian Grand Prix in the FW14.

LEFT Alternator location and drive from right-hand cylinder-bank inlet camshaft at the gearbox end of the RS3 engine. *(Renault Sport/DPPI)*

Vehicle Control and Monitor module (VCM)

In 1992, the electronic systems on the FW14B were the most complex seen on an F1 car up to that point. The 'master' electronic control unit, which was designed in-house at Williams, is the Vehicle Control and Monitor module (VCM), known internally at Williams as the

BELOW Alternator location and drive from the left-hand cylinder-bank inlet camshaft at the timing end of the RS4 engine. *(Renault Sport/DPPI)*

117

ANATOMY OF THE WILLIAMS FW14B

Stage 2C VCM. This controls the systems for active suspension, gearshift, traction control and data logging. The VCM communicates with the engine-management Electronic Control Unit (ECU), supplied by Magneti-Marelli, using a then-new serial communications standard known as Controller Area Network (CAN). CAN is now universal throughout motorsport, as well as the road-car world, and is also used in many other complex electronically controlled systems.

Steve Wise, who, along with Paddy Lowe, developed the electronic control systems for the car, recalls the details of the CAN: "Our use of CAN was the first in F1. When Paddy and I started in '87, we spent a while deciding which microprocessor to use, and we settled on an Intel device called a 196 – there were various versions of it. When the Intel guys came over, because it was interesting for them to talk to us, they said: 'Well, why not use this CAN BUS that we've developed a chip for?' The original system I think had been developed by Bosch for the road-car industry, but Intel suggested: 'Why don't you take this up because it's going to be the next big thing.' So we thought: 'Well, let's put hardware in the box and then we've got it there in case we ever want to use it.' I think we persuaded Magneti-Marelli to fit CAN into their new engine controller as well, to run at that same time, specifically so we could communicate between the two boxes."

Another important function of the VCM was data logging, which was very much in its infancy in motorsport in 1992, as Steve Wise explains: "Right from the beginning with the new electronics, we were keen to have a lot of visibility with the data, because that was one of the things that hobbled the old system – the data we obtained was really minimal and difficult to visualise. So quite a lot of effort went into being able to visualise the data on a graph or a screen, and also recording data all around the lap, not only what the sensors were doing but also how the intermediate software was set up; things like switch positions and what they mapped to were very easy for us to interpret from the data.

"We wanted to integrate data logging. Road-car people did it rather differently, for very good reasons: they had a control system and then a separate data logger, so that's what everyone had

CONTROLLING THE FW14B – THE VCM SET-UP FILE

As described in the main text, the VCM set-up file contained data for various parameters relating to the car's set-up, including gearchange points, clutch settings, suspension ride heights, 'push-to-pass' set-up, and the allocation of functions to the cockpit switches.

Different circuits have different ride-height requirements, wing-level requirements, gear ratios, traction-control requirements, and so on, and the set-up file enables these circuit-specific parameters to be catered for in terms of active-suspension control set-up, gearbox-control set-up, traction-control set-up, and so on.

The engineers can send the set-up file to the VCM over a serial link.

The example text set-up file shown here – for Nigel Mansell's car at the season-closing Australian Grand Prix in November 1992 – is annotated (in red) to explain the various codes, but here are a few further notes to aid interpretation of it:

- DRH (Down Ride Height) isn't the actual ride height, but is a set-up parameter measured from a reference point on a set-up plate mounted on top of the gearbox. The DRH is the master datum point for suspension ride-height set-up.
- At different speeds, target ride heights are set for front on-throttle (FONtgt), and front off-throttle (FOFFtgt) conditions, and similarly for rear on-throttle (RONtgt) and rear off-throttle (ROFFtgt) conditions. These settings help to minimise pitching under braking and acceleration. The rear of the car will try to squat under acceleration (on-throttle conditions) and the front of the car will try to dive under braking (off-throttle conditions), so the target ride heights enable the system to compensate, maintaining a consistent ride height as the driver moves from on-throttle to off-throttle and vice versa.

```
> START >>>>>>>>>>>>>>>>>>>>>>>>>>>>>>>>>>>>>>>>>>>>>>>>>>>>
> SETUP 106ADL2R      07:08  08-Nov  1992      106ADL2R = Chassis 1, setup no 6, Adelaide, 1992, R race.
>          NM Race LAST RACE this year
Setup   Loading      NM Race LAST RACE this year
New
Ident       1   Chassis 1

> BSE >>>>>>>>>>>>>>>>>>>>>>>>>>>>>>>>>>>>>>>>>>>>>>>>>>>>>>
BSEDef    Barrel Shift Encoder – definitions, or gearbox settings, it could all get a bit childish when trying to think of different three letter
accronyms!
> STRATEGY      UP    1 /  DOWN    1
> BAR SPEED        14700 rpm    Max speed allowed in target gear when changing down to prevent over revving
> F.DRIVE       12   /  52    Final drive ratio
> RATIO   N   1st.   2nd.   3rd.   4th.   5th.   6th.   Error
> INPUT        13   16    16    20    21    23    Number of teeth on input shaft
> OUTPUT       37   38    32    32    30    29    Number of teeth on output shaft
Max     349.6  50.0  130.5  156.4  185.7  232.2  260.0  349.6 kmh   Max permitted downchange speed as calculated from above
Auto    144.0  144.0  144.0  144.0  144.0  144.0  144.0 rpm
UPspeed 149.0  84.4  85.2  81.0  90.3  89.3  100.0  89.3 %
UPmid   149.0  84.4  85.2  81.0  90.3  89.3  100.0  89.3 %
DNspeed 149.0  149.0 100.0 100.0 100.0 100.0 100.0 100.0 %
DNmid   149.0  149.0 119.8 118.8 125.0 112.0 113.3 113.3 %
> SELECT    0   1   2   3   4   5
Mode       0    0 = Race mode 1 = Test mode, changes function of some buttons, e.g Data to Drink
UPlift    3.50    Clutch lift target for upshifts = 3.5mm
DNlift    3.50    Clutch lift target for downshifts = 3.5mm
Bite      2.50    Clutch bite point, determined after garage boxrun
PrePulse  7.00    Clutch moog valve current for initial lift = 7mA
> VARS.:  BG   ES   EM   EG   RG   TG
Gilbert 0102h  0100h  0304h  0202h  0020h  0020h    Gearchange timing parameters, nicknamed "Gilbert" settings as the engineer
responsible was nicknamed "Gilbert gearchange"

BSElock        BSE parameters locked to the new settings above, if this is not done at the end of each setup entry the new setttings are
lost after a power cycle.
> RRS >>>>>>>>>>>>>>>>>>>>>>>>>>>>>>>>>>>>>>>>>>>>>>>>>>>>>>
RRSDef       Reactive Ride Suspension Definitions
> DATUM  Front   Rear
DRH     -11.0   10.0 mm.    Reference Down Ride Height
Target ride height maps, different targets at different speeds and with throttle ON or OFF.
> SPEED   0   50   100   150   200   250   300   350 kmh
FONtgt0  5.0  5.0  5.0  5.0  6.0  7.0  8.5  8.5 mm.
FOFFtgt0 5.0  7.0  7.0  7.0  7.0  8.5  8.5  8.5 mm.
RONtgt0  48.0  23.0  23.0  24.0  25.0  25.0  25.0  25.0 mm.
ROFFtgt0 48.0  32.5  30.6  28.7  26.8  25.0  25.0  25.0 mm.
FONtgt2  5.0  7.0  9.0  9.0  7.0  8.5  8.5  8.5 mm.
FOFFtgt2 5.0  7.0  7.0  7.0  7.0  8.5  8.5  8.5 mm.
RONtgt2  48.0  23.0  23.0  24.0  25.0  25.0  25.0  25.0 mm.
ROFFtgt2 48.0  32.5  30.6  28.7  26.8  25.0  25.0  25.0 mm.
FONtgt4  5.0  5.0  5.0  6.0  7.0  8.5  8.5 mm.
FOFFtgt4 5.0  7.0  7.0  7.0  7.0  8.5  8.5 mm.
RONtgt4  48.0  23.0  23.0  24.0  25.0  25.0  25.0  25.0 mm.
ROFFtgt4 48.0  32.5  30.6  28.7  26.8  25.0  25.0  25.0 mm.
> SELECT   0   1   2   3   4   5
FLDtgt   8.5      = Front Low Drag target ride height
RLDtgt   16.0  16.0  16.0  16.0  16.0  13.0    = Rear Low Drag target ride height
FDcomp   0.0
FBcomp   0.0
RScomp   0.0
RBcomp   0.0
> SELECT  DRY   DRY   DRY   WET   WET   DRY    Compensation settings for different tyre rolling radii
Ftcomp   11977  11977  11977  9514  9514  11977
Rtcomp   15348  15348  15348  14349  14349  15348
Ltcomp   100.0  100.0  100.0  122.0  122.0  100.0
> SELECT   0   1   2   3   4   5
Pfilter  0404h
GfiltS   0000h
GfiltF   0101h
Bfilter  0101h
Ffilter  0101h
Lfilter  0101h

> COEFF.   a10   b10   b20   a11   b11   b21
>         7.2 Hz.  /  0.9  0.0 Hz.  /  0.0
Gnotches -29472 -26524  13271   0   0   0
> SUNDRY settings              150 kmh 0.0 mm
Odds    10000  3000  10000  3000  14044  15168   Odd settings that don't sit anywhere else
PDS2    25  6554   0   0   -951  1902   Puncture Detection Settings
> SELECT   0   1   2   3   4   5   Matrix for Dash selector switch optional settings to change the suspension settings.
FXgain   100.0
FIgain   200
RXgain   100.0
RPgains  12.0  12.0  0.0  0.0  0.0  0.0
RIgain   200
FVgain   16.0
RVgains  12.0  12.0  0.0  0.0  0.0  0.0
FAgain   3200.0
RAgain   3200.0
FSgain   -5568
RSgain   2644
RBgain   5560
RGgainS  125.0
RGgainF  125.0
ADgain   6470
RRSlock
> TCM >>>>>>>>>>>>>>>>>>>>>>>>>>>>>>>>>>>>>>>>>>>>>>>>>>>>>>
TCMdef      Traction Control Module definitions
> SELECT   0   1   2   3   4   5
Maxcut  100h  106h  106h  106h  106h  106h   Traction Control settings vs selector switch positions
SlipCut  400.0
SlipLim  107.0
SlipInt   0
SlipDer   0
SpdCut  300.0
SpdLim   70.0
Cfilter  8101h
TCMlock
> PMF >>>>>>>>>>>>>>>>>>>>>>>>>>>>>>>>>>>>>>>>>>>>>>>>>>>>>>
Rate     0.02 s     Logging rate 0.02 s = 50hz, optional fast logging of 100hz available but memory size limits data size. Note in 2015 a
fast logging rate is considered to be 100Khz.
GITlog     Global Integral Task – set logging
RRSlog     Reactive Ride Suspension – set logging
BSElog     Barrel Shift Encoder – set logging
TCMlog     Traction Control Module – set logging
>Define FC.pres.  C       0 psi     0.00 1015.00  0.00 1000.00
>Define Log1   C     1 Volt    0.00  5.00  0.00  5.00
>Define Log2   C     2 Volt    0.00  5.00  0.00  5.00
>Define Log3   C     3 Volt    0.00  5.00  0.00  5.00
>Define Lat2acc.  A   E307h  g     -5.00  5.00 -5.00  5.00
>Define RF1strut  A   E311h  mm.   0.00 68.83 -20.00 80.00
>Define RF.strut  A   E31Fh  mm.   0.00 68.83 -20.00 80.00
>Define LF1strut  A   E329h  mm.   0.00 68.83 -20.00 80.00
>Define LF.strut  A   E337h  mm.   0.00 68.83 -20.00 80.00
>Define RR1strut  A   E341h  mm.   0.00 71.98 -20.00 80.00
>Define RR.strut  A   E34Fh  mm.   0.00 71.98 -20.00 80.00
>Define LR1strut  A   E359h  mm.   0.00 71.98 -20.00 80.00
>Define LR.strut  A   E367h  mm.   0.00 71.98 -20.00 80.00
>Define S.Trim    I   E2CDh  Clic  -13.00 13.00 -20.00 20.00
>Define F.Trim    I   E2D9h  Clic  -13.00 13.00 -20.00 20.00

>Define R.Trim    I   E2E5h  Clic  -13.00 13.00 -20.00 20.00
Extra logging channels setup for this run
> LOCK >>>>>>>>>>>>>>>>>>>>>>>>>>>>>>>>>>>>>>>>>>>>>>>>>>>>>
Setup  106ADL2R      NM Race LAST RACE this year
Clear
> END >>>>>>>>>>>>>>>>>>>>>>>>>>>>>>>>>>>>>>>>>>>>>>>>>>>>>>>
```

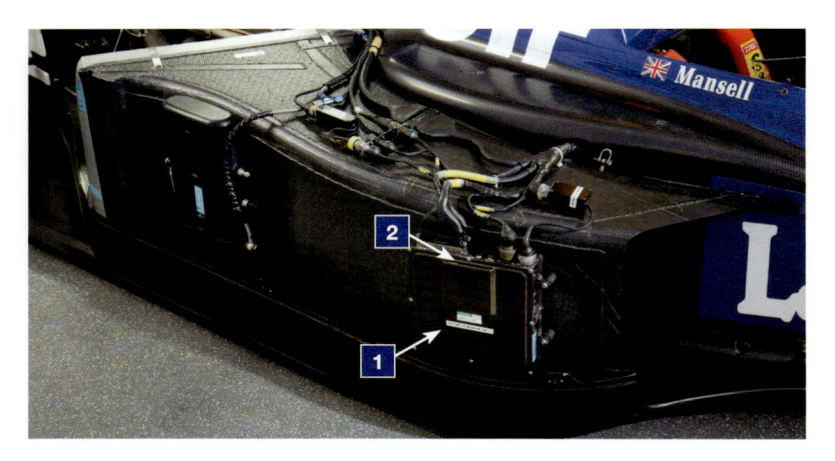

ABOVE The Vehicle Control and Monitor module (VCM) location (1) in the right-hand sidepod, with the memory-card slot (2) visible at the top of the casing. *(John Colley)*

BELOW A view of the VCM with the cover removed, showing the internal components. *(John Colley)*

1. Main processor
2. Stiffener bar
3. Temperature indicator
4. Components programmable at the factory
5. Carbon lid (blue connector mates with corresponding connector in VCM)
6. 'Wire-wrap' connections to Raychem external wiring connector

in their minds. But, where I came from, with a military background, we were already getting into the idea of having a combined data logger and control system. That way, not only do you get the data from the sensors, but you get visibility of what the software is doing and how the flow of information is going through the system, and absolutely everything is there to see.

"We had a little memory card, a bit bigger than a credit card, and certainly a lot fatter. There was a little hatch in the VCM, and we just pulled the card out, put a fresh one in, and put the card into the PC and read it."

The VCM circuit boards use mainly through-hole mounted components for reliability, although surface-mounted electronic components were beginning to appear from the late 1980s. Internally, a stiffener bar is fitted across the centre of the VCM casing, and silicon is used extensively to prevent components vibrating. Steve Wise recalls: "We have been told subsequently by test houses that the vibration profile we typically see on an F1 car [until the recent change to V6 engines] is higher than on any civil or military equipment, other than the nozzle of an Arianne rocket!"

Certain components were programmed at the factory, to define the basic functionality of the VCM, but at a circuit the engineers had the option of programming both the main code and the set-up from a PC. This was novel at the time, and provided unrivalled flexibility. The norm was for most ECUs (Electronic Control Units) to have their main programs changed by inserting different chips into sockets on the circuit boards.

Interestingly, the connections between the external, military-specification connectors and the circuit-board wiring were made using 'wire-wrap' techniques, rather than soldering or crimping. With this method, the wire is tightly wrapped around a square terminal post, with no additional means of retention.

The VCM housing, located in the right-hand sidepod, was cast from magnesium, with carbon lids, and the complete assembly weighed around 1kg. The main processor was an Intel 80C196 microcontroller.

Various parameters for the car's operating systems – ride heights, gearchange points, 'push-to-pass' system set-up, allocation of functions to various cockpit switches, and so on – were set up via a 'set-up file' that was downloaded to the VCM by the engineers. This set-up file was circuit specific, and contained coding to provide commands to the control software (see panel on pages 118–119 for details).

It is easy to forget how rapidly computer systems have developed since the early 1990s. At the start of 1992, the FW14B's VCM had 250KB of memory contained on a removable card, which can be pulled from its slot in the top of the VCM in order to download data. Towards the end of the season, the Williams team advanced to a 'massive' 1MB memory card for recording data during testing! By contrast, a typical F1 car today has around 2GB of memory to record telemetry data. It is worth pointing out, however, that the number of sensors, logging rates and data bandwidths were far lower in 1992, with, for instance, many items of data logged at 8 bits rather than the 16 bits in universal use today.

During testing, extra data loggers could be added, and these were normally fitted in the left-hand sidepod.

The Magneti-Marelli engine ECU is fitted on the rear of the monocoque behind the roll structure, under the airbox.

Traction control

The traction-control system on the FW14B was developed in-house at Williams, and was designed to reduce wheelspin by cutting engine power. The system is useful not only for improving traction but also for reducing tyre degradation.

The reduction in engine power is achieved by temporarily cutting the ignition to a number of engine cylinders. The automatic (closed-loop) traction-control system is controlled by the VCM according to signals received from wheel-speed sensors fitted at all four wheels. The front wheel-speed sensors provide a reference speed, and the software then compares the signals from the front and rear wheel-speed sensors to determine when the rear wheels are overspeeding, indicating a loss of traction. The VCM sends a signal via the CAN link (see page 118) to the engine ECU to reduce engine power by cutting cylinders. This monitoring and computing process is carried out at a frequency of 100Hz (100 times per second).

The number of cylinders (sparks) to be cut to achieve the required reduction in engine power is determined by the VCM, but the Renault (Magneti-Marelli) engine ECU determines which cylinders in the engine to cut. The cuts are sequential and progressive on all cylinders, to prevent the build-up of potentially damaging crankshaft oscillations.

The driver can switch the traction-control system on and off and adjust the system strategy using a switch on the right-hand side of the dashboard (see pages 126–127). By this means the driver can adjust the degree of rear-wheel overspeed permitted before the system begins to cut in, in addition to adjusting how fast the cylinder cutting intensifies as the rear-wheel overspeed increases.

Puncture Detection System (PDS)

At the 1992 Monaco Grand Prix, Nigel Mansell famously suffered a puncture that cost him the race, leaving Ayrton Senna to win. The team's failure to spot the puncture, ironically, was due to the efficient operation of the active suspension system, as Chris Dietrich recounts: "We didn't see it until it was too late. We could see the positions of the four struts from the data, and the reason the puncture wasn't detected was that the car compensated for the tyre deflating – basically by jacking itself back up."

A Puncture Detection System was therefore developed using the sensors incorporated in the active-suspension control system. Again, Chris Dietrich explains: "We had a target ride height – an actively calculated target ride height – so that the car should travel round the average of the circuit in a certain plane, and if that plane started to move off, you knew that something was wrong with a corner of the car. So, you'd set that number, which we called PDS in the set-up file (see pages 118–119), and if the car deviated from that by a certain amount, a little red light at the top of the dash warned the driver."

ABOVE The location of the Magneti-Marelli engine ECU (arrowed), on the monocoque, under the airbox. *(John Colley)*

LEFT Removing the front-left wheel-speed sensor from the upright. *(John Colley)*

RIGHT The fire-extinguishant reservoir (arrowed) under the driver's legs in the cockpit, viewed with the seat removed. *(John Colley)*

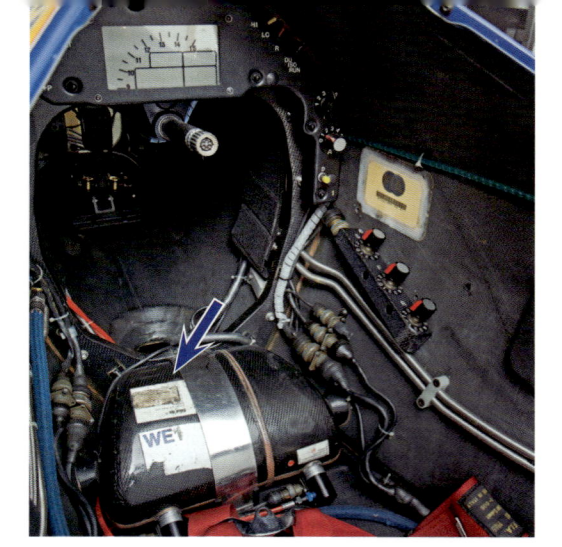

RIGHT The fire-extinguisher/electrical master cut-off switch (arrowed) for emergency use. *(John Colley)*

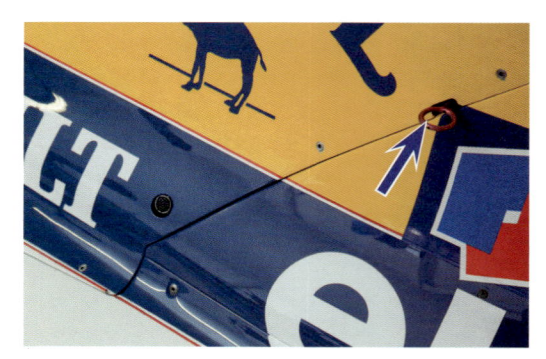

RIGHT The driver's fire extinguisher switch (arrowed) in the cockpit. *(Steve Rendle)*

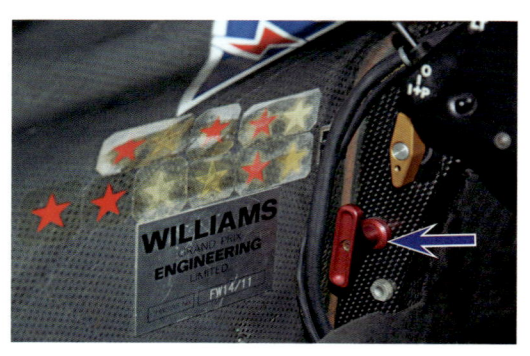

RIGHT In this view, Mansell's race harness can be clearly seen. Note the padding under the shoulder-strap buckles, the excess webbing tucked into the shoulder straps, and the quick-release buckle. *(John Townsend)*

Hydraulic system

The hydraulic system on the FW14B is used to operate the gearbox and the active suspension system, and, later during the 1992 season, the 'throttle blipper' system. The braking system hydraulic circuit is entirely independent.

The hydraulic system is described as part of the active suspension system, beginning on page 90.

Safety equipment

Fire extinguisher system

The fire extinguisher system comprises a pressurised reservoir containing the extinguishant, which is fitted on the floor of the cockpit, under the driver's legs, and discharge nozzles in the cockpit and on the rear monocoque bulkhead.

Two switches are fitted to operate the extinguisher system. One switch is activated via a pull ring on the right-hand side of the car at the rear of the monocoque, and can be activated by marshals and team members from outside the car. Pulling the ring operates a cable, which is connected to a switch on the 'power box' described previously. This switch activates the extinguisher system and also the electrical cut-off master switch, as specified in FISA regulations.

The other (red) switch is located on the left-hand side of the cockpit for use by the driver.

Electrical cut-off master switch

Two master electrical cut-off switches are fitted to the car, to cut the electrical supply to the ignition and fuel pumps by means of an electrical circuit breaker. These switches are integral with the fire extinguisher switches described previously.

There is also a separate power switch (for use by the mechanics, rather than for emergency use), accessible through a small hole in the engine cover – see pages 116–117.

Driver's harness

The six-point harness is manufactured by Sabelt, and is mounted on anchor plates bolted to the monocoque. The harness is fitted with a quick-release mechanism operated by turning a lever on the buckle.

Driver's seat

The seat was custom-moulded for each driver to ensure a comfortable and anatomically correct fit. With the driver sitting in the car, quick-setting foam was used to take a cast from which the seat was moulded.

The seat is split into left and right halves to enable it to be removed from the cockpit. The two halves are secured to the sides of the monocoque with Allen bolts. The left-hand half is embossed with the relevant driver's initials for identification. The seat assembly contains slots for the harness straps.

The seat extends from the top of the cockpit opening along the sides of the cockpit – at approximately the driver's thigh level – to a point forward of the dash roughly in line with the driver's knees, effectively forming protective padding for the driver's legs along the cockpit sides.

Medical air system

In 1979, a regulation was introduced stipulating that a driver's helmet must be fed with a 'medical air' supply to ensure that there was a supply of breathable air in the event of fire. A helmet of the time, therefore, contained a pipe on the left-hand side to which a white air hose was connected during races, though not always during practice and qualifying. In later years, the regulations were amended and a medical air system was no longer required.

Rather than being pure oxygen, which would be extremely dangerous in the event of a fire, 'medical air' is dry 'normal' air with a little added nitrogen to maintain its dryness. The system was triggered using the same circuit as the fire-extinguisher system.

Cockpit controls

Compared with F1 cars of the 1970s and 1980s, the FW14B's cockpit controls are relatively complicated, although far simpler than those found on F1 cars today.

The controls on the steering wheel and several of the controls in the cockpit can be allocated specific functions using the set-up file loaded in the VCM (see pages 118–119). This means that the functions of various switches could change according to the wishes of the

LEFT Dickie Stanford removes the right-hand seat half from FW14B/11. *(John Colley)*

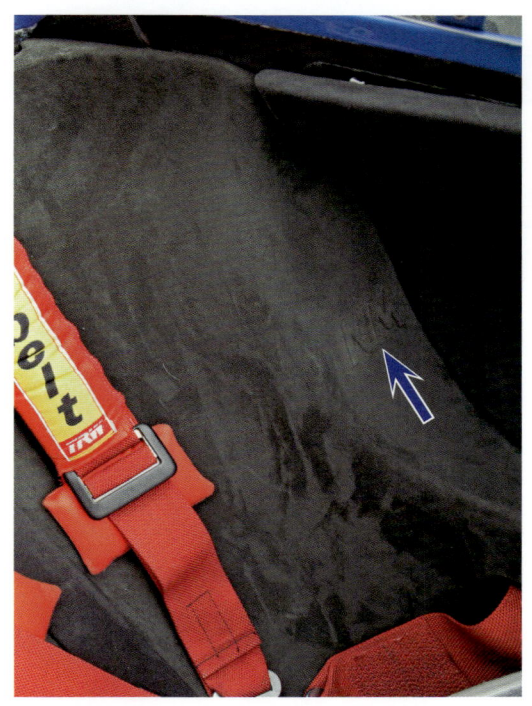

LEFT In this view of the left-hand section of Mansell's seat in FW14B/11, the 'NM' (arrowed) embossed on the seat for identification is visible. *(John Colley)*

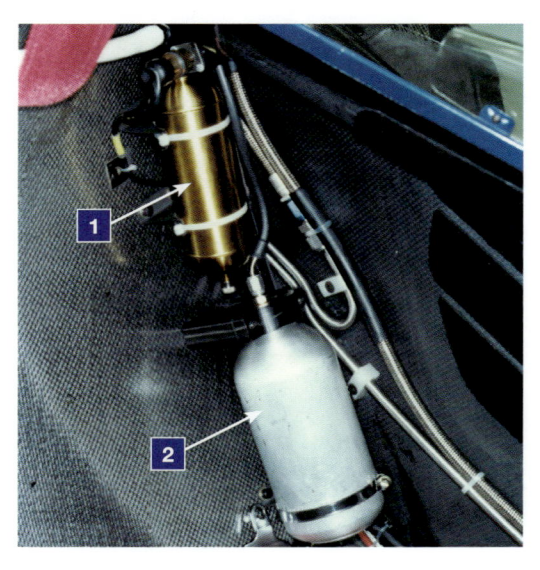

LEFT Driver's seat removed to show the medical air bottle (1) and engine pneumatic valve air bottle (2). *(Tony Matthews)*

ABOVE Nigel Mansell's steering wheel in FW14B/11. The functions of the three buttons could be changed, but one was always the push-to-pass button, and one the radio push-to-talk button. *(John Colley)*

RIGHT FW14B/11's steering wheel removed to show the gearshift paddles. The right-hand paddle changes up, and the left-hand paddle down. *(John Colley)*

RIGHT The digital dashboard module was supplied by Renault. *(Steve Rendle)*

engineers and drivers, and in some cases these functions changed from race to race.

The controls were designed to be accessible for the driver, and foam padding is fitted to various areas on the cockpit sides to protect the driver's elbows.

Steering wheel

The steering wheels were custom-made by Italian manufacturer Personal to Williams's specifications. Each wheel was tailored to the specific driver's preferences.

During the 1991 season, the FW14s were fitted with aluminium steering wheels, but for the FW14B carbon-fibre wheels were introduced. The rim of both types of wheel had a foam covering wrapped in a layer of suede.

Mansell's wheel was of a noticeably smaller diameter than Patrese's. Williams engineering drawings show that the overall diameters were 259mm for Patrese and 248mm for Mansell in the FW14 (1991, aluminium), and 246mm for Patrese and 237mm for Mansell in the FW14B (1992, carbon).

The steering wheel attaches to splines on the end of the steering column via a quick-release mechanism. To remove the steering wheel, the driver pulls a collar on the rear face of the wheel boss. The wiring harness runs down through the column, with a single turn around the top of the column to allow for the single turn of the steering wheel from lock to lock.

Paddles on the rear of the steering wheel allow the driver to change gear. The paddle set-up is the same regardless of driver: the right-hand paddle is pulled to change up, and the left-hand paddle is pulled to change down. With the car stationary and neutral selected, reverse is selected by holding in the left-hand paddle. This set-up was the norm for most drivers at the time, but some years later, in 1996, Jacques Villeneuve preferred single-paddle operation, using the right-hand paddle for changing both up and down, pulling back for upchanges and pushing forwards for downchanges.

Three buttons on the steering wheel can be set up using the software to activate various functions according to driver and engineer preference.

Digital dashboard display

The FW14B is fitted with a Renault-supplied digital dashboard display, which shows engine revs – from 9,000 to 15,000rpm – as a bar graph.

Four numbers can be displayed below the bar graph, this information being dependent on whether the car is in the garage (information relevant to mechanics) or out on the track (driver information). Typically, the display shows the engine pneumatic-valve system air pressure when in the garage, and the engine water temperature, oil pressure and lap delta when out on the circuit.

Dashboard lights

At the top of the dashboard are three warning lights. The large rectangular warning light at the top centre of the dashboard is the gearchange indicator light, while the two smaller red LED lights comprise a serious system fault warning light and a puncture warning light (operated by the Puncture Detection System – PDS).

Pedals

A conventional three-pedal set-up is used, with alloy pedals mounted on a pedal box fitted to the floor of the monocoque. All the pedals pivot at their bottom ends.

The pedal components and set-up were specific to each driver, with different travel-stop settings, but in terms of the pedals themselves only the brake differed between the two race drivers. Interestingly, a significantly larger brake pedal footplate was manufactured for test driver Damon Hill, who has size 12 feet!

For access to the pedals, once the front monocoque cover panel has been removed (see page 80), an access panel can be removed from the top of the monocoque to allow access from above. During 1992 a Renault telemetry transmitter was located in the recess in the access panel.

The brake and clutch pedals act directly on the relevant master cylinder pushrods (two pushrods for the brakes – front and rear), with a brake-bias adjustment cable acting on the brake-bias bar attached to the brake pedal.

The throttle cable is attached to a stud fitted towards the top of the pedal.

A 'drive-by-wire' throttle system was tested on the FW14B during 1992, but was not raced until the FW15C was introduced in 1993.

Driver's drink system

The driver's drink system comprises an electric pump located under the seat back, on the right-hand side. A bladder containing the drink sits below the pump. The system is operated by pressing a button on the dashboard (see photo overleaf), which activates the pump, supplying fluid through a tube to the driver's helmet.

Suspension control switches

There are a number of switches fitted in the cockpit that control various active-suspension parameters. All the suspension-control switches are mounted on the right-hand side of the cockpit. The precise functions of these switches, and the degree of adjustment available, can be altered by the engineering team, using the set-up file loaded in the VCM.

A three-position black toggle switch at the upper right-hand side of the dashboard controls various hydraulic-system functions:

DU   Dump – discharges pressure from the hydraulic system.

ISO   Isolate – prevents a gear being selected

ABOVE Removing the panel from the front of the monocoque to enable access to the pedal assembly. *(John Colley)*

LEFT The pedal assembly viewed through the access hole in the top of the monocoque. The steering column can be seen above the pedals. *(John Colley)*

LEFT A view of the dashboard showing: (1) Engine control switch; (2) Black toggle switch controlling various hydraulic-system functions; (3) Red toggle switch controlling radio; (4) Yellow engine 'overtaking' toggle switch. *(Steve Rendle)*

RIGHT The three multi-position suspension-control multi-switches on the right-hand side of the cockpit – see text for details. *(Steve Rendle)*

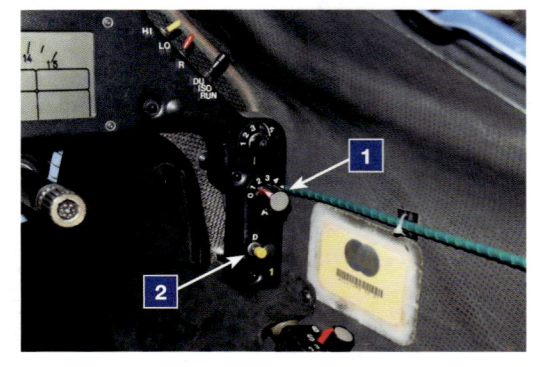

RIGHT The traction-control switch (1) and drink/data-stop switch (2) on the right-hand side of the dashboard. *(Steve Rendle)*

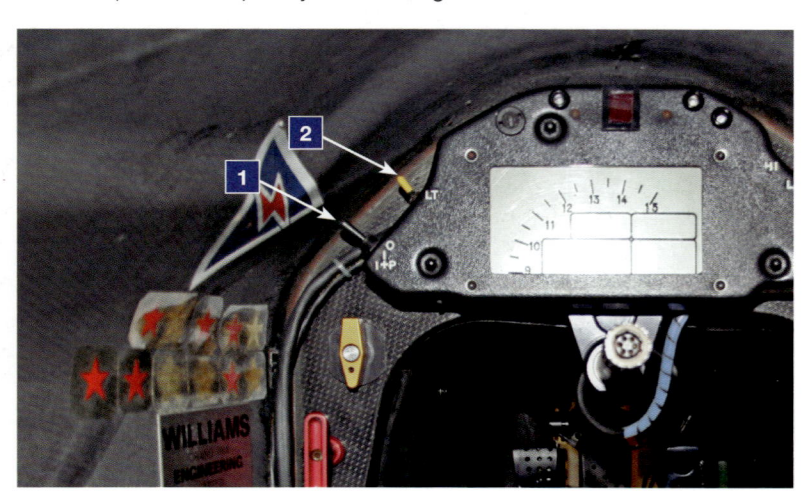

BELOW The ignition/fuel-pump switch (1) and rear-light switch (2) on the left-hand side of the dashboard. *(Steve Rendle)*

and the suspension dropping to the target ride height, in order to allow the car to be moved around easily by the team or marshals in the garage, paddock, or during recovery.

RUN Run position for normal use, which enables gear selection and suspension ride-height control.

Three multi-position selector switches located in a carbon housing on the right-hand side of the cockpit are used to control the target ride height for the active suspension system. During 1992 the driver would use these switches infrequently when out on the track, but could make adjustments to compensate for factors such as tyre degradation or lightening fuel load. The switch functions are as follows:

S Slow-corner ride height (up to 150kmh)
F Fast-corner ride height (above 150kmh)
R Rear ride height (used for fine adjustment of rear ride height)

Chris Dietrich provides an insight into the use of these three switches: "There were three knobs for the driver that changed the ride height, and that was basically all he did with the active system. You had a strategy selector that could change gains in the control system to make the car more or less responsive, but primarily they were just playing with the ride heights, and you could give them as much adjustment or as little adjustment as you wanted.

"The three controls were a slow-speed ride height, fast-speed ride height and just the rear ride height independently. You could set the threshold between the slow-speed and the high-speed corners, which I think was 150kmh, so you'd have the car with probably a higher ride height for the slow-speed corners, and you could adjust that up or down by two or three millimetres – it was a six-position switch. You'd have another ride height where the car would come down to get the diffuser working at high speed, and again you could play with that a little bit if the car was touching, just to tweak it up a little. Then you had the rear adjustment to rebalance the car, which effectively adjusted understeer/oversteer. In the set-up file, you could give the driver a big amount of adjustment, or a small amount of adjustment, or nothing, so he just thought he was playing with it and he wasn't!

"Nigel used to play with it quite a bit – he used to come in and he'd twiddle the switches around in the cockpit so that Riccardo didn't know what settings he'd run. It didn't actually matter, because it was all in the data.

Engine 'overtaking' switch

A two-position yellow toggle switch at the upper right-hand side of the dashboard allows an increase in maximum engine revs to aid overtaking:

Lo Normal position
Hi Raises the engine's maximum rev limit by approximately 200rpm to aid overtaking

Engine control switch

A multi-position selector switch located on the right-hand side of the dashboard (the upper of two switches) allows adjustment of various engine-related functions – such as engine mapping and fuel mixture – according to the maps stored in the Magneti-Marelli engine management ECU.

Traction control switch

A multi-position selector switch (marked 'A') located on the right-hand side of the dashboard (the lower of two switches) controls traction-control strategies (see page 121).

Radio switch

A two-position red toggle switch at the upper right-hand side of the dashboard activates the radio system.

Rear-light switch

A two-position yellow toggle switch at the upper left-hand side of the dashboard activates the rear rain light.

Ignition/fuel-pump switch

A three-position black toggle switch located at the upper left-hand side of the dashboard activates the ignition, VCM and fuel pumps as follows:

O   Off
I   Ignition and VCM on
I+P   Ignition, VCM and fuel pumps on

Drink/data-stop switch

A yellow push button on the right-hand side of the dashboard has two functions. When used during testing it suspends the data-logging process, and when used during races it activates the driver's drink pump.

When the button is used for data, it records a snapshot of data up to the point when the switch is pressed. As the VCM has a limited data memory, if there is a problem or incident, the driver presses the switch and data recording stops, so that the problem cannot be overwritten. In 1992, this function was used mainly for testing, as a race duration was too long to capture all the data. For a race, therefore, the button operated the driver's drink system, which was only fitted for races.

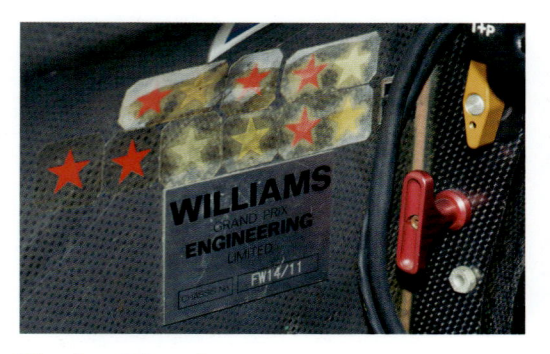

Brake bias lever

A gold-coloured lever on the lower left-hand side of the dashboard is used to adjust the front/rear brake balance, via a cable connected to the pedal assembly.

Chassis identification plate

The chassis identification plate is on the left-hand side of the cockpit. On the project car featured in this manual, the plate carries the chassis number 'FW14/11', although the car is recorded in all the team's records as 'FW14B/11'. It was built as an FW14B, and was used for the first time in June 1992 as a T-car at the Canadian Grand Prix.

Above the chassis plate, the mechanics placed 'star' stickers to keep a tally of the car's results. A red star denotes a pole position, a gold star a race win, and a silver star a second place. No sticker was used for a third place. The history of FW14B/11 is given in the 'Chassis history' appendix on page 170.

An FIA homologation plate is fitted on the right-hand side of the cockpit. A barcode on the plate identifies the specific chassis and was used for scrutineering and data recording.

LEFT Chassis identification plate on the left-hand side of the cockpit. The significance of the coloured 'star' stickers applied above the plate is explained in the text. *(John Colley)*

BELOW FIA homologation plate (arrowed) on the right-hand side of the cockpit. *(John Colley)*

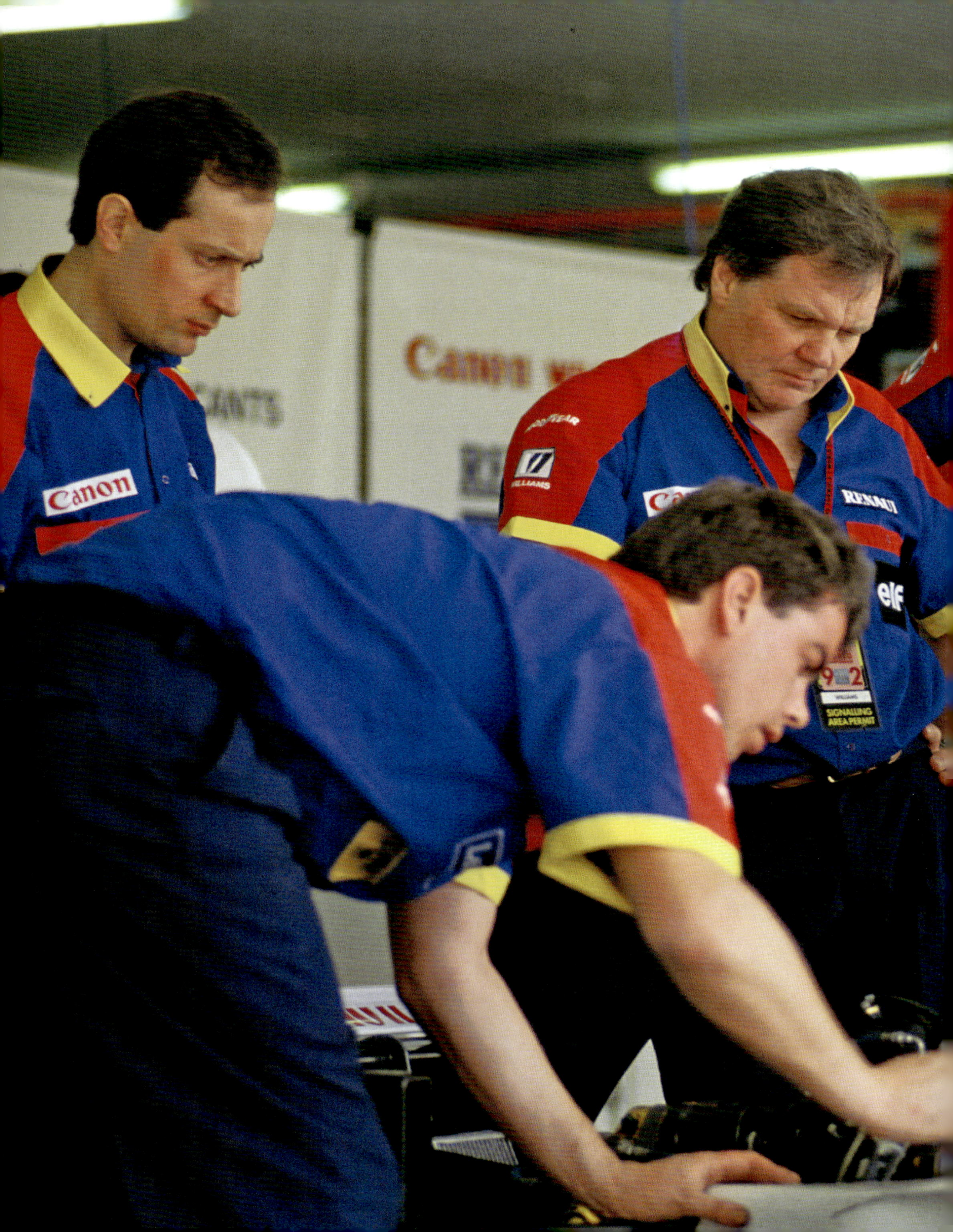
Canon
Canon
WILLIAMS
elf
SIGNALLING AREA PERMIT

Chapter Five

The engineers

The FW14B was designed, manufactured, developed and run in-house by the engineering team at Williams – a team with a strong thread of innovative engineering running through its DNA. However, the Williams engineers were assisted by many other outside engineers working for the team's partners and suppliers, including Renault Sport, Elf fuels, Goodyear tyres, Vickers Hydraulics, AP Racing (brakes) and Carbon Industrie (brakes). The cooperative efforts and sheer hard work of all these engineers and support staff saw the FW14B become one of the most successful F1 cars of all time.

OPPOSITE Puzzled looks from the engineering team in the Williams garage during the Portuguese Grand Prix weekend in September 1992, possibly after Mansell's excursion into the gravel trap due to a momentary hydraulic problem during Friday-morning practice. Looking on in the background are, from left, Steve Wise, Patrick Head and Adrian Newey, and in the white shirt, Renault engineer Denis Chevrier. *(Schlegelmilch/Getty Images)*

ABOVE Patrick Head watches the monitor in the garage at the season-opening South African Grand Prix, along with Frank Williams and other members of the team. *(John Townsend)*

Providing due credit to everybody involved in the FW14B project – all of whom contributed to its success and to the team lifting the 1992 Constructors' and Drivers' World Championships – would take a book in itself, so the following sections outline the roles of some of the key engineers at Williams and Renault Sport, along with reminiscences from some of the key Williams engineers.

Patrick Head

Patrick Head first began to work with Frank Williams in late 1975, and became co-founder and Designer for Williams Grand Prix Engineering in 1977. His first car design for Williams, the FW06, raced during the 1978 season and finished second at the United States Grand Prix at Watkins Glen. Head's second car for Williams, the FW07, gave the team its first victory, in the hands of Clay Regazzoni, at the 1979 British Grand Prix, and in 1980 the FW07B took Williams to both the constructors' and drivers' championships.

Head assumed control of the Williams team temporarily after Frank Williams's road-car accident in 1986.

In terms of the FW14B, Head oversaw the design of the car, from its birth as the FW14, through its evolution to the FW14B, and took personal charge of the design and development of the semi-automatic gearbox.

He oversaw the design, development and construction of all Williams F1 cars, including the FW14B, up until 2004, when he relinquished his role as Technical Director to become Director of Engineering, retiring from the team at the end of 2011.

In 2015 Patrick Head received a knighthood in recognition of his services to engineering and motorsport in Britain.

"When Adrian came to Williams in the middle of 1990," says Head, "he was employed as Chief Aerodynamicist and I was titled Chief Designer, but after a week it was clear to me that Adrian could go much beyond the role defined by his title, so I transferred him to the Chief Designer role, and I became Technical Director. I specified with Adrian the areas that he would be responsible for, and those that I would look after, as I continued in a number of areas to still act as Chief Designer. That covered most mechanical elements – transmission, in-wheel assemblies, brakes and suspension systems. I also continued to lead some development programmes, which included active ride, a programme which we had been working on since 1985. Paddy Lowe was directly responsible for the active-ride programme, with David Lang leading the mechanical design of the parts.

"We started on the active ride programme in 1985, on an FW09, but very soon conducted a complete redesign of the control system, changing from the initially fully mechanical system from Automotive Products (from where the initial programme came). At this stage, the programme was managed by Frank Dernie.

"We first raced the system on an FW11B at Monza in 1987 with Nelson Piquet driving. On reflection, the system was not really ready to be raced, although it did win this race. We brought the system in for committed racing for 1988, our year with the Judd engine. Although it had its moments, it proved still not ready, mostly because the control strategy was not sufficiently developed, but also as we had problems with 'aeration' within the hydraulics.

"At the end of that year, Frank Dernie left Williams to go to Lotus, and Paddy Lowe, now with Mercedes, took over direct responsibility. Paddy was very strong on control strategy, so David Lang was responsible for the mechanical design. After Frank Dernie left, late in 1988, I took overall responsibility for the programme, as Paddy, although very capable, had little experience of the full system and its integration into the car. Paddy had only recently joined us from outside the motor racing industry.

"During the development of the active suspension there were many trials, and many test days on which the car was on its way home after almost no running. However, we could see that it had great potential, as proved in later years. We had Paddy Lowe, Mark Blundell and Simon Wells running a 'mini' active-ride dedicated test team. Mark Blundell has a fine sense of humour – it was a happy test team making steady progress on their special project. I reviewed each test and development with Paddy Lowe, and we decided upon the next steps together.

"At Silverstone in 1988, Nigel expressed that he had lost confidence in the active system, saying that the car was unpredictable, meanwhile we did not have ready solutions. The rear of the car was very easy to convert to conventional suspension, but the front required the hydraulic struts to be converted to spring/damper units, and the decision and resulting design changes were only implemented after second practice on the Friday – it was an 'all-nighter' for many of us. We were lucky that the race was wet, conditions in which Nigel excelled. The second place in the race for the team was a real lift, which we very much needed.

"The FW14 was clearly a very good car, and quite possibly we could have won the 1992 championship by running an uprated version, even without the active ride. We were always concerned that introducing something as complex as the active ride could result in poor reliability and not winning the championship. We were really not fully comfortable with our decision to run it until after the first few races of 1992, all won by Nigel Mansell. It was always developed with the intention to race, if there was any doubt that was the ultimate aim, we would have stopped the programme.

"In terms of gearbox development, we had a motorcycle-type barrel-selector transmission programme underway in the mid-'80s, but then we heard that Ferrari were running an automated system, which seemed a very good idea, mainly due to the driver being able to maintain both hands on the steering wheel at all times.

"We had a test gearbox with electro-hydraulic selection running in the factory on rigs early in 1990, and tested with a transmission successfully fitted in an FW13B in mid-1990. However, that transmission did not have suitable geometry to fit within the aero geometry that Adrian required [for the FW14], so we needed to start a new gearbox to be ready to run when the FW14 was available. The quickest way to achieve this was for myself to conduct the design, and I did this within a 6-week period late in 1990. The transmission was the TG3 (for Transverse Gearbox 3!). We had some initial problems, which resulted in poor reliability at the start of 1991, due to a trivial build-specification problem, but apart from that the gearbox was quite trouble-free.

"Considering all the car designs I have been involved with at Williams, I think the FW14B was close to the top. Inevitably, because the FW07 was more from my own pen, that is probably 'at the top'. The FW11 was a very good car, and helped to bring the Honda engine through to being very competitive – thanks to Honda obviously, but with much assistance from ourselves. The FW14B was a fine car, but the origin of the shape was from Adrian Newey – the relationship to the Leyton House is plain to see – but there is much Williams and my own input into that car.

"On one hand, 1992 was a very successful year, but there are always challenges, one being that Riccardo Patrese did not get on well with the active car. In the FW14 the year before, he had been pretty much as fast as Nigel nearly everywhere.

"I think the FW14B was effective because the car was aerodynamically strong, but had many other attributes – it was not weak in any area.

"The car was excellent, the engine was strong, relations between Renault and Williams were strong, results were good, how could one not enjoy?"

ABOVE Patrick Head (right) and Adrian Newey (centre) in discussion with Riccardo Patrese at the 1992 Portuguese Grand Prix.
(John Townsend)

Adrian Newey

Adrian Newey joined Williams from March during 1990, and the first Williams car on which he carried out design work was the 1991 FW14. Newey's talent as an aerodynamicist was evident on the FW14, and in 1992 the active suspension system provided the stable platform that enabled Newey to maximise the aerodynamic performance of the FW14B.

Newey formed an outstanding design partnership with Patrick Head, and between 1991 and 1997 both men were instrumental in designing cars that took Williams to 59 race victories, five constructors' titles (1992, 1993, 1994, 1996 and 1997) and four drivers' championships (1992, 1993, 1996 and 1997).

During 1996, Newey left Williams for McLaren, where he enjoyed further success with championship-winning cars in 1998 and 1999, before moving to Red Bull Racing in 2006, where he oversaw the design of cars that won four consecutive World Championships from 2010 to 2013.

Paddy Lowe

Paddy Lowe graduated with a degree in engineering, and worked as a control engineer developing control systems for packaging machinery, before joining Williams in 1987, along with Steve Wise, to oversee the development of the F1 team's electronic systems. Lowe was heavily involved in the development of the FW14B's electronic control system, including writing the control software and designing the control system for the suspension.

Lowe left Williams in 1993 to join McLaren's R&D department, progressing to become the team's Technical Director in 2011. He left McLaren at the end of 2012 to become Executive Director (Technical) at the Mercedes F1 team.

Recalling his time at Williams, Lowe says:

"I got the job at Williams by writing in. I actually wrote to three teams – Williams, Toleman and Arrows – and only Frank Dernie wrote back. Coincidentally, he was looking for an electronics technician to help with the active suspension project, because he realised they'd bitten off more than they could chew. Having interviewed me and Steve Wise, he realised that he needed an engineer, rather than a technician – in fact he realised that he should have both of us, so we both started on the same day. Steve was stronger on electronics hardware design, and I was stronger on software, so it was broadly split along those lines.

"It was an exciting time, as we created a whole new capability that was absent within Formula 1 teams at that point. None of the teams had an electronics capacity in those days. The engine people did have an ECU, so in a way they were ahead of the teams.

"The 'leek' incident at Pembrey in 1989 [see page 43] was one massive wind-up! I hadn't worked out what was happening until they pulled the leek out – they completely had me! They were all in on it. The background was that in the early tests we had problems, and the car was always springing a leak, so I was overly sensitised towards hydraulic leaks. Of course, they knew that, and they'd set it all up, with Mark in on it. He went out and did the install lap, and then he called on the radio and said, 'I've got to come in, there's a massive leak in the cockpit.' I'm thinking, 'Oh, ****, not again!' So, then he limped in and they took the cover off and told me it was really bad and I'd better have a look myself, so I looked in, and there was this vegetable! It's always like that in Formula 1, it's still the same today – you work very hard, and there's a certain humour in the way we work, to keep everybody going.

"When we picked up the active-suspension development programme in 1988, the system was programmed to provide a constant ride height all the time, but with the more sophisticated system that we developed for '92, the ride-height targets were cnstantly scheduled, to optimise the downforce and the balance of the car according to speed or various other signals.

"The car relied a lot on feed-forward control, and a good example of its use was during cornering. When you turn in to a corner, you get a huge shift of weight from the inside to the outside wheels, and a passive car will tend to roll away from the corner. With the active car, we could schedule the ride height, so that if you wanted it would actually roll *in* to the corner, and in fact we did that to compensate for the tyre deflection. So, in mid-corner, the car would still be flat, because you'd rolled it the opposite way to compensate for the tyre squash. According to lateral acceleration and your prediction of tyre deflection, from the loads you were measuring, you could put some anti-roll in to the ride-height targets, using the actuators, so that the chassis was level, even though the outside tyre was massively more deflected vertically than the inside tyre. That was the steady, quasi-static target-setting aspect, but then we used feed-forward during the transient stage, so as the driver actually turned in towards that state, even in the dynamic, as we saw that change in acceleration, we would pump fluid into the outside actuators to stop the car leaning out of the corner, even momentarily. The drivers so liked that feel, that we pumped extra fluid into the outside actuators at the point of turn-in, so that the car momentarily banked in to the corner, rather than rolling out of the corner, which gave the drivers a great feeling of response and confidence at turn-in and during direction change.

"Traction control came a bit later, and was one of the key systems on the FW14B. Looking at the big picture, we'd spent from 1988 through to the end of 1991 developing towards the FW14B, and a lot of that time was spent on the infrastructure – such as the VCM and software, and the ability to make harnesses, instrumentation, and hydraulics – in parallel developing the suspension itself. All that work went into making something that was worth about a second a lap. At the 11th hour, we added in traction control, which only took about a month, towards the end of 1991, and that gave us another second a lap! The traction control

ABOVE Paddy Lowe sits in the cockpit of a Renault-engined FW12 test mule during a pre-season test at Rio de Janeiro in 1989. *(Paddy Lowe)*

LEFT One of the Psion Organisers used by the mechanics to send commands to the FW14B VCM. A Psion was part of the standard mechanic's tool kit for an FW14B. *(Paddy Lowe)*

LEFT Paddy Lowe at work using Williams's very first PC during pre-season testing at Rio de Janeiro in 1989. *(Paddy Lowe)*

and active suspension meant that we came into 1992 with, in round numbers, two seconds a lap advantage over everybody else. As soon as you added those two elements to the FW14, which was already a good car, we were unbeatable.

"We used a Psion Organiser, which was well ahead of its time in some ways. It was a small, programmable personal organiser, with which you could write little programs and save them to EPROMs, which you plugged in, so you could get it to do little calculations for you. An extra was a port that allowed you to connect it to other devices. We wrote little programs that created menus, and when you selected things within the menus, it would send commands to the VCM. We were therefore able to use the Psion Organiser as a hand-held tool for managing certain operations on the car, and we wrote the code and engineered it in such a way that the mechanics could use it. It was completely menu-driven, and very simple to use.

"The South African Grand Prix [the first race of the season] was my favourite race of 1992, because it was the culmination of all the work over four or five years. We had the two cars on the grid, and it was the first time they were actually going to race. All I could think about were the things that could go wrong. I actually remember feeling physically sick on the grid because it was almost too much to bear! Somebody was trying to comfort me saying, 'Don't worry mate, it'll be all right!'

"An interesting point about Kyalami was that the traction control had been introduced very late, and Renault weren't keen because they hadn't been able to do any work to test the resilience of the engine to the cutting of cylinders. We were pretty blasé in thinking that it was just a misfire, so what could go wrong? In reality of course, it could probably be very damaging to the engine, so they were correct to be cautious. We agreed we wouldn't use it in the race, because it wasn't race-proven. So, Nigel didn't use the traction control at Kyalami – he didn't need it. Ayrton kept catching up with Riccardo in the race, and every time he came close, Riccardo would switch the traction control on, and then open a gap, at which point the Renault engineer would come running out to the pit wall and ask us to tell Riccardo to turn the traction control off. We'd tell him to turn it off, Ayrton would catch up again, and then Riccardo would switch the traction control on again. The race went on like that!

"We got the 1–2 at Kyalami, and we were celebrating when I got a call from Patrick to say that I'd better go down to *parc fermé*, as there was an issue. I went down, but I'd never been in *parc fermé* before, and it was the first time I'd met Charlie Whiting. What had happened was that they'd brought the cars in to the top end of the pitlane, by the podium, parked them there and then switched them off. When you switched the car off, valves sealed the fluid in the actuators, so the car stayed at the current ride height. The stewards had then wheeled the cars all the way down the pitlane to *parc fermé* at the other end. When you wheeled the car along, the effect of little bumps was to move fluid from one hydraulic circuit to another. What happened was that the front of the car jacked itself in the air, and the rear jacked itself down, because the fluid moved from the rear to the front, so by the time they were in *parc fermé*, the cars were nose-up. This resulted in the top rear edge of the rear wing being illegal – it was outside the legality box, because the car was so highly pitched. So Charlie wanted an explanation, and I said, 'Well, Charlie, it would be alright if you let me fire the engine up, and then I just need to move this switch to re-enable the car, and it will sort itself out and put it to the proper ride height.' Which all seemed a bid dodgy! It probably sounded as if I was saying, 'I want to move this special legality switch!' It was actually just an enabling switch to switch on the suspension. So he let us do it and then the rear wing was fine. He said that he was happy, and that he wouldn't exclude us, but that it had better not happen again! I think we modified the position of the rear wing, so even if the car was pitched up, the wing was still within the legality box. In those days, the cars were measured relative to the ground, with the car at its static ride height. Today, we wouldn't have the same problem, because the cars are measured relative to a reference plane, so the wheels don't come into it.

"I think around the time of the FW14B, the motor racing industry moved itself forwards into the modern era, because it had been very late in bringing in electronics. 1992 was the beginning of the era we're in today.

"It was very rewarding, and I feel very fortunate to have come in at that point, because for the young guys now, it's very difficult to get the breadth of experience that we had in those days."

Brian O'Rourke

Brian O'Rourke joined Williams in early 1982, after working in the aerospace industry, latterly with Northrop in the US, where he worked on the design of composite structures for what would become the F/A-18 Hornet.

He was recruited by Patrick Head to bring his composites experience to the team in order to oversee the design and manufacture of Williams's first carbon-composite chassis, for the 1985 FW10.

O'Rourke was closely involved in the design, manufacture and testing of the monocoque for the FW14 and FW14B, in addition to the composite aerodynamic components and bodywork.

He is still Chief Composites Engineer at Williams today.

Chris Dietrich

Chris Dietrich began working at Williams in 1988, and is still with the team today, as Lead Engineer – Car Systems, Sensors and Wiring. He was closely involved in developing and testing the FW14B's control systems and wiring, and worked closely with Paddy Lowe, Steve Wise and Dave Lang during the development of Williams's active suspension system.

Steve Wise

Steve Wise joined Williams from the defence industry in 1987, in the same week as Paddy Lowe, and was responsible for designing the electronic hardware for the FW14B's active-suspension control system, and writing the

ABOVE Brian O'Rourke poses with the FW14B (right) and FW15C (left) behind him in the Williams Grand Prix Collection. *(Brian O'Rourke)*

LEFT Chris Dietrich gives advice to Karun Chandhok during his run in an FW14B at Turweston in July 2012. *(Mark Loasby)*

ABOVE Steve Wise (left) talks to Paddy Lowe (right) during an active-suspension test with an FW12 at Pembrey in 1989. *(Dave Lang)*

software and designing the control system for the semi-automatic gearbox control system. He is still with Williams today, as Head of Electronics R&D.

"When Paddy and I joined," says Wise, "we both had this idea that there were all sorts of things we could do on a racing car that had been opened up for us because of the fact that electronics and software were mature enough at that stage, whereas a few years before it was really not very practical.

"Paddy and I weren't there at the beginning. Before we joined, Frank Dernie worked with Kurt Borman to develop the very first realistic electronically controlled system in the mid-to-late 1980s. Simon Wells was involved in the original system that Frank Dernie had conceptualised, so it was really the three of them, with John Cadd and Phil Farrand, who developed the original systems on the FW11 and FW12.

"The reason Paddy and I were recruited was because at Williams they were mainly dependent on Honda or other external contractors for gathering data and doing trick new things. So, Patrick and Frank Dernie decided that they needed a bit more electronics knowledge in-house. Paddy always had an interest in active ride, and so that's why he gravitated towards writing the software for that project. But it was all built on the same concept as Frank Dernie's original three-legged system.

"The controller in the mid-to-late 1980s was a lot more basic, simply because electronics progressed in the intervening years. Kurt Borman was a contractor, rather than an employee, so Paddy and I progressively took over his role, though he continued to do bits of work for us right up until a couple of years ago.

"We eventually reached the conclusion, in the middle of 1988, when we had the Judd engine, that the active system was really difficult to understand. We had very little data from the original computer system on the car, and we didn't really know enough about what was happening. We thought there was scope for improving the safety side of the system as well. We spent quite a lot of time developing and refining the hardware and the software to make sure, for example, that if a sensor failed, the car would carry on in its original way. It probably took more effort to introduce that high degree of safety, which everyone takes for granted nowadays – not only in racing cars, but even more so with road cars and aircraft – than was involved in developing the actual control system. So that's why we had that long gap between 1988 and 1992, when we started racing the active car properly.

"The electronics hardware was finished by 1990, so that freed me up to work on the gearbox software. Patrick was very keen on the autoshift gearbox. I came from a background where you had a fairly rigorous process of development, validation testing, etc, by the book, but we ran the gearbox at Croix-en-Ternois in northern France, just to test it, and Patrick said: 'Right, let's get it on a race car.' That was pretty scary, but it raced for the first time on the FW14 from the start of 1991."

Dave Lang

Dave Lang joined Williams in 1986, and worked as a design engineer on the development of the active suspension system. He was instrumental in the 'overnight' conversion of the FW12 from active to passive suspension during the Friday night of the 1988 British Grand Prix – details of which he recalls below. He is currently Design Engineer at Williams.

"Before the race, we had no contingency plan whatsoever to convert the car to passive.

"I was back here [at the factory], and had my dog with me. They'd had the morning session on Friday, and Gary Thomas, who was the drawing office manager in those days, had a phone call from Patrick saying that he was on his way back from Silverstone in Jonathan Palmer's helicopter because Nigel had said that he was not going to go out again the following day if the car was going to remain active. He said he didn't want to drive it any more because he had no confidence in it.

"So, we were going to try to convert it overnight to a standard car. Well, the big problem was that it wasn't so bad at the back, because we'd still got bellcranks where the dampers could go. So we could rework the back and put in some Penske dampers – which was fine – but the front suspension had no bellcranks, and the actuators were on the ends of the pushrods, so they bolted straight into a casting in the tub. We thought: 'How are we going to do that?'

"Patrick arrived back mid-afternoon, and we had to decide how we were going to convert the front struts into a damper assembly, and also a spring unit, within that package, as that's all we'd got. I worked on converting the strut assembly into a damper assembly. I drew up some new components so we could actually insert a Penske piston into some new parts and put some shims

LEFT Dave Lang (right) in discussion with Mark Blundell during the test with the FW12 active car, at which the 'leek' appeared, at Pembrey in August 1989.
(Dave Lang)

BELOW A photograph taken by Dave Lang at the Pembrey test in August 1989. From left: Simon Wells (just in view), Chris Dietrich, Steve Wise, Paddy Lowe and John Cadd (with leek in hand).
(Dave Lang)

either side of it, and then connect up the porting to a Penske reservoir. Gary Thomas and Enrique [Scalabroni] worked out how they were going to do the springing unit, which was a little pack of disc springs that were going to be below the strut. Once they'd decided which ones they were going to use, and the rate and all the rest of it, they phoned, I think, Springmasters in Redditch, and they arranged to supply the ones we wanted. If I remember correctly, this was late in the afternoon, and we needed them the following day, so they agreed to leave them somewhere so that we could send up a driver to pick them up.

"We had to get the drawings for the new bits done, and two or three guys were kept back in the machining shop. I think we'd finished the first of the detailed drawings by around about teatime, so they were starting to cut metal just after teatime. We stayed all night, to make sure the bits and pieces went together, and then Simon [Wells] and I had got the first pair of struts ready to go on a damper dyno – to see if we had a damper curve – early in the morning. I think it was before nine o'clock, so by that time the first pair was on its way up to Silverstone. I think by lunchtime the second pair was on the way as well.

"So, I went to work on the Friday morning, at about 8.30am, and I never went home until Saturday evening at about 7.00pm – we just worked all the way through. Enrique, Gary and I did the drawings for the new components, two or three guys in the machine shop made all the parts, and then Simon and I got the assemblies ready, and they went to Silverstone! Then on the Sunday it was a wet race and Mansell came second!

"We had to use whatever components we had at the factory, then anything else we had to get made or converted. We converted the active strut assembly to turn it into the damper. It all fitted in the original package space.

"Two or three races later we then converted the chassis to bellcranks, and it went back to a more conventional set-up."

Simon Wells

Simon Wells joined Williams in 1983, and worked on the Williams active-suspension project from its very earliest days. He is currently Operations Director at Williams.

"I joined Williams in 1983 to work in the R&D department and worked on the very first active suspension system. In 1984 a mechanical system was installed on an FW09, which Nelson Piquet drove at Silverstone, but unfortunately it caught fire when both turbos failed – the actual turbines sheared off and disappeared down the exhausts, resulting in a flame thrower due to the turbo oil having ignited.

"My early job was to oversee the testing of R&D parts in the test lab, to create test rigs, conduct the analysis, as well as overseeing the build on the hydraulic side of the car. We worked in conjunction with the Test Team, who were responsible for running the car at the track and who then gave feedback to the R&D department. I then oversaw the changes that were needed in the test lab.

"After the active FW11B, the decision was taken to put it onto the FW12 race car which had the Judd engine. It was a fully integrated system, so there were no front bellcranks, as it was all directly coupled into the chassis. After the first few races of the season, we soon realised that we were running into problems that we didn't quite understand. All the development was being done at the track and there was no test lab work as such back then. This resulted in the system being taken off halfway through the season (at the British Grand Prix) and it was at that point that the decision was taken to build more in-house test rigs to accelerate development. This became a full-time commitment for me.

"The FW13 was the next car used for development, which went to Estoril for a test shortly after the race there. It was at this point we really started to make progress, and the control system strategy led by Paddy Lowe started to extract the maximum out of the aero package. Essentially the same system was then packaged onto the FW14 which we ran during 1991 to continue development and fine tuning.

"In terms of the FW14B, we had to gear up to run the system as part of the normal production and assembly process. My role was to continue with development and set-up a more advanced test lab. I was tasked to come up with the assembly running processes and procedures. These had to be documented to make sure that during assembly technicians and race mechanics knew what to do. It was a true Haynes Manual.

"The challenges with the FW14 and FW14B were mainly around the packaging. We knew from the FW12 that there were problems with air (in the hydraulic system), so a lot of emphasis went into solving this. It was mainly caused by cavitation due to the low pressures in the system, which you could see at high wheel velocities. When you hit a kerb, you'd see a negative pressure on the unloaded side of the damper valve and you'd get air coming out of the solution as tiny air bubbles which then affected the damper valve and gave the suspension a soggy feel.

"Managing the minimum pressures in the system became the biggest challenge. We did a lot of detailed design on the internal hydraulics and raised the low-pressure side of the system, which was pressurised with nitrogen. Our reservoir design was one of the most complicated you could imagine. If you looked at a section through the reservoir you would see many devices to manage entrained air. One was an inclined small mesh screen, which is a common method for removing air bubbles from the fluid. The downward moving bubbles sit on the top side of the mesh and rise above the fluid level. The way that the fluid return fed back in was really carefully designed, so it wouldn't cause a lot of turbulence and froth the fluid. The way we charged it with nitrogen to 50psi was also carefully thought out. That one component was key to the operation of the system and had particular design input from Patrick Head.

"The other challenge was the failsafe we put in the system to improve safety and reliability. We basically put dual sensors on critical channels. A lot of the potentiometers were twin-track devices and if you started seeing a deviation between the two channels the software would detect which one to use. Paddy Lowe was responsible for the redundancy built into the system and the control software. I dealt with all the hardware and testing, and Dave Lang looked after the hydraulic design.

"Where we really made the big gain with the FW14B was Paddy working with the aero package in terms of the ride-height mapping.

This consisted of low, medium and high-speed corner mapping to provide the ultimate aero platform. We also looked at stall characteristics on the diffuser and altering our braking ride-height map versus acceleration. Once we'd got all that ironed out, that really optimised the aero package.

"The FW14 aero package was already pretty good, but on passive springs and dampers you'll get parts of the aero map that are more sensitive to ride height, so it's always going to be a compromise with the car's set-up. What we did with the FW14B was to make sure that it was always optimised at all speeds and ride heights, and that's what really gave us the advantage. With the active system not only were we able to maximise the aerodynamic package, we were also able to run very low wheel rates, which gave us a huge grip advantage for low speed corners. The traction on the active car was pretty awesome."

David Brown

David Brown was Nigel Mansell's Race Engineer at Williams in 1992. He joined the team in 1981 as a draughtsman in the drawing office. In 1987, he became Race Engineer on Mansell's FW11B, and took on the same role with Thierry Boutsen when Mansell left to join Ferrari at the end of 1988.

When Mansell returned to Williams in 1991, Brown was again appointed as his Race Engineer, before carrying out the same role for

ABOVE Another photograph taken during the Pembrey test in August 1989, showing Simon Wells (right) and Dickie Stanford (left) during a break in on-track activity. *(Dave Lang)*

ABOVE David Brown discusses 'Green Sheet' data with Nigel Mansell at the 1992 Hungarian Grand Prix. *(John Townsend)*

RIGHT John Russell and Nigel Mansell at the 1994 Australian Grand Prix, which proved to be Mansell's final F1 victory. *(Sutton Motorsport Images)*

RIGHT Dickie Stanford positions the timing monitor on Mansell's FW14B during qualifying for the 1992 San Marino Grand Prix. *(John Townsend)*

Alain Prost, Ayrton Senna and Damon Hill, until he left for McLaren at the end of 1995.

Brown went on to work for Jordan, before moving to the US and working for a range of US-based race teams. He is currently a race engineer with Porsche North America.

John Russell

John Russell was Riccardo Patrese's Race Engineer during 1992, after joining Williams in that role in 1989. He became Damon Hill's Race Engineer for 1993 and early 1994, before switching to engineer David Coulthard's and Nigel Mansell's cars later in the season.

At the end of 1994 Russell transferred to become Chief Engineer at Williams Touring Car Engineering, before moving to become Chief Engineer for the Williams BMW Motorsport Le Mans project of 1998 and 1999. In mid-1999 Russell rejoined the Williams team briefly before moving to the Jaguar Racing F1 team as Chief Designer, where he remained until 2003.

Since 2011 he has worked in the Australian V8 Supercar series for Triple Eight Race Engineering as Director of Engineering and Production.

Dickie Stanford

Dickie Stanford worked as Chief Mechanic on the Williams race team running the FW14B during 1992. He joined the team in 1985, as Race Mechanic on Nigel Mansell's FW10, and became Chief Mechanic in 1990.

In 1995 he was promoted to become Team Manager, a role in which he remained for ten years before taking a factory-based job in order to spend more time with his family.

Stanford returned to the role of Team Manager in 2010 before stepping down ahead of the 2014 season to become General Manager of Williams Heritage, where he is responsible for the care, maintenance and, where appropriate, running of the cars in the Williams Grand Prix Collection.

Bernard Dudot

Bernard Dudot was Technical Director of Renault Sport in 1992, a role that he had held since 1980. He led the design and development of Renault's 1.5-litre turbo V6 engine before being instrumental in the design and development of Renault's new 3.5-litre V10 to suit the F1 technical regulations introduced in 1989. He remained as Renault Sport Technical Director until 1997, when Renault left F1.

After spells as Technical Director at Prost Grand Prix and Project Manager with the Nissan Infiniti Indy Racing League engine project, Dudot returned to Renault Sport in 2003. He left in 2005 to set up a motorsport technology consultancy, which he still runs today.

Jean-Jacques His

Jean-Jacques His joined Renault in 1972 to work on road-car engine projects, eventually moving to the Renault Sport R&D department, working for Bernard Dudot.

When Renault withdrew from F1 in 1985, he moved to Ferrari's motorsport department, where he worked until Renault Sport regrouped to develop a new V10 engine for F1 in 1988, when he rejoined. When Renault Sport again withdrew from F1 at the end of 1997, he transferred back to the parent company to become head of engine design.

In 2000, His returned to Renault Sport as Technical Director, but left the company during 2003 to join Maserati, before moving to his current position as Chief Powertrain Engineer at Ferrari's road-car division.

Philippe Coblence

Philippe Coblence joined Renault Sport in 1983, after three years with Matra Sport (Formula 1 division). He was Design Office Coordinator at the Viry-Châtillon headquarters of Renault Sport during the design and development of the Renault V10 3.5-litre engine, and worked extensively on the design and development of all Renault's V10 F1 engines, including the RS3C and RS4 used in the FW14B.

Coblence went on to become Project Leader, and then Head of Design Department at Renault Sport, and in 2003 moved to the road-car division at Renault, where he became Design Manager for Powertrains until he retired in 2015.

LEFT Bernard Dudot pictured in 1992 during his time as Renault Sport Technical Director. *(Renault Sport/DPPI)*

LEFT Jean-Jacques His, head of Renault Sport R&D department during 1992. *(Renault Sport/DPPI)*

LEFT The very first test of a Renault V10-powered Williams, at Paul Ricard in October 1988, with an FW12. From left: Renault Sport's Jean-Marc Brepson, Bernard Dudot and Philippe Coblence, with Patrick Head. *(Renault Sport)*

Harrods
CREATEONE
クリエイトワン
CAMEL
elf
Labatt's
Nigel Mansell

Chapter Six

The drivers

The FW14B came from an era of F1 when a car was rarely raced for more than a single season. As a consequence, other than regular race drivers Nigel Mansell and Riccardo Patrese, and test driver Damon Hill, very few people have experienced an FW14B on-track. All the drivers who are known to have driven an FW14B are listed over the following pages, along with brief biographies, while Mansell and Patrese provide their thoughts about their experiences of developing and racing the FW14B.

OPPOSITE Nigel Mansell talks to Riccardo Patrese in the garage during the 1992 Japanese Grand Prix weekend – a race that Patrese won. *(Sutton Motorsport Images)*

Nigel Mansell

After a number of setbacks and sacrifices, Nigel Mansell's determination and driving skills saw him rise through the junior formulae to catch the attention of Lotus founder and team principal Colin Chapman, who signed him as Lotus's F1 test driver for 1980. Mansell's testing skills impressed the team sufficiently to earn him his F1 race debut in a Lotus 81B at the 1980 Austrian Grand Prix, following which he was promoted to a full-time race seat with Lotus for 1981.

Mansell drove for Team Lotus for four full seasons, until the end of 1984, when he moved to Williams. His first podium finish came at the 1981 Belgian Grand Prix, where he was third, and he achieved four more third-place finishes with Lotus.

Partnering Keke Rosberg, Mansell made his Williams debut in the Honda turbo-powered FW10 at the 1985 Brazilian Grand Prix. Towards the end of that season the Honda package came good and Mansell took fastest lap at the Italian Grand Prix, then second place in Belgium, and finally achieved his first F1 victory at the European Grand Prix at Brands Hatch, following this up with another win at the following round in South Africa.

Mansell continued to drive for Williams in 1986 and 1987, and was in contention for the World Championship during season-long battles with Brazilian team-mate Nelson Piquet, in the FW11 and FW11B. The 1988 season was a challenging one with the Judd V8-powered FW12, and at the end of the year Mansell left to join Ferrari.

For 1991, Mansell was persuaded to return to Williams. With Riccardo Patrese as his team-mate, he won five races and finished second in the World Championship, to McLaren's Ayrton Senna. He then dominated the 1992 championship with the FW14B, becoming World Champion.

Mansell is the only man to have driven every FW14B chassis produced, an honour that falls to him because no one else drove chassis FW14B/11 (the 'project car' for this book), the car he used to win the 1992 British, German and Portuguese Grands Prix.

Nigel reflects on his experiences driving for Williams with the FW14B:

"In 1991 we went through a lot of pain and anguish to get the gearbox right, and of course the wheel came of at Estoril, and it's a great shame, because I think '91 could have been a championship year as well. It was all on the hoof, and I think that was the fascinating thing with Formula 1 then – unlike now in some ways – you could make some gains with some good basic changes within the rules and regulations, so if you weren't really competitive, you could actually do something mechanically. The epic one was in 1985 with the turbo car, when they changed the rear suspension to provide some more anti-squat, and we found three-quarters of a second a lap – it was marvellous!

"The biggest gain I think I found between 1991 and '92 was in myself, because I knew that this was the last chance at the OK Corral. I had a one-year contract left, the age I was, I knew I was going to be replaced and I wasn't probably required going forward, and I put the limits out there – I extended my envelope of driving, and the relationship I had with the car. I think it would be fair to say that Williams did too. I knew this was the last chance, and that's why I drove the whole year with a broken foot! How many drivers drive all year with a broken foot? I did. Because you know this is the one time, when you taste it and feel it, touch it and

RIGHT Nigel Mansell pictured during 1992 by his personal photographer, John Townsend. *(John Townsend)*

live it, and so personally I worked so hard with the team – the engineers, the mechanics – and we didn't leave any stone unturned. I was on a high with adrenaline.

"If you look at weight, that was another element, because I've always been at a disadvantage there. Prost, Senna and Piquet always had half a second a lap in their pockets. Because the driver and the car weren't weighed together, I was always at a disadvantage being a heavy driver. So I lost upwards of 20 pounds that winter and I was the lightest I've ever been, and able to compete on a more level playing field.

"I came out of the starting blocks on a mission that year. I've been a driver my whole life, and I can only say that basically I was a man possessed, refusing to take anything for granted. I used to almost sleep with the car, and Patrick Head used to say to me: 'Nigel, go to the hotel, everything's fine.' I said: 'I'm just looking at things, I'm just making sure everything's right.' I just micro-managed everything – everything!

"You don't win a championship in a car that isn't great, but it would be so wrong not to congratulate Renault, for what they did with the engine, and Elf, because it was a power-boosting fuel – the fuel got better and better. So with Renault, with Elf, with Patrick Head and Adrian Newey, and the whole team, and even Riccardo and myself, the package got put together brilliantly well. The perfect storm came together: it started back in the mid-to-late '80s, then it came to fruition for me in '92.

"Just like Ayrton Senna with McLaren, Alain Prost with McLaren, Michael Schumacher with Ferrari, it's the team – and Williams got everything absolutely perfect. Some of these drivers had the opportunity to win and defend year after year with their teams, but for whatever reason, not just personal to me, Williams then changed things.

"I wrote in the contract it had to be fun, and I wrote in the contract that we had to do whatever testing we needed, whatever was necessary to get the job done – the facilities, the finances, and the backing to do it – and we went on so many extensive programmes to make sure we were good to go.

"In those days – no disrespect to the drivers and teams today – we used to go testing all the time. It was hardcore testing. If something went wrong, you went off and had an accident, or a spin, or you had a scare, but, you know, none of this bloody simulation stuff, where they can do everything in real-time and all the rest of it. They very rarely have to go testing any more – it's just astonishing it can all be done in the simulator. Riccardo and I, with a fantastic team – the Williams team, and all their incredible employees and engineers – worked tirelessly together, and it was a blast, it was fun. It was tough at times, to understand how it was working, and what we could do about problems. For example, what filter you could put in so the suspension wouldn't jump up and down so much at the wrong time – and basically it was hard work.

"It was at the end of '91, before we went into the winter, when we had to make a decision about whether we were going to go active. There was a mighty test, and then we had to decide: 'Shall we give it a go or not?' You had to commit to the programme, and it was a tough decision. I remember the test very, very well, but at the end of it we said, 'You know what? There's got to be potential with this if we can sort some things out.'

"The thing that was quite extraordinary with the FW14B was the sheer brute force required from the driver to hang on to the car. Because there was no power steering, the physicality of driving the car was brutal, and that's what the current drivers will never experience in the present era of Formula 1, because they have power steering, and various other things.

"Once Riccardo said to me: 'Look, just help me out here, how can you go through this corner so much faster, it's crazy!' And I said: 'Well, first of all you've got to carry the speed in, and then the thing is having the confidence that when it kicks out on you, which it will… the car is never in a perfect balance… when it kicks out on you, you have the strength, the presence of mind and obviously the skill and the *belief* – and I think that's the single biggest word to use – the *belief* that you can catch it, and then not have an accident. And on some corners, you know, where there was a bit of run-off, or the barrier wasn't so close to the circuit, Riccardo was really, really good, quicker than me in certain places, but in the real fast corners he just couldn't trust the car. I wouldn't say I trusted it, but I knew its limits. I pushed the envelope and the limits of the car to the full.

"I had a minute steering wheel. That was because as soon as the car kicked out, on a one-to-one steering lock I could twitch it back. My arms, wrists and upper body were very strong, and without that I wouldn't have been able to control the car. In those days we did opposite-lock a car, and you had to catch it. You had to drive, if you like, in front of the car, and know what the car was going to do. If you waited for the car to do something to you, then all you were doing was reacting to it, and you'd be too slow. Any great champion anticipates what a car's going to do before it does it, so then you're actually quite quick. You're driving the car, the car's not driving you. You're trying to be one step ahead of the car – or ten steps ahead!

"I think the biggest area where I found the advantage was the balance in the slower-speed corners. I felt there was more potential in the slower-speed corners than the medium-to-high-speed ones. It was the blown diffuser. The blown diffuser was totally reliant on the driver keeping his foot on the throttle, so that the exhaust sucked the car down. As soon as you came off the throttle, you'd lose that to a large degree. That's why it was sometimes so important to be braver than you wanted to be and to trust it. If you feathered the throttle or came right off it, you would actually break the grip level – and that was instantaneous!

"As I showed with Ferrari, because we had the blown diffuser in 1989 and '90, with the famous overtake on Gerhard at the Peraltada [Berger in the 1990 Mexican Grand Prix], if you kept your foot in, you could definitely get more grip. The problem was, if you didn't make it, you had the most horrendous accident.

"I don't know whether I'd use words like brave, foolish, aspiring, trusting… but it was... it was a knife-edge all the time. If you were willing to push the parameters, sometimes – not all the time, this is what the difficult thing was, you were always gambling – sometimes you thought: 'Wow, that really worked, I'll try that again.' And then you'd come round and do it again, and it didn't work! The anticipation level, the anxiety level, driving the car was more than it should have been. I know Riccardo suffered more than I did.

"What we had then was the brute force of the engine, the tyres, and the aerodynamics. So, not blowing my own trumpet, but as Riccardo will tell you, and any other driver, I could manhandle the car. You could put your spirit, you could put your technique, you could put your energy and you could put your personality into the car to get it round some of the corners. And that's what I loved about the car. Equally, it could bite you in the arse too!

BELOW Nigel Mansell crosses the line to win the 1992 British Grand Prix – his home race – to a rapturous reception.
(John Townsend)

"I don't think the active suspension was as big an influence on the performance as people think. It was part of it, but it was only one element of maybe ten. The year before, we lost the championship because of the gearbox – the gearbox is a significant element. The engine's incredibly significant, the fuel, the car and the set-up – with the active obviously – is so, so mega-important. And the people who made sure that it was set up right – David Brown, the engineers and the mechanics. Whatever suspension you want on the car, you're screwed unless the aerodynamics are right, so Adrian Newey with the aerodynamics was absolutely fantastic. Then, of course, you need the right tyres, and we then still had to balance the car both aerodynamically and mechanically, and the active suspension doesn't really do that for you, you actually had to input data. It's like a computer, it's only as good as the input you give it. And those things I've just listed, if any one of those drops out, then you ain't going to win. And if you like, one of the last elements is that the driver in the car must not screw up!

"In terms of season highlights, I think the British Grand Prix for me was always incredibly special, but I don't think you can ever say there's a more special moment than actually winning a World Championship and standing on the top step with Ayrton. Winning the championship in Hungary wasn't straightforward – we had a puncture, we had other problems – but to come second, with Ayrton winning, and then to be crowned World Champion there was just electrifying.

"I think also we worked so hard for so long. It wasn't just about 1991, '92, it was about the 12, 13, 14 years before that. It was like, 'Oh my goodness me!' – it was just an amazing feeling. Even talking with you now, you pinch yourself and say: 'Thank goodness that we're part of an incredibly exclusive club in the world, to be a World Champion.'

"I'm grateful that Riccardo and myself, and the Williams team, pioneered part of the package that presented the team with such great success for a number of years, and the evolution of it certainly was something special to be part of. I'm really pleased and proud that it's been part of my history. I think it's been a journey of evolution throughout my whole career, with different teams and different cars, and I'm just so delighted that with Sir Patrick Head, Sir Frank Williams and the Williams team – David Brown, Paddy Lowe, Adrian Newey, and lots of other great people within the team, that we got a fantastic job done.

"I think the biggest thing is that when you think you've got all things covered, you find out very quickly you haven't! You keep bouncing back, you never give up, you keep focused, and just because you think you've done a great job, and you might have won a race, it doesn't mean you can't do it better. If you want to be there at the top, you have to keep pushing the envelope.

"It wasn't just the FW14B car that won the championship, it was a whole load of elements that came together, and that should not be overlooked."

ABOVE World Champion at last – the relief is palpable as Nigel Mansell celebrates on the podium in Hungary with race winner Ayrton Senna and third-placed Gerhard Berger. *(John Townsend)*

Riccardo Patrese

After much success in the lower formulae, Riccardo Patrese made his F1 debut with Shadow at the 1977 Monaco Grand Prix. Later in 1977 he went to Arrows, where he stayed until his move to Brabham for 1982 to partner Nelson Piquet for two seasons. Famously, Patrese took his first F1 victory at the 1982 Monaco Grand Prix – crossing the line first after a race of both attrition and confusion.

For 1984 and '85, Patrese moved to Alfa Romeo. The cars suffered disastrous reliability, although he managed third place at his home grand prix, at Monza, in 1984.

After returning to Brabham for 1986 and '87, poor reliability again hampered Patrese's results,

RIGHT Riccardo Patrese pictured in 1992. *(John Townsend)*

his best finish being another third place, at the 1987 Mexican Grand Prix.

Patrese joined Williams for the final round of the 1987 season, in Australia, standing in for the injured Nigel Mansell in the FW11B. This led to a full-time race seat at Williams for 1988, alongside Mansell. Patrese stayed at Williams for five full seasons.

In 1989, Patrese scored four second places and two thirds, taking third place in the drivers' championship. In 1990, he won the San Marino Grand Prix – his only visit to the podium that season – and by the end of the year his career tally of race starts made him the most experienced driver in F1 history.

Patrese took two wins with the FW14 in 1991, along with two second places and four thirds, plus four pole positions and two fastest laps. At the end of the season, he finished third in the drivers' championship behind World Champion Ayrton Senna and Williams team-mate Nigel Mansell.

Riding shotgun to Mansell in 1992, Patrese won the Japanese Grand Prix, and took six second and two third places, to finish runner-up to the team leader in the drivers' championship.

A move to Benetton for 1993, to partner rising star Michael Schumacher, proved to be Patrese's final season in F1, his best results being third place in the British Grand Prix and second in Hungary.

In the 16-year period from 1977 to 1993, Patrese competed in 256 grands prix, a record that stood until Brazilian driver Rubens Barrichello passed Patrese's landmark in 2008.

In addition to his F1 career, Patrese combined his F1 commitments with a sports-car racing schedule for seven years between 1979 and 1985, driving for the works Lancia team at the World Sportscar Championship rounds that did not clash with F1 races, including Le Mans in 1981 and 1982. Over that period he co-drove a Lancia to eight outright wins, including at Silverstone and Nürburgring in 1982 and Spa in 1985.

After his retirement from F1, Patrese returned to Le Mans with Nissan in 1997, but the car failed to finish. He dabbled in touring cars at various points during his career and also competed in the short-lived Grand Prix Masters series during 2005 and 2006.

Patrese drove all the FW14B chassis except for FW14B/11 and covered extensive test mileage during 1991 and 1992. He holds the distinction of being the last driver to win a race in an FW14B – the Japanese Grand Prix in October 1992 – which he won in chassis FW14B/10, its only race victory.

Riccardo reflects on his experiences driving for Williams with the FW14B:

"I started to drive the FW14B during the winter of 1991/92, after they'd done a lot of testing with Damon. I started at Estoril, and immediately the impression was very good. I felt the grip was at a higher level than the FW14. We had traction control, we had the possibility to control the suspension with all the electronic controls, and it was immediately good.

"The key was that the car was always at the same ride height, and because of that the bottom of the car was always flat – parallel – it was not rolling or pitching, so the active suspension optimised the downforce 100%, and we had the maximum in every corner. To find the best set-up we had to test very hard. It was good to have so many possibilities for the set-up, but it was also difficult to find the right direction to go. In those days the driver was very important in choosing the right direction to go, because you could lose a lot of time if you didn't give the team the right information and the right feedback.

"During the winter Nigel was not available, so between me and Damon, I think we did at least

20,000km of testing. We were going all week in one place, especially Estoril, which we used a lot because in the winter time the weather there was not so bad. We would be testing all day – sometimes maybe 500km in the morning, and 500km in the afternoon. We were getting a lot of practice driving the car.

"In the corners there could sometimes be a problem due to the fact that if you lifted you could lose the downforce. Also, compared with the 1991 FW14, the car was a little bit more unpredictable. With the FW14 you could feel a little bit more what was happening, especially in the corners, so you could understand when you were reaching the limit. With the 14B, the grip was really massive, but the moment it went away, it really was going! So, it was a little bit more difficult to find the limit in the high-speed corners.

"The challenge that I had with the car, compared with the FW14, was that in the high-speed corners the steering wheel was getting very, very heavy, because of the downforce that the car was producing. You really needed the strength to manage the steering wheel, and I think one of my problems during 1992 against Nigel was that he was stronger than I was, and in those days we didn't have power steering. You had to really have the strength to handle the steering wheel, and I think Nigel had a little bit of an advantage in the fact that he was stronger than I was, and he was more agile with the steering wheel because he had more strength.

"If you remember with the FW14, against Nigel, especially during the first part of '91, I was very competitive. I think the difference between the 14 and the 14B, which gave Nigel the performance advantage over me was the steering, and the traction control. In '91, I could see from the telemetry that I was coming out of slow corners as good as, or sometimes better than Nigel. I was managing with my foot – my throttle control – to have better traction out of slow corners. In the high-speed corners I was very similar to Nigel. In '92, the traction control made coming out of a slow corner easier, so we were equal because the electronics were doing the job, but in high-speed corners Nigel was usually a bit quicker than I was. So, because of this, in '92 you could see that Nigel was quicker than I was most of the time. The car was fantastic, but from the driving point of view, I had some small disadvantages against my team-mate, because we were equal on the speed out of slow corners, and Nigel was better on the high-speed corners.

"When we first tested the 14B, of course we were doing lap times quicker than the '91 car, but in the straights the car was always slower than the FW14, and we couldn't understand this. The thinking was that maybe a little bit of power was taken from the engine because of the hydraulic pump, but that was not the answer. What happens with a car with normal suspension is that when the speed increases, the rear goes down, and because of that, the diffuser stalls, and you gain speed, but if you always keep the attitude of the car with the nose down and rear up, it's as if you have a parachute, and so the car was slow on the straight. When we discovered this, we introduced a little button [the 'push-to-pass' button], and to begin with we had a little label

BELOW Riccardo Patrese leads the 1992 Japanese Grand Prix. He went on to take victory – his only win in the FW14B.
(John Townsend)

THE DRIVERS

ABOVE Riccardo Patrese at his home race – the Italian Grand Prix at Monza – leading Nigel Mansell. Patrese retired from the lead, five laps from home, with hydraulic-pump drivebelt failure. *(John Townsend)*

with 'Turbo' written on it, and from the in-car camera you could see 'Turbo', so all the other teams were worrying because you could see that we were pushing this 'Turbo' button on the straight, but it was a joke of course! What it was doing was just raising the front and dropping the back, and if you remember in the straights the car was throwing showers of sparks, and everybody was asking why. It was because we were touching at the rear, but we were increasing the ride height at the front, so the attitude of the car was like a boat – nose up, rear down. Using this system, the car could gain up to 10kph on a long straight by stalling the diffuser, and the car was a rocket! We would hold the button down, and then before the braking area we released it.

"On the FW14B we had the possibility to come out from a first-gear corner and to go up to sixth gear by just pressing a button, and the gearbox would change up without us doing anything. And, if for a corner after a straight we wanted, say, fourth gear, when we were at full throttle we could pull the left paddle twice to call that we wanted the gearbox to go to fourth in the braking area, and when we were braking at the end of the straight, without touching anything, the car would automatically go to fourth gear. It was really an automatic gearbox – it was a big advantage, and very easy – almost too easy. If we wanted, we could do nothing and the gearbox would change up and down itself. We had the option to use the paddles, or not. For example, at Spa, for Eau Rouge [after exiting La Source hairpin] I could keep the throttle down, and pull the paddle, and the car would change up – first, second, third, fourth, fifth, sixth – without touching anything, then before the braking area after Eau Rouge [approaching Les Combes] I wanted to have third gear, so still fully on the throttle I would make three calls on the left paddle, and I didn't have to worry about touching the paddles any more, I could just brake and the car would automatically go to third gear. I didn't use these options all the time, and I used the automatic upchanges more, as I preferred to change down manually. Although we had the option for fully automatic operation, we didn't always use all the options.

"In '92, we could also have the clutch on the steering wheel if we wanted, and we had the option to drive the car with two pedals, as they do now. I tested that option, but I didn't like to brake with my left foot, so I kept the normal clutch. There were many options electronically speaking.

"With all the technology, there was one thing we overlooked that gave me a big problem at the Imola test before the grand prix, at Tamburello. The week before the race, we were doing a test, and I was doing a grand prix simulation for fuelling and tyres. After 20 or 30 laps I had the accident. I was going through the corner all the time, and for us, Tamburello was like a straight – it was a very quick corner, nothing special, because the downforce on the car was keeping the car on the line very easily. I lost the car and I had a big crash. I went to the medical centre, and I didn't really remember what happened because of the big impact. My helmet touched the wall. We wanted to understand what happened, because I seemed to lose the car without a reason. With the telemetry, we discovered that I had a puncture in the right rear tyre, and because the tyre was losing air, the [active suspension] system was correcting the ride height, and because of that I couldn't feel the puncture. When I went into the corner, the tyre had lost enough air that it came off the rim. So the system was correcting for something that was going wrong – a puncture. In a normal car, if you have a puncture you can feel that something is wrong. I could not feel anything wrong, so I had a big crash. So, after that problem, we had a big red light in the cockpit, in front of the steering wheel, so that if there was a problem in the system, the light came on to advise the driver for safety reasons to be careful. The light did not come on very often, as the car was very reliable.

"Before the Japanese Grand Prix, Nigel came to me, and because he was already champion, he said: 'Riccardo, thank you very much for your help and support, we are a fantastic team and so, this grand prix is for you. I'll slow down a little bit and you go ahead and win the grand prix. OK, this is between us.' He was on pole, so he started, and I was behind him. On the straight I could see that he eased off the throttle a little bit and I could overtake, as he said. The problem was that when I went in front he was straight into my back pushing hard like hell, and every lap we were beating the lap record! Ayrton was 30 seconds behind, and I said: 'Bloody Nigel, you said that you'd let me win this bloody grand prix and you push, and every single lap we are beating the lap record.' It's not as if Senna was two seconds behind, he was 30 seconds behind! Nigel was pushing, pushing, pushing, pushing, and at the end his engine broke, and finally I could breathe! But he'd been pushing, pushing, all the way. That was the only grand prix I won in '92.

"I survived in Formula 1 for 17 years, with highs and lows, because I think my attitude with the teams was always really very professional. I never really did polemics, and I also respected what I signed, because I signed that I would obey what the team was saying.

"The 14B was the best car that season, and in my opinion maybe the best car since the beginning of Formula 1. I was very proud of that car, because I did a lot of work on that project. I was very happy, even though I didn't win the championship. At the end of the season everybody was very satisfied with the work we did. I was proud and happy to be there. Results are important, but what you give to the place you work, and that everybody appreciates you, is important too, so I'm happy because of that."

Damon Hill

Damon Hill is by far the most experienced FW14B driver not to have raced the car. He covered significant testing mileage in both the FW14 and FW14B during 1991 and 1992, impressing the team sufficiently to secure a race seat for 1993, alongside Alain Prost.

Hill remained with Williams until the end of 1996, and rose to the challenge of becoming lead driver in 1994, after the tragic death of Ayrton Senna.

He narrowly lost out in the drivers' championship, to Michael Schumacher, in 1994 and 1995, but became World Champion with Williams in 1996.

Mark Blundell

Mark Blundell should be regarded as another test driver of the FW14B, although at the time the car he experienced was still technically an FW14, before it was 'officially' designated an FW14B.

Having tested extensively for Williams during 1989 and 1990, Blundell made a brief return to test chassis FW14/06 at Estoril in October 1991, during his debut year as an F1 race driver for Brabham.

For 1992, Blundell combined F1 testing duties for McLaren with driving for Peugeot in the World Sportscar Championship, winning Le Mans.

He returned to F1 from 1993 to 1995, driving for Ligier, Tyrrell and McLaren respectively, before moving to the US to drive in the CART championship from 1996 to 2000, taking three wins during 1997.

LEFT Damon Hill poses outside the garage during testing with an FW14B at Silverstone in April 1992. *(John Townsend)*

ABOVE Mark Blundell pictured in the FW12 active-suspension development car during the test at Pembrey in August 1989 where a 'leek' was discovered in the footwell (see page 44). In this photograph, the leek has been placed in the engine air intake. *(Dave Lang)*

BELOW Gil de Ferran pictured during his FW14B test at Silverstone in November 1992. *(Sutton Motorsport Images)*

In 2001, Blundell returned to Europe to race sportscars alongside his new role as a commentator. He finished second at Le Mans in 2003, helping Bentley to a 1–2.

He now runs a sports management and marketing business.

Gil de Ferran

Gil de Ferran drove FW14B/06 at a Silverstone test in November 1992, as part of a prize for winning the British Formula Three Championship with Paul Stewart Racing. He progressed to drive for Paul Stewart Racing in F3000 during 1993 and 1994, before forging a career in the US, in the CART series, taking the drivers' championship in 2000 and 2001, and winning the Indianapolis 500 in 2003.

After a spell as Sporting Director for the BAR-Honda F1 team from 2005 to 2007, de Ferran returned to driving in 2008, in the American Le Mans Series. He finished runner-up in the 2009 championship, with five wins, before retiring from driving for good to concentrate on running a team in the IndyCar championship.

He currently works as an ambassador for the FIA Formula E Championship.

John Robinson

John Robinson drove FW14B/06 in June 1992 at the Goodyear tyre test track at Colmar-Berg in Luxembourg. He had previously driven an FW13 for a Renault film at Estoril in December 1991, and was invited back to drive at the Goodyear event.

Robinson went on to race in Europe and the US, and today runs a successful automotive events company.

Alain Prost

Alain Prost, then a triple World Champion, drove FW14B/09 during a four-day test session at Estoril at the end of September 1992. This was his first test as a Williams driver, prior to testing the FW15 in preparation for the 1993 season.

Prost began his F1 career with McLaren in 1980, then drove for Renault from 1981 to 1983 before returning in 1984 to McLaren, where he won three drivers' titles, in 1985, 1986 and 1989.

He then moved to Ferrari for two seasons, followed by a sabbatical during 1992.

Prost took the FW15C to the Drivers' World Championship in 1993, and helped Williams to that year's Constructors' World Championship, winning seven races, with team-mate Damon Hill taking three wins. The 1993 championship title was Prost's fourth, and last, as he retired as an F1 driver at the end of that season.

In 1997, Prost took over the Ligier F1 team, which he ran until 2002, and in 2014 he joined forces with the DAMS racing team to form a new operation – e.dams Renault – to compete in the FIA Formula E Championship, with his son, Nicolas, as one of the drivers, alongside Sebastian Buemi. The team went on to win the inaugural Formula E teams' championship.

RIGHT New signing Alain Prost, in his Williams overalls, gives advice to Gil de Ferran during his FW14B test in November 1992, a month after Prost's first FW14B test. *(Sutton Motorsport Images)*

Karun Chandhok

Karun Chandhok drove FW14B/06 briefly in July 2012 at Turweston airfield in preparation to run the car at a Renault promotional event. Unfortunately, the test was cut short because problems were encountered with the engine-management system, thought to be due to an incompatibility between the ex-Ligier engine and engine ECU fitted to the car, and the CAN link that connects the VCM and engine ECU (see page 118).

Chandhok raced in F1 for HRT and Lotus in 2010 and 2011, and has since competed in the FIA World Endurance Championship, including Le Mans, and in the FIA Formula E Championship.

Valtteri Bottas

Current Williams driver Valtteri Bottas drove FW14B/06 at Turweston in September 2012, when he was the team's test driver, as a follow-up to the July test with Karun Chandhok. The intention was to solve the problem encountered at the earlier test and the personnel on hand included Renault engineers, but unfortunately it was not possible to diagnose the problem conclusively. FW14B/06 has not run since.

Bottas joined Williams as test driver in 2010, after impressive success in Formula Renault and Formula Three between 2007 and 2009. In 2008, he won the Formula Renault Eurocup and the Formula Renault Northern European Cup, and in both 2009 and 2010 he won the Masters of Formula Three event at Zandvoort.

Bottas continued as test driver for Williams for 2011 and 2012 before being promoted to a race seat for 2013. He finished fourth in the drivers' championship for Williams in 2014, and fifth in 2015.

Private owners

On two occasions FW14Bs have run while in private ownership – in 1997 in Brunei and in 2009 at Donington.

ABOVE Karun Chandhok during his brief run in FW14B/06 at Turweston in July 2012. *(Mark Loasby)*

BELOW Current Williams driver Valtteri Bottas, pictured in 2015, briefly drove FW14B/06 at Turweston in September 2012. *(Williams)*

FW08B
1982
FW11
1986
Nigel Mansell
Nelson Piquet
Marlboro
Mobil
Techniques
d' Avant Garde
CHAMPION
CAMEL
RENAULT
elf
5
MAGNETI
MARELLI
GOODYEAR
EAGLE
Canon
Canon
Bull

Chapter Seven

Williams Heritage

Williams Heritage was created in 2014 to manage the team's collection of historic Formula 1 cars. The division is tasked with maintaining and curating the Williams Grand Prix Collection, in addition to showcasing and, where appropriate, running the fleet of cars owned by Williams, from the team's first F1 season as a fully fledged constructor – in 1978 – to the cars most recently retired by the race team.

OPPOSITE FW14B/11 in the Williams Grand Prix Collection, with other cars from Williams's history in the background. From left: FW08, FW08B, FW11, FW10, FW09. *(John Colley)*

The Williams Grand Prix Collection at Grove contains an example of every F1 Williams car since 1978. From the mid-1980s onwards, there are often two examples, and coming up to date virtually all of the F1 cars manufactured by Williams have been retained. There are also some specific test cars, such as the FW08B, the six-wheeler, and the FW15D, which was Ayrton Senna's test car, the FW15 converted to passive suspension in preparation for the 1994 season. In addition to caring for the cars on display in their purpose-built museum on the factory site, Williams Heritage is also responsible for looking after a treasure trove of cars and documentation that remains in storage, rarely seen by the public.

Williams Heritage is headed by Jonathan Williams, Sir Frank's son. He is supported by Dickie Stanford as General Manager, and Toby Norrell as Archive Specialist. Jonathan Williams provides the following insight into the operation:

"In the very early days, the whole of Williams was housed in a space with less square footage than our race bay today. Old racing cars just got in the way, and the revenue from selling them bolstered the team's income for the year to come. There was a market in those days because you could enter the World Championship without being a constructor. In 1980, for example, there was an independent team, RAM, running the previous year's FW07As in World Championship races, and the UK also had a domestic Formula 1 series, the Aurora championship.

"At that time I don't imagine Dad and Patrick were thinking: 'We've just won the World Championship, so in ten years' time let's have a museum.' They were probably thinking it would all be over after five years! After all, they'd already experienced everything they'd done coming to an abrupt end. So we were missing a few 'heavy hitters' from our collection.

"Two very important FW07s were missing but eventually we were able to acquire them. One was chassis 2, which was Regazzoni's race-winning car from the 1979 British Grand Prix. That was one of the cars sold to RAM, and raced in 1980 in the Aurora championship, and occasionally in the World Championship. We brought it back in 1993 from San Francisco. Chassis 9 was Jones's car from the 1980 Canadian Grand Prix, where he sealed his drivers' championship and our constructors' championship – the first World Championships for Williams. That car was bought back in 1997 from John Fenning, the founder of Willans, the seat-belt company.

"Nowadays we take a great deal of care in selecting the cars we add to the Williams Grand Prix Collection. Fortunately, the pickings became somewhat richer with the FW36 than we had been used to for several years. So it is a case of sorting through the podium finishes to select an important example, and also trying to keep a balance so that the right drivers are represented in our museum. Valtteri Bottas had been with the team for quite a while before we had a car of his in the museum, so our FW36 is one of his. The best results to choose from were three second places, one of which was the home grand prix, Silverstone, so we have that car. In the 2015 season we had four third places – two for each driver – and Felipe Massa took one of his third places at Monza, probably the most iconic circuit of those four third-place finishes. We want to give Felipe representation, so the FW37 that comes into the museum will be his.

"Spares and parts to go with cars are not always physically transferred to Heritage. We still go into the factory stores, for example, for sub-assemblies, such as gearbox and transmission components for cars going back a couple of years. It's more efficient for those components, if they're not getting in the way, to stay within the logistical spread of the relevant departments in their stock rooms. For the bigger components – bulky items such as wheels and bodywork – Heritage will usually take delivery of those quite quickly, but will have various embargoes placed on what we do with them. Because the factory never knows what requirement may be thrown at them, they always keep the best couple of sets of everything for recent cars, just in case an FW37, or an FW36, is needed for any running programme.

"Regarding engines, not every car in the collection has an engine, because prior to 2009 a lot more cars were being produced each year. The greatest number in a year was in 2001, when nine cars were produced, whereas since 2009 it has been four cars per year. An engine supplier isn't going to give you nine engines, so when we've had works partners – such as BMW and Renault – we've always looked to keep at least two engines from each year, and they've been very obliging about that. Honda, however, were rather protective at the time, and because the termination of the partnership in 1987 occurred early, we weren't able to retain any engines, although 12 years later, after much effort, we were finally able to get two. Likewise, Toyota have generously given us two engines to cover that three-year period with us.

"The newer the cars are, generally the more you need to have support from the engine technicians – the software and hardware technicians – in order to run them. Renault, for example, are very helpful and very honest with us and say: 'Hey guys, we don't have a heritage department', but they'll try and help us, even if it's difficult. The further back you go, the simpler the cars are and the more self-sufficient you can be.

"We've got some clever people here, and I'm sure if someone said: 'Get this BMW working!', we'd usually get the help we need. Some of the guys are so good at being hands-on, rolling up their sleeves and fiddling with wires and plugging laptops into things. We have a number of Williams 'lifers' here, guys who go back to the 1980s, and they are such a valuable resource – probably more valuable than any hard data you could get from any laptop or spreadsheet. But we have all that too and there's great value in the archive that Toby has organised.

"We're very well supported by the company's Support Team, which is a group within the factory that provides mechanical services, people who don't usually go racing. Tim Newton heads that up, and he has a lot of Williams history. He has mechanics who are available to us when we need them, and likewise his group are very enthusiastic and very knowledgeable about the cars. The new, younger guys he recruits are quite starry-eyed and it's exciting for one of them if he's told: 'Right, can you just go across to Heritage today because they need some help on Damon Hill's championship-winning car.' This might be a 25-year-old who watched that car as a kid, and now he's actually being asked to go and pull the gearbox off it!"

BELOW Another view of the Williams Grand Prix Collection, showing the cars from the mid-to-late 1990s. The FW16, from 1994, is in the foreground. *(Williams)*

Appendix 1

The rival cars

During the 1992 season, arguably there were no challengers to the FW14B's superiority, and cars from only three other teams – McLaren, Benetton and Ferrari – finished on the podium.

A total of 16 teams competed during the season, with the controversial Andrea Moda team joining the championship at the third round in Brazil. With 26 cars permitted to start the race, and 30 cars allowed to take part in qualifying, pre-qualifying took place for seven of the 16 rounds.

The closest challengers
McLaren MP4/6B and MP4/7A

McLaren began the 1992 season with the MP4/6B for Ayrton Senna and Gerhard Berger. Senna had been with McLaren since 1988, while Berger joined for the start of the 1990 season, replacing the departing Alain Prost, who moved to take Berger's seat at Ferrari alongside Nigel Mansell.

The MP4/6B was an updated version of the 1991 MP4/6, which took Senna to the 1991 Drivers' World Championship, and McLaren to the Constructors' Championship, beating Williams's FW14. The MP4/6 became the last F1 car to win a World Championship with a manual gearbox and the last World Championship winner to use a V12 engine. The manual gearbox and Honda V12 engine were retained for the MP4/6B, which was only used for the first two rounds of 1992, with a best result of third place for Senna at the opening race in South Africa.

The original intention was for the all-new MP4/7A to make its debut at the fourth round of the championship, the Spanish Grand Prix, but such was the dominance of the FW14B that McLaren Team Principal Ron Dennis decided to introduce the car a race earlier at the Brazilian Grand Prix, a month before the Spanish round.

The MP4/7A was the first McLaren to feature a semi-automatic transmission. The car continued to use a Honda V12 engine, and also featured a 'fly-by-wire' throttle system, which allowed full-throttle gear changes.

The new car was unable to answer the speed of the FW14B, and its challenge was also hampered by poor reliability, Senna and Berger each retiring from six races during the season. The MP4/7A proved to be consistently the fastest of the FW14B's challengers, Senna winning three races (Monaco, Hungary and Italy) and Berger two (Canada and Australia).

Senna and Berger finished fourth and fifth respectively in the drivers' championship, while McLaren was second in the constructors' championship.

During the latter part of the season, an MP4/7A was modified to test McLaren's prototype active suspension system, which was used for races from the start of the 1993 season on the MP4/8.

BELOW The Honda V12-powered McLaren MP4/7A first appeared at the Brazilian Grand Prix and proved to be the most consistent challenger to the FW14B's dominance, with five victories – three for Ayrton Senna (seen en route to winning at Monaco) and two for Gerhard Berger. *(John Townsend)*

Benetton B191B and B192

Benetton drivers Michael Schumacher and Martin Brundle used the B191B for the first three races of the season. Schumacher was competing in his first full season of F1 racing, having made his debut with Jordan at the 1991 Belgian Grand Prix, before controversially being 'poached' by Benetton for the rest of the season. Brundle joined the team for the start of 1992 after a frustrating year hauling an uncompetitive Brabham-Yamaha into the points.

Designed by John Barnard and Mike Coughlan, the B191B was a lightly updated version of the 1991 B191, powered by a Ford HB V8 engine. The car was quick enough to challenge the McLarens, and Schumacher finished third in Mexico and Brazil, before the new B192 was introduced for the fourth round of the championship, the Spanish Grand Prix, which was the first European race.

The B192 was an all-new car designed by Ross Brawn and Rory Byrne – a pairing that would go on to achieve great things in F1 with Michael Schumacher at both Benetton and Ferrari. Although the B192, which retained the Ford V8 engine and used a manual six-speed gearbox, was a step forward for Benetton, it was underpowered compared with the Renault V10-powered Williams and the Honda V12-powered McLaren.

The B192 chassis proved to be very nimble, allowing both drivers to score regular podium placings, and the car also allowed Schumacher to take his debut F1 victory, at the Belgian Grand Prix in changeable conditions. This win, supported by three second places and two thirds, enabled Schumacher to beat Senna to third place in the drivers' championship, despite Senna winning three races. Brundle took a second place and four thirds to end up sixth in the drivers' championship, while Benetton finished third in the constructors' championship.

Ferrari F92A and F92AT

The Ferrari F92A, powered by Ferrari's V12 and featuring semi-automatic transmission, was an all-new car for the 1992 season designed by Steve Nichols and Jean-Claude Migeot. During the early 1990s Ferrari was going through a period of management upheaval, and this resulted in a design philosophy that favoured aerodynamics at the expense of mechanical

ABOVE Michael Schumacher in the Benetton B192 at the Italian Grand Prix at Monza. The B192 gave Schumacher his debut F1 victory, at the Belgian Grand Prix. *(John Townsend)*

BELOW The Ferrari F92AT at speed, in the hands of Jean Alesi at Suzuka for the Japanese Grand Prix. The F92AT, and its predecessor, the F92, were fragile, with Ferrari achieving only 12 finishes from a possible total of 32. *(John Townsend)*

performance, a trait that was to prove the car's Achilles heel.

The F92A featured a 'twin-floor' layout, with the sidepods effectively isolated from the lower floor, enabling the air to flow unimpeded over the top of the lower floor to the rear diffuser, increasing downforce. Although the aerodynamic principle was sound, the mechanical set-up was compromised, and politics within the team prevented a coherent development programme.

Ferrari retained Jean Alesi for 1992. The French Sicilian had joined the Scuderia in 1991 after showing his potential during a season and a half with the underfunded Tyrrell team. Alesi was partnered by Italian Ivan Capelli, who struggled throughout the season, and was replaced for the final two races by compatriot Nicola Larini.

The F92A was used for the first 11 rounds of the championship, before the revised F92AT was introduced at the Belgian Grand Prix. The F92AT was fitted with a new seven-speed transverse gearbox (hence the 'T' appended to the car's revised type number) in place of the F92's six-speed longitudinally mounted unit. The F92AT also featured revised front suspension and improved engine mountings to reduce flex, but the updated car fared little better than its predecessor. Reliability was initially poor, with neither of the F92ATs finishing their first three races, but both did complete the last two races, in Japan and Australia.

When Larini was brought in to replace Capelli, he was tasked with driving a revised F92AT fitted with Ferrari's prototype active suspension system, which came with a significant weight penalty. While Alesi took the passive-suspension F92A to fifth place in Japan and fourth in Australia, Larini was unable to finish any higher than 12th and 11th respectively in the active car.

Alesi only finished six of the season's 16 races, scoring two third places (in Spain and Canada), two fourths and two fifths, taking him to a distant seventh in the drivers' championship. Capelli only finished four races, his best result being fifth place in Brazil. Ferrari finished fourth in the constructors' championship, 70 points behind third-placed Benetton.

The other 1992 runners and riders
Lotus 102D and 107

The Lotus 102D was little changed from the ageing 1991-season 102B, with the exception of a Ford (Cosworth) HB V8 engine in place of the previous Judd EV V8. (Although the Lotus 102C tested with an Isuzu V12 engine, it was never raced.)

The Lotus drivers for 1992 were Johnny Herbert, who was in his second full year with the team after making his F1 debut driving for Lotus at the last two races of 1990, and F1 debutant Mika Häkkinen.

The best results for the 102D were sixth place in South Africa (Herbert) and Mexico (Häkkinen), before the all-new Lotus 107 made its debut at the fourth round at San Marino in Herbert's hands, and from Monaco onwards both drivers used the new cars. The

BELOW Johnny Herbert driving the Lotus 107 at its debut race in San Marino. Herbert finished only five races during 1992. *(John Townsend)*

107 retained the Ford HB V8 engine, but with Lotus's first semi-automatic gearbox.

The 107 proved to be a significant step forward from the 102D, taking Häkkinen to fourth places in France and Hungary, along with a fifth and two sixth places. However, it suffered from reliability problems and Herbert finished only three races, his best result a sixth place in France.

Tyrrell 020B

The Tyrrell 020B was an update of the 1991 020 designed by Harvey Postlethwaite. Whereas the 020 was powered by a Honda V10, the 020B used an Ilmor V10 developed by Mario Illien and Paul Morgan, who would later form a partnership with Mercedes-Benz to develop engines for the Sauber and McLaren F1 teams. The V10 engine was mated to a Hewland six-speed semi-automatic gearbox.

The 020B was driven by Italian Andrea de Cesaris and Frenchman Olivier Grouillard. De Cesaris scored eight points, thanks to a fourth place in Japan, two fifths and a sixth, while Grouillard failed to score, with a best result of eighth in San Marino.

Footwork FA13

The Japanese Footwork logistics company took over the Arrows team in 1991, and the team was renamed accordingly. The FA13 was designed by Alan Jenkins, and was powered by the Mugen-prepared Honda V10 mated to a manual six-speed gearbox. The car was driven by Michele Alboreto and Aguri Suzuki.

The combination of straightforward design and Mugen-Honda power resulted in a reliable and consistent performer, although the car was well off the pace of the front-runners. Suzuki failed to score, while Alboreto took two fifth and two sixth places, giving the team six points, which took them to seventh place in the constructors' championship.

Ligier JS37

The Ligier JS37 used Mecachrome-prepared Renault V10s – initially the RS3B, and later the RS3C. Ligier was the only Renault-powered team other than Williams.

The JS37 was designed by ex-Williams man Frank Dernie and Gérard Ducarouge. The car

ABOVE Italian F1 journeyman Andrea de Cesaris in the Ilmor V10-powered Tyrrell 020B during the British Grand Prix at Silverstone. *(John Townsend)*

BELOW Michele Alboreto drives the Footwork FA13 at the Hungarian Grand Prix, where he finished seventh. The car was reliable, but well off the pace of the front-runners. *(John Townsend)*

BELOW The Ligier JS37 was the only car other than the FW14B to use the Renault V10 engine during 1992. Erik Comas is seen here at the team's home race – the French Grand Prix – where he finished fifth. *(John Townsend)*

ABOVE Paul Belmondo in the March CG911B during qualifying for the Monaco Grand Prix. Belmondo failed to make the cut in Monte Carlo, while his team-mate, Karl Wendlinger, retired from the race. (John Townsend)

was not a success, and suffered from both aerodynamic and handling issues, which were particularly apparent on bumpy circuits such as Mexico and Monaco. The car also suffered from poor reliability, with a finishing record of less than 50%.

Drivers Thierry Boutsen and Erik Comas both scored points, Boutsen with fifth place at the final round in Australia and Comas with fifth at his home race in France, plus sixth-place finishes in Canada and Germany. Ligier finished the season equal with Footwork on points, Footwork finishing one place ahead in the Constructors' Championship by dint of a higher number of seventh-place finishes.

March CG911B

For 1992, the former Leyton House team was rebranded as March, and the CG911B was an updated version of the 1991 Leyton House CG911 designed by Gustav Brunner and Chris Murphy following the departure of Adrian Newey for Williams. The car was powered by an Ilmor V10 – the same engine used by Tyrrell for 1992.

Struggling for funding, the team retained Mercedes-Benz-backed driver Karl Wendlinger, who had driven for the team in the final two races of 1991, and signed French driver Paul Belmondo as his team-mate.

Reliability was poor, with Wendlinger finishing only six out of 14 races before he was replaced by Dutchman Jan Lammers for the last two rounds. Wendlinger scored the team's best result of the year with fourth place at the Canadian Grand Prix. Belmondo struggled, and failed to qualify in six of 11 attempts, with his best result a ninth place in Belgium. Emanuele Naspetti took Belmondo's seat from the Italian Grand Prix, but fared little better, with a best result of 11th in Spain.

The team finished ninth in the constructors' championship, with three points from Wendlinger's fourth place in Canada.

Dallara F192

The Dallara F192 was run by BMS Scuderia Italia, and was an update of the team's 1991 Dallara F191, reworked around a 1991-specification Ferrari V12 engine rather than the previous Judd V10.

Designed by Gian Paolo Dallara, the F192 suffered from poor handling throughout the season, possibly in part due to the relatively high front-wing mainplane, which featured deep endplates. A range of modifications during the season failed to improve the car's competitiveness.

RIGHT The Dallara F192, seen at the Brazilian Grand Prix with JJ Lehto at the wheel, scored only two points during 1992. (John Townsend)

The driver line-up comprised Finn JJ Lehto, who drove for the team during 1991, and new signing Pierluigi Martini, who joined from Minardi.

The team scored only two points, thanks to two sixth places for Martini in Spain and San Marino, resulting in tenth place in the constructors' championship.

Jordan 192

After a headline-grabbing debut season in 1991, with the fabulous-looking 191 designed by Gary Anderson, Jordan had hoped to retain Ford V8 power for 1992. However, there was a late switch to Yamaha V12 power after design of the 192 had begun, and the car ended up compromised. The team also had an all-new driver line-up, with Italian Stefano Modena and Brazilian Mauricio Gugelmin.

The Yamaha engine proved to be unreliable and down on power compared with its rivals, and the team suffered a disastrous season. Between the two cars there were only nine finishes and a solitary point, for Modena's sixth place at the final round in Australia.

Minardi M191B and M192

Minardi started the 1992 season with the M191B, an updated version of its 1991 car, revised by designer Aldo Costa to take the team's new Lamborghini V12 engine in place of the previous Ferrari V12. The M191B was used for the first four races, and then the M192 was introduced for the San Marino Grand Prix.

Gianni Morbidelli stayed with the team for 1992, having joined for the last two races of 1990, while F1 rookie Christian Fittipaldi was signed after winning the 1991 International F3000 Championship. After Fittipaldi suffered a fractured vertebra following an incident with Michele Alboreto's Footwork during a wet practice session at the French Grand Prix, Alex Zanardi stood in for three races.

The team finished the season with a single point, courtesy of sixth place for Fittipaldi in Japan.

Venturi-Larrousse LC92

The French Larrousse team first appeared in F1 in 1987, using a Lola chassis. In late 1991, March co-founder Robin Herd's design consultancy was signed to design the 1992 car, the LC92A, while a controlling stake in Larrousse was sold to the Venturi road-car company, hence the car's name. A deal was signed to use Lamborghini V12 engines, which the team had used previously in 1989 and 1990 before switching to Ford V8 power for 1991.

ABOVE The Jordan 192 struggled to match the performance of its predecessor, which had stunned the F1 community in the team's debut year. Mauricio Gugelmin, seen at the German Grand Prix, failed to score a point. *(John Townsend)*

LEFT Gianni Morbidelli pilots the Minardi M191B at the Mexican Grand Prix, where he retired. His best result of the year was seventh place at the following race, in Brazil. *(John Townsend)*

ABOVE The Venturi-Larrousse LC92 reverted to Lamborghini V12 power, but proved to be fragile. Japanese driver Ukyo Katayama is seen at the Belgian Grand Prix, where he finished 17th.
(John Townsend)

BELOW The Fondmetal GR02 in action with Belgian Eric van de Poele at the Hungarian Grand Prix on its way to tenth place – the team's best result of the season.
(John Townsend)

Bertrand Gachot was retained, having driven for the team at the final round of 1991 in Australia, while Ukyo Katayama was hired to partner the Belgian. Gachot finished only four races, having to retire from 11 rounds and suffering disqualification in Canada after receiving a push-start. However, his sixth place at Monaco, albeit a lap down on the leaders, secured the team's only point of the season. Katayama's best result was ninth in Brazil.

Fondmetal GR01 and GR02

The Fondmetal GR01 was an evolution of the still-born Fomet 1 designed by Robin Herd's design consultancy and used by Fondmetal for the 1991 season. The ungainly car was powered by a Ford HB V8.

Andrea Chiesa used the car for the first seven rounds, but failed to qualify at five of them, and retired from the two that he started. Chiesa also used the car for the British Grand Prix, but again failed to qualify. Chiesa's teammate, Gabriele Tarquini, used the GR01 for the first six rounds, but retired from every race. Chiesa was replaced by ex-Brabham driver Eric van de Poele for the Hungarian, Belgian and Italian Grands Prix.

An all-new car, the GR02, appeared at the Canadian Grand Prix in the hands of Tarquini. Designed by Sergio Rinland's consultancy, the GR02 retained the Ford HB engine but appeared to have significantly more potential than its predecessor. However, it was introduced after insufficient testing and reliability issues, plus a series of on-track incidents, meant only two finishes before Fondmetal owner Gabriele Rumi pulled the plug on the team following the Italian Grand Prix, due to mounting debt.

Fondmetal only managed three finishes during the entire season, the best van de Poele's tenth place at the Hungarian Grand Prix.

Brabham BT60B

The Brabham BT60B had the ignominious distinction of being the last F1 car raced under the Brabham name. By 1992, the team was owned by Japanese investment group Middlebridge, and was struggling for funding.

The BT60B was a revised version of the team's 1991 challenger, the Yamaha V12-powered BT60Y. As Yamaha switched to Jordan for 1992, the BT60B was adapted to use a Judd V10.

Belgian Eric van de Poele was signed to drive alongside Italian female F1 rookie

Giovanna Amati, but both struggled to qualify, van de Poele only managing it for the opening round in South Africa, where he finished 13th (and last). Amati failed to qualify for the first three races before being replaced by Williams test driver Damon Hill, who also struggled with the uncompetitive car. Hill qualified for the first time at the British Grand Prix at Silverstone, where he finished 16th (and last), four laps behind winner Nigel Mansell! Hill also qualified for what became Brabham's final grand prix, in Hungary, where he gave the team its best result of the season with 11th place, which was again last and again four laps behind the race winner, Ayrton Senna. So ended Braham's F1 history.

Andrea Moda C4B and S921

The Andrea Moda team appeared solely for the 1992 season. It was owned by Italian shoe designer Andrea Sassetti, the team taking its name from his fashion company. Andrea Moda was essentially a rebranded version of the spectacularly underperforming Coloni outfit, which failed to qualify for a single race during 1991.

For the first round in South Africa the team used an updated version of the 1991 Coloni car, the C4, which had used a Ford DFR V8. The car was modified to take the team's Judd V10 and designated the C4B. Italians Alex Caffi and Enrico Bertaggia were signed to drive.

The team's debut at Kyalami descended into farce when both cars were excluded due to Sassetti having failed to pay the required championship entry fee. At the second round, in Mexico, the comedy of errors continued, with the team's two cars freighted in pieces and failing to arrive in time to be assembled for first practice. Following this misfortune, Caffi and Bertaggia were fired for publicly criticising the team. The replacement drivers were the experienced Brazilian Roberto Moreno and British F1 rookie Perry McCarthy.

In Brazil, the team finally had two complete new S921 cars available. This car was basically a chassis designed in 1990 by Nick Wirth's Simtek consultancy for an aborted BMW F1 project, and updated to take the Judd V10. Despite the new car, the team's ineptitude continued, with Perry McCarthy failing to qualify for a single race due to a catalogue of disasters, most of which could be put down to the team's appalling organisation. Moreno fared little better, although he was responsible for the highlight of the team's short existence, when he qualified at Monaco, starting the race from last place, and retiring after 11 laps with a blown engine.

At the Belgian Grand Prix, Sassetti was arrested in the paddock for alleged financial irregularities. The team was then refused entry to the paddock at the following round at Monza, after the FIA took action to ban the team for bringing the sport into disrepute. The team sank without trace.

ABOVE Italian driver Giovanna Amati in the Brabham BT60B during qualifying for the Brazilian Grand Prix – her final attempt to qualify for an F1 race. *(John Townsend)*

BELOW Alex Caffi at Kyalami during practice for the South African Grand Prix – a rare appearance on-track for the Andrea Moda C4B. The team was excluded from the event for failure to pay the championship entry fee. *(John Townsend)*

Appendix 2

FW14B 1992 race results and statistics

Race results

Grand Prix	Nigel Mansell		Riccardo Patrese	
	Qualifying	Race	Qualifying	Race
South Africa	Pole	1st, FL	4th	2nd
Mexico	Pole	1st	2nd	2nd
Brazil	Pole	1st	2nd	2nd, FL
Spain	Pole	1st, FL	4th	Rtd
San Marino	Pole	1st	2nd	2nd, FL
Monaco	Pole	2nd, FL	2nd	3rd
Canada	3rd	Rtd	2nd	Rtd
France	Pole	1st, FL	2nd	2nd
Britain	Pole	1st, FL	2nd	2nd
Germany	Pole	1st	2nd	8th, FL
Hungary	2nd	2nd, FL	Pole	Rtd
Belgium	Pole	2nd	4th	3rd
Italy	Pole	Rtd, FL	5th	5th
Portugal	Pole	1st	2nd	Rtd
Japan	Pole	Rtd, FL	2nd	1st
Australia	Pole	Rtd	3rd	Rtd

Pole = Pole position; Rtd = Retired; FL = Fastest lap

FW14B 1992 season statistics

Races	16
Wins	10 (Mansell 9, Patrese 1)
1–2 finishes	6 (all Mansell 1st, Patrese 2nd)
Podiums	21 (Mansell 12, Patrese 9)
Fastest laps	11 (Mansell 8, Patrese 3)
Pole positions	15 (Mansell 14, Patrese 1)
Points scored	164 (Mansell 108, Patrese 56)

Appendix 3

FW14B specifications

Chassis

Front suspension	Upper and lower wishbones, with pushrod-operated, hydro-pneumatic actuators and remote damper valves and disc-spring pack
Rear suspension	Lower wishbone and upper arm, with pushrod-operated, hydro-pneumatic actuators and remote damper valves and disc-spring packs
Active-suspension components	Williams
Wheel diameter	Front: 13in Rear: 13in
Wheel rim widths	Front: 11.4in Rear: 16.3in
Tyres	Goodyear
Brakes	Calipers: AP Discs: Carbon Industrie
Brake pads	Carbon Industrie or Hitco
Steering	Williams
Radiators	Williams/Behr
Fuel tank	ATL
Battery	Yuasa
Instruments	Renault

Transmission

Gearbox	Williams six-speed transverse semi-automatic
Driveshafts	Williams
Clutch	AP

Engine

Type	Renault RS3C/RS4
No. of cylinders	V10 (67°)
Maximum rpm	Approx 14,400
Fuel and oil	Elf
Spark plugs	Champion
Fuel injection	Magneti-Marelli
Ignition system	Magneti-Marelli

Dimensions

Wheelbase	2,921mm
Track	Front: 1,803mm Rear: 1,676mm
Gearbox weight	50kg
Chassis weight (tub)	50kg
Overall weight of car (without driver)	505kg
Fuel capacity	230 litres

Appendix 4

FW14B individual chassis histories

Courtesy of Toby Norrell

Note: *Chassis FW14B/06 and FW14B/07 were originally constructed and used as FW14 chassis in 1991, and were later upgraded to FW14B specification, hence the FW14B series of chassis starts at FW14B/06. Chassis FW14B/08 to FW14B/11 inclusive were built as FW14B chassis from the outset.*

FW14B/06

Currently owned by Williams Grand Prix Collection, on loan to private museum

Date	Venue	Race/Test	Driver	Qualifying	Race
23/07/91	Silverstone*	Test (Active)	D. Hill	–	–
20/08/91	Silverstone*	Test (Active)	D. Hill	–	–
28–29/08/91	Monza*	Test (Active)	D. Hill/R. Patrese	–	–
05/09/91	Brands Hatch*	Test (Active)	D. Hill	–	–
02–04/10/91	Estoril*	Test (Active)	M. Blundell/N. Mansell/R. Patrese	–	–
08/10/91	Paul Ricard*	Test (Active)	D. Hill	–	–
01–03/11/91	Adelaide*	**Race**	N. Mansell	–	T-car
18–22/11/91	Estoril*	Test (Active)	D. Hill/R. Patrese	–	–
09–13/11/91	Barcelona*	Test (Active)	N. Mansell/R. Patrese	–	–
17–18/12/91	Paul Ricard*	Test (Active)	D. Hill	–	–
17–19/01/92	Paul Ricard*	Test	R. Patrese	–	–
03–09/02/92	Estoril*	Test	D. Hill/R. Patrese	–	–
28–31/05/92	Monaco	**Race**	R. Patrese	–	T-car
02–05/06/92	Magny Cours	Test	N. Mansell/R. Patrese	–	–
10/06/92	Luxembourg	Test	J. Robinson	–	–
24–26/06/92	Silverstone	Test	R. Patrese	–	–
15–17/07/92	Hockenheim	Test	N. Mansell/R. Patrese	–	–
11/08/92	Silverstone	Test	N. Mansell/D. Hill	–	–
19–21/08/92	Monza	Test	D. Hill/R. Patrese	–	–
02–04/09/92	Monza	Test	D. Hill/R. Patrese	–	–
28/09–01/10/92	Estoril	Test	D. Hill	–	–
07–09/10/92	Paul Ricard	Test	D. Hill	–	–
21–22/10/92	Long Marston	Test	D. Hill	–	–
11/11/92	Silverstone	Test	G. de Ferran	–	–

*For these events, the chassis identity was FW14/06, the car later being converted to FW14B specification as FW14B/06

OPPOSITE FW14B/08 won the first five races of the 1992 season in the hands of Nigel Mansell, and is seen here at the first round, at Kyalami in South Africa. *(John Townsend)*

FW14B/07
Currently owned by Williams Grand Prix Collection

Date	Venue	Race/Test	Driver	Qualifying	Race
18–22/11/91	Estoril*	Test (Active)	D. Hill	–	–
09–13/12/91	Barcelona*	Test (Active)	D. Hill/N. Mansell/R. Patrese	–	–
17–18/12/91	Paul Ricard*	Test (Active)	D. Hill	–	–
17–19/01/92	Paul Ricard*	Test	D. Hill	–	–
18/02/92	Silverstone	Test	D. Hill	–	–
27/01–01/03/92	Kyalami	**Race**	N. Mansell	–	T-car
11–12/03/92	Silverstone	Test	D. Hill	–	–
20–22/03/92	Mexico	**Race**	N. Mansell	–	T-car
03–05/04/92	Interlagos	**Race**	N. Mansell	–	T-car
13–15/04/92	Silverstone	Test	D. Hill/N. Mansell	–	–
22–24/04/92	Imola	Test	R. Patrese	–	–
01–03/05/92	Barcelona	**Race**	R. Patrese	4	T-car
06–08/05/92	Imola	Test	R. Patrese	–	–

*For these events, the chassis identity was FW14/07, the car later being converted to FW14B specification as FW14B/07

FW14B/08
Privately owned

Date	Venue	Race/Test	Driver	Qualifying	Race
03–09/02/92	Estoril	Test	N. Mansell	–	–
18/02/92	Silverstone	Test	D. Hill	–	–
27/02–01/03/92	Kyalami	**Race**	N. Mansell	1	1
20–22/03/92	Mexico	**Race**	N. Mansell	1	1
03–05/04/92	Interlagos	**Race**	N. Mansell	1	1
01–03/05/92	Barcelona	**Race**	N. Mansell	1	1
15–17/05/92	Imola	**Race**	N. Mansell	1	1
28–31/05/92	Monaco	**Race**	N. Mansell	1	2
12–14/06/92	Montréal	**Race**	N. Mansell	3	DNF (spin)
03–05/06/92	Magny Cours	**Race**	N. Mansell	–	T-car
10–12/07/92	Silverstone	**Race**	R. Patrese	–	2
24–26/07/92	Hockenheim	**Race**	R. Patrese	2	8
14–16/08/92	Budapest	**Race**	R. Patrese	1	DNF (engine)
28–30/08/92	Spa	**Race**	R. Patrese	4	3
11–13/09/92	Monza	**Race**	R. Patrese	4	5
25–27/09/92	Estoril	**Race**	R. Patrese	2	DNF (collision)

FW14B/09
Privately owned

Date	Venue	Race/Test	Driver	Qualifying	Race
18/02/92	Silverstone	Test	R. Patrese	–	–
27/02–01/03/92	Kyalami	**Race**	R. Patrese	4	2
20–22/03/92	Mexico	**Race**	R. Patrese	2	2
03–05/04/92	Interlagos	**Race**	R. Patrese	2	2
01–03/05/92	Barcelona	**Race**	R. Patrese	–	DNF (spin)
15–17/05/92	Imola	**Race**	R. Patrese	2	2
28–31/05/92	Monaco	**Race**	N. Mansell	–	T-car
03–05/06/92	Magny Cours	**Race**	N. Mansell/R. Patrese	1	1
10–12/07/92	Silverstone	**Race**	N. Mansell	–	T-car
15–17/07/92	Hockenheim	Test	N. Mansell/R. Patrese	–	–
24–26/07/92	Hockenheim	**Race**	N. Mansell	1	T-car
14–16/08/92	Budapest	**Race**	N. Mansell	–	T-car
28–30/08/92	Spa	**Race**	N. Mansell	–	T-car
11–13/09/92	Monza	**Race**	N. Mansell/R. Patrese	–	T-car
25–27/09/92	Estoril	**Race**	N. Mansell	–	T-car
28/09–01/10/92	Estoril	Test	A. Prost	–	–
23–25/10/92	Suzuka	**Race**	N. Mansell	–	T-car
06–08/11/92	Adelaide	**Race**	N. Mansell	–	T-car

FW14B/10
Currently owned by Williams Grand Prix Collection, on loan to Donington Museum

Date	Venue	Race/Test	Driver	Qualifying	Race
13–15/04/92	Silverstone	Test	N. Mansell	–	–
01–03/05/92	Barcelona	**Race**	N. Mansell	–	T-car
06–08/05/92	Imola	Test	N. Mansell	–	–
15–17/05/92	Imola	**Race**	N. Mansell	–	T-car
28–31/05/92	Monaco	**Race**	R. Patrese	2	3
20–21/05/92	Silverstone	Test	D. Hill/N. Mansell	–	–
12–14/06/92	Montréal	**Race**	R. Patrese	2	DNF (gearbox)
03–05/06/92	Magny Cours	**Race**	R. Patrese	2	2
10–12/07/92	Silverstone	**Race**	R. Patrese	2	T-car
23–25/10/92	Suzuka	**Race**	R. Patrese	2	1
06–08/11/92	Adelaide	**Race**	R. Patrese	3	DNF (fuel pressure)

FW14B/11
Currently owned by Williams Grand Prix Collection

Date	Venue	Race/Test	Driver	Qualifying	Race
12–14/06/92	Montréal	**Race**	N. Mansell	–	T-car
24–26/06/92	Silverstone	Test	N. Mansell	–	–
10–12/07/92	Silverstone	**Race**	N. Mansell	1	1
24–26/07/92	Hockenheim	**Race**	N. Mansell	–	1
14–16/08/92	Budapest	**Race**	N. Mansell	2	2
28–30/08/92	Spa	**Race**	N. Mansell	1	2
11–13/09/92	Monza	**Race**	N. Mansell	1	DNF (hydraulics)
25–27/09/92	Estoril	**Race**	N. Mansell	1	1
23–25/10/92	Suzuka	**Race**	N. Mansell	1	DNF (engine)
06–08/11/92	Adelaide	**Race**	N. Mansell	1	DNF (collision)

Formula One seasons
   1969–1980 seasons 11–15
   1981–1990 seasons 15–21
   1991 season 21, 30–7
   1992 season 50–73
      rival cars 158–165
      Williams results 166
   1993–2000 seasons 21–23
   2001–2015 seasons 24–27
Formula Two racing 10
Frank Williams (Racing Cars) Ltd 10–13
French Grand Prix
   1991 race 35
   1992 race 60–1, 161, 166
Frentzen, Heinz-Harald 23
front spring pack, active-ride system 94
front suspension 87–8, 167
front wings 83
frontal impact tests 78
fuel system 110–11
fuel tanks 79, 163
fuel-pump switch 127
fuels 64, 101, 103–4, 111, 167

Gachot, Bertrand 61, 164
Galli, Nanni 12
Ganley, Howden 12
gearbox 112–15, 131, 150, 167
Gené, Marc 24–5
German Grand Prix
   1975 race 12
   1991 race 35
   1992 race 62–4, 163, 166
Gomm, Maurice 11
Goodyear tyres 52, 115–16, 167
Grand Prix Collection 154–7
Grand Prix Masters series 148
Grand Prix seasons see Formula One seasons
Green Sheets 44, 61, 140
Grouillard, Olivier 161
ground-effect cars 40
Gugelmin, Mauricio 30, 163
gurney flaps 83

Häkkinen, Mika 60, 65, 160–161
Hamidy, Egbhal 87
harnesses 122
Hauty, Gilles 102
Head, Patrick 9, 12–14, 18, 30, 40–1, 48, 66, 100, 112, 128–32, 134, 141, 145
Heidfeld, Nick 25
Henry, Alan 116
Herbert, Johnny 60, 71, 160–161
Herd, Robin 163–164
Hesketh Racing 13
Hill, Damon 21–3, 48, 52–3, 69, 125, 140, 148, 151, 165
   FW14B chassis histories 168–170
His, Jean-Jacques 103, 141
Hitco 98
homologation plates 127
Honda engines 19, 131
Horsley, Anthony 'Bubbles' 10
Howard, Keith 40
Hülkenberg, Nico 26
Hungarian Grand Prix
   1991 race 36
   1992 race 64–6, 86, 103, 111, 161, 164, 166

hydraulic actuators 38–40
hydraulic fluid/pump, active-ride system 91–3
   fluid accumulator 95
   fluid cooler 96
   gearbox 113
hydraulic system 122
hydraulic valve block, active-ride system 95

Ickx, Jacky 12–13
identification plate 127
ignition switch 127
ignition system 99, 111, 167
Illien, Mario 161
impact tests 78
injectors 110, 167
Italian Grand Prix
   1987 race 19, 42, 130
   1991 race 36
   1992 race 67–8, 83, 150, 159, 166

Japanese Grand Prix
   1987 race 19
   1991 race 37
   1992 race 70–1, 149, 151, 159, 166
   1996 race 23
Jenkins, Alan 161
Jones, Alan 8–9, 14–16
Jordan 192 F1 car 163
Judd engines 19, 45, 130

Katayama, Ukyo 164
Kermorvan, Alex 102
Kirby, Gordon 41–2

Laffite, Jacques 12, 15–17
Lammers, Jan 162
Lang, Dave 42–5, 48, 91–4, 96, 130–1, 136–8, 139
Larini, Nicola 73, 160
Larrousse, Gérard 102
launch control 112
leek prank 44
Lehto, JJ 58, 162–3
Leyton House CG901 car 30, 131
Ligier F1 team 101
   JS37 F1 car 161–162
Loasby, Mark 113
Lombardi, Lella 12
Lotus active suspension system 40, 42, 46
Lotus F1 cars 160–161
Lowe, Paddy 38, 44, 47–8, 84, 90, 130–9, 171
lubrication system 108–9
   gearbox 114

McCarthy, Perry 165
MacDonald, John 48
McLaren F1 cars
   M26 car 8–9
   MP4/4 car 19, 42
   MP4/6 car 37
   MP4/6B car 159
   MP4/7A car 55, 67, 158
Magee, Damien 12
Maldonado, Pastor 26
Malivin, Gérard 102
Malshar, David 52–3, 61
manifold 111

Mansell, Nigel 17–22, 31–8, 42, 45–9, 84, 86, 126, 131, 139, 142–51
   1992 season 50–73
   results 166
   FW14B chassis histories 168–170
Mansell, Rosanne 59
March racecars 11–14, 30
   CG911B F1 car 162
Martini, Pierluigi 163
Martini sponsorship 27
Massa, Felipe 27, 156
Matthews, Tony 76
Mecachrome engines 23, 101
medical air system 123
Mehl, Leo 116
memory cards 120
Menrath, Jean-Pierre 102
Mercedes engines 27
Mercier, Jean-Philippe 102
Merzario, Arturio 12
Messier foundry 105
Mexican Grand Prix
   1986 race 19
   1991 race 34
   1992 race 39, 50–1, 54–5, 163, 166
   2015 race 27
Migeot, Jean-Claude 159
Minardi F1 cars 163
Modena, Stefano 33, 163
Monaco Grand Prix
   1977 race 147
   1980 race 15
   1982 race 147
   1991 race 33
   1992 race 57–9, 83, 166
   1993 race 21
   2003 race 24
monocoque 77–80
Montoya, Juan Pablo 24–5
Morbidelli, Gianni 163
Moreno, Roberto 33, 165
Morgan, Paul 161
Motion Technology 41
Motor Sport magazine 40, 48, 52–3, 61
Murphy, Chris 162

Nakajima, Kazuki 25
Naspetti, Emanuele 162
Nève, Patrick 13–14
Newey, Adrian 21, 30–2, 47, 53, 128–32, 145, 147, 162
Newton, Tim 157
Nichols, Steve 159
Norrell, Toby 156, 168
nosebox 83
   frontal impact tests 78

oil coolers 109
oil pressure pump 109
oil tank 109
   gearbox 113
O'Rourke, Brian 28–9, 40–1, 77–8, 82–3, 87, 135
overtaking switch 126–7

Pace, Carlos 11
paddles (on steering wheel) 124
Palfroy, Michel 102
Pasquier, Paul 102

Patrese, Riccardo 19, 21, 31, 33–9, 47, 82–4, 86, 100, 126, 131–2, 134, 140, 142–51
   1992 season 50–73
   results 166
   FW14B chassis histories 168–170
PDS (Puncture Detection System) 116, 121
pedals 125
Pelletier, Patrice 102
Pembrey test (1989) 44, 132, 136, 137, 139, 152
Pescarolo, Henri 11, 12
Peterson, Ronnie 11
Piola, Giorgio 40
Piquet, Nelson 15, 18–19, 41–2, 137, 130, 144
Piquet Jnr, Nelson 25
Pirelli tyres 52, 116
pistons 105–6
Pizzonia, Antonio 25
pneumatic valve mechanism 107
Poele, Eric van de 164–165
Portuguese Grand Prix
   1991 race 36
   1992 race 69–70, 166
Postlethwaite, Harvey 14, 161
power box 116–17
pressures (tyres) 116
Prost, Alain 18, 21, 31, 33, 35, 42, 64, 69, 71, 140, 152–3
   FW14B chassis histories 170
Prost, Nicolas 152
Psion Organiser 133–4
pump fuel 101, 104, 111
Puncture Detection System (PDS) 116, 121, 150–151
push to pass button 87
pushrods 38–9

Race of Champions (1969) 11
radiators 81, 110, 167
radio activation switch 127
radio aerial 80
reactive suspension 40
   FW11B car 19
   FW12 car 19–20
rear diffuser 84–5
rear spring pack, active-ride system 94
rear suspension 88–9, 167
rear wing 85–7
rear-light switch 127
rear-wing endplates 86
Red 5 race number 18
Redman, Brian 11
refuelling 79
Regazzoni, Clay 14–15
regulations (FISA)
   1993 season 21
   1995 season 22
   2014 season 26
   active suspension 38
   fire extinguisher/electrical cut-off 122
   fuels 64, 101, 103–4, 111
   medical air system 123
   wings 83
Renault engines 20–1, 26, 30, 49, 52, 76, 92–3, 99–112, 141, 167
Renault Sport 49, 99–103, 104, 131, 140–41

Index

Abingdon airfield 40–1
Abu Dhabi Grand Prix (2014 race) 27
accelerometers, active-ride system 95
active-ride/active suspension system 38–47, 90–7, 131–3, 147, 167
  control switches 125–6
actuators 38–40, 93–4
aerodynamics 38–9, 82–7
air system 123
airbox 110
airbox cover 80–1
airflow 81–2
Alboreto, Michele 42, 161, 163
Alesi, Jean 56–8, 60, 66–8, 159–160
Alonso, Fernando 25
alternator 117
Amati, Giovanna 165
Anderson, Gary 163
Anderson, Ian 44
Andrea Moda F1 cars 165
Andretti, Mario 16
anti-lock braking (ABS) 48, 98
Arrows F1 team 132
Australian Grand Prix
  1986 race 18
  1991 race 37–8
  1992 race 71–3, 166
    VCM set-up file 118–19
  1994 race 22
Austrian Grand Prix
  1979 race 8–9
  1980 race 144
Automotive Products (AP) 39–40, 130
Autosport magazine 40–2, 84

Babonnaud, Patrick 102
Bailey, Len 11
Barnard, John 30, 159
Barrichello, Rubens 26, 148
Belgian Grand Prix
  1981 race 144
  1990 race 30
  1991 race 36
  1992 race 66–7, 86, 164, 166
Belmondo, Paul 162
Benetton F1 cars 159
Berger, Gerhard 35, 37, 42, 146–7, 158
  1992 season 54–66, 68–73
Bertaggia, Enrico 165
blown diffuser 84–5, 111, 146
Blundell, Mark 20, 44, 47–8, 131–2, 137, 151–2, 168
BMS Scuderia Italia 162
BMW engines 23–4
bodywork 79–82
Borman, Kurt 41–2, 136
Bottas, Valtteri 26–7, 153
Boutsen, Thierry 20–1, 100, 139, 162

Brabham racecars 10–11
  BT26A F1 car 10
  BT60B F1 car 164–5
brakes 98–9, 167
  bias lever 127
  pedal 125
Brawn, Ross 159
Brazilian Grand Prix
  1976 race 13
  1985 race 144
  1989 race 100
  1992 race 55–6, 162, 166
  1994 race 22
  2010 race 26
Brepson, Jean-Marc 141
British Grand Prix
  1979 race 14
  1988 race 20, 45, 131, 136–8
  1991 race 35
  1992 race 61–2, 146, 161, 166
Brown, David 59, 61, 63, 139–140, 147
Brundle, Martin 20, 33, 159
  1992 season 55, 59, 61–2, 65–8, 71, 73
Brunner, Gustav 162
Buemi, Sebastian 152
bulkheads 77
Button, Jenson 23–4
Byrne, Rory 159

CAD (Computer Aided Design) system 77–8
Cadd, John 44, 136–7
Caffi, Alex 161
calipers, brake 88–9, 98–9, 169
camber angle adjustment
  front 88
  rear 89
camshafts 99, 108
CAN (Controller Area Network) 115, 118
Canadian Grand Prix
  1989 race 100
  1991 race 33–4
  1992 race 59, 166
Capelli, Ivan 160
Carbon Industrie 98
Cesaris, Andrea de 161
Chandhok, Karun 135, 153
Chapman, Colin 46, 144
Chasselut, Philippe 102
chassis 76–9
  identification plate 127
  specification 167
Chiesa, Andrea 164
Ciral foundry 105
clutch 112, 167
  pedal 125
Coblence, Philippe 102, 107, 110, 141
cockpit controls 123–7
  view inside 98
Comas, Erik 61, 66, 161–162

Computer Aided Design (CAD) system 77–8
connecting rods 105
Constructors' World Championship 132 see also Formula One seasons
  1979–1990 seasons 15–21
  1991 season 37–8
  1992 season 67, 73
  1993–2015 seasons 21–27
Controller Area Network (CAN) 115, 118
controls, cockpit 123–7
cooling ducts 81
cooling system 109–10
Cooper, Adam 52–3, 61
Corbeau, Georges 102
Costa, Aldo 163
Cosworth engines 10–11, 14, 17, 25–6
Coughlan, Mike 159
Coulthard, David 21, 140
Courage, Piers 10–11
crankcase/crankshaft 105
crash tests 78
cylinder heads 106–8
  scavenge pumps 109

Dallara, Gian Paolo 11, 162
Dallara F192 F1 car 162–163
Dallas Grand Prix (1984 race) 17
Daly, Derek 16
damper valves, active-ride system 94–5
dashboard display 124–5
data logging 118, 120–1, 127
de Cesaris, Andrea 161
de Ferran, Gil 152–3, 168
De Tomaso racecars 11
Dennis, Ron 158
Dernie, Frank 40–1, 47, 130–132, 136, 161
Dietrich, Chris 38, 44, 91, 121, 126, 135, 137
diffuser 84–5, 111, 146
digital dashboard display 124–5
dimensions of FW14B car 167
discs and pads 98, 167
Distribution Pneumatique 107
Drag Reduction System (DRS) 87
drink system 125
  activation switch 127
drive-by-wire throttle system 125
driver's harness 122
driver's seat 123
Drivers' World Championship 132 see also Formula One seasons
  1980–1990 seasons 15–21
  1991 season 37, 144
  1992 season 65–6, 71, 73, 147
  1993–2015 seasons 21–7
driveshafts 115, 167
Ducarouge, Gérard 102, 161

Dudot, Bernard 48–9, 100, 102–3, 140–1
Dutch Grand Prix
  1970 race 11
  1980 race 15
dynamometer 104

ECU 111–12, 121
electric starter 113
electrical cut-off master switch 122
electrical system 116–17
Elf fuels 31, 64, 101, 104, 111, 145
endplates
  front wing 83
  rear wing 86
endurance engine testing 104
Energy Recovery System (ERS) 26
engine control switch 127
engine cover 80–1
engine management system 111–12
engines 99–112 see also Renault engines
  specification 167
ERS (Energy Recovery System) 26
European Formula Two Championship 10
European Grand Prix (1985 race) 17–18, 144
exhaust system 111
  blown diffuser 84–5
expansion tank, hydraulic fluid 97

Fargues, Jean-Paul 102
Fearnley, Paul 52–3, 61
Ferrari F1 cars 159–160
FIA Formula E Championship 152–3
FIA homologation plate 127
fire extinguisher system 122
FISA regulations
  1993 season 21
  1995 season 22
  2014 season 26
  active suspension 38
  fire extinguisher/electrical cut-off 122
  fuels 64, 101, 103–4, 111
  medical air system 123
  wings 83
Fisichella, Giancarlo 23
Fittipaldi, Christian 163
floor/rear diffuser 84–5
fluid cooler, hydraulic 96
fluid filters, active-ride system 96
Fondmetal F1 cars 164
Fondmetal wheels 115
foot pedals 125
Footwork FA13 F1 car 161
Formula E Championship 152–3